Contexts of Education

DEVELOPMENT IN LEARNING

———

I: THE REGULATION OF BEHAVIOUR
II: DEVELOPMENT IN HUMAN LEARNING
III: CONTEXTS OF EDUCATION

DEVELOPMENT IN LEARNING
BEHAVIOUR : LEARNING : EDUCATION
III

Contexts of Education

—

EDITED BY

J. F. MORRIS

AND

E. A. LUNZER

STAPLES PRESS

First published 1969 by Staples Press
3 Upper James Street Golden Square London W1
Copyright © Staples Press 1969
Printed in Great Britain by
Cox & Wyman Limited
London, Reading and Fakenham

SBN 286 62119 3

CONTENTS

PART II: ENVIRONMENT AND THE LEARNER

CHAPTER 6. THE SOCIAL PSYCHOLOGY OF LEARNING *by J. F. Morris*

PREFACE

Development in Learning has been designed to serve as a comprehensive introduction to the problems of educational psychology. Its primary purpose is to serve as a basic text for students preparing for higher diplomas and degrees, especially in the field of education. It is addressed, secondarily, to all those students of psychology who retain an interest in the development of children, and even real children in schools, not just children in laboratories. It is addressed, finally, to all those who have sufficient common sense to dare expose its prejudices to the searing (though still rather diluted) acid of scientific analysis.

Volume I, *The Regulation of Behaviour*, concentrates on the most fundamental problem of psychology, and especially human psychology, the role of learning and its nature. We have tried to show up the sham of what once passed for super-science, the pure empiricism of associationist stimulus-response learning theories. We also tried to sketch in the outlines of a more adequate foundation for behavioural studies. We tried to do this not by inventing something new, but rather by spreading a sheet wide enough to capture some of the best thinking and research which has begun to permeate the psychological atmosphere, especially here in Britain, and by attempting a distillation, however crude.

Volume II, *Development in Human Learning*, is in both senses the central volume of this work. For the project was conceived in the belief that the central aim of education is to teach, or, which is the same thing, to provide the optimum conditions for learning. Crucial to educational psychology is the study of how children learn, and how their powers of learning develop. Although much of the book deals with the important contribution of Piaget, considerable attention is given to social learning, to language, to the role of programming, and so on.

Then what of the present volume? The title *Contexts of Education* suggests that we are now turning aside from the central 'text', the process of learning, to look at things more peripheral, things which modify the learning process in the school situation. This is deliberate. In Part I we are concerned with individual differences in abilities, in aptitudes, in personality, in temperament and in adjustment. In one sense at any rate, such differences are parameters to the system we envisage as learning. They affect the efficiency of the process, causing it to range very widely, as widely as the gap that separates the extremes of maladjustment

(Chapter 4) or of mental handicap (Chapter 5) from the 'high-fliers' in Britain's controversial selective schools. Likewise in Part II we see how the efficiency of learning is modified by the attitudes which pupils and teachers bring to their roles in the learning situation, whether absorbed from the cultural milieu (Chapters 6 and 8), or elaborated through an intricate series of identifications and cross-identifications, of self-delineation and complementary delineation of the reciprocal other, operating within the microenvironment of the school itself (Chapters 6, 7). Here too the gap in the efficiency of the system, even with ability and temperament not too greatly different, can yet be made to vary from near zero, as in Hargreaves' D stream pupils, to near-maximal as in his A stream. Nor is this cause for wonder, since there should be nothing surprising about the fact that the output of a system (here, the pupil's learning) must approach zero as the co-efficient of one of its parameters reaches zero.

Not surprising in theory, but how often do we find this recognized in standard textbooks on educational psychology? For although the present volume deals with parameters to the learning process or *contexts* in which it occurs, it is in no sense an appendage or an afterthought. Individual differences are related to learning much as the design of a motor-car engine and its capacity are related to its performance, while social contexts relate to it much as the quality of the fuel and lubricants as well as the nature of the terrain on which it is driven relate to the other. Theoretically such factors must come second to how the machine works; in practice they are all-important. That is why it is entirely appropriate that *Development in Learning* was conceived from the start as involving a necessary collaboration of two editors, one whose primary interest is in the nature of the learning process itself, while the interests of the other extend widely enough to include everything in the individual and in society that impinges on it.

Finally, a word about the chapters in this book. Little need be said here about Part II, the integration of which reflects a measure of praiseworthy collusion on the part of its authors, the more so since one of us has provided a separate introduction and overview. But the chapters in Part I were conceived separately, to cover the field. On the whole there is little overlap. At the same time each of the contributors approaches his topic from his own point of view. These do not always coincide, and at least in one case they may appear to conflict. Butcher's incisive yet thoughtful study of special abilities and of creative ones in particular complements Clarke's masterly survey of general intelligence with special reference to the interaction of nature and nurture. The picture is further filled out in Cashdan's excellent survey of learning handicap and its attendant problems. However, Chapters 3 and 4 reflect a more radical difference in approach. For Warburton's deceptively engaging chapter is essentially an extremely learned and professional distillation of a vast body of research results gained from what Allport called the *normative* approach to personality: when we survey a sufficiently representative population of individuals all of whom differ recognizably from one another as people, what personality traits go with what? What are the dimensions that make them different? Conversely, Stott's highly original and penetrating study of adjustment, reflecting as it does the author's long experience in individual casework with delinquents, is an expression of Allport's historic or *idiographic* approach, concentrating on each individual in turn: by what processes do his innate endowments and propensities combine with one another, and how are they transformed in the course of his own particular experiences to make him the particular individual that he is? Both approaches are legitimate. We do not ask the reader to choose between them, because in the final analysis both will surely be integrated within a more satisfactory theory of personality than any which we can compass as of now. Indeed, we cannot refrain from shedding an editorial tear over the admittedly occasional aspersions cast by each on the camp of the other. But it makes things come alive. For, as Warburton sagely remarks, in the field of personality assessment, we are still at the Eocene age.

This brings us to our last point. It was certainly the intention of one of us (E.A.L.) to provide a glorious editorial chapter, to explain just how individual differences in the various aspects of ability and personality enter into the function of the learning process, conceived as a system, as we conceived it in Volumes I and II. This chapter does not appear. The task remains beyond his competence. This is partly a reflexion of personal inadequacy. But in part it may suggest that we need to learn much more than is now known about the nature and origin of individual differences before we can attempt an integration of all these topics within a general theory of behaviour.

But once again, this does not lessen their importance. Science must lean towards the empirical before a master theory becomes possible. But neither theory nor practice can be served by ignoring hard facts for want of elegant interpretations. The facts presented throughout the chapters of this volume are as hard as any.

Preface

In concluding this preface, we have the greatest pleasure in expressing our heartfelt thanks to our contributors, not only for lending their scholarship, but also for their patience and understanding. Most of these chapters were projected several years ago, and in all these cases the authors have very willingly amended their earlier drafts, often more than once. Thanks are due also to the excellent work of our indexer, Miss Ann Stewart.

E.A.L.
J.F.M.

CONTRIBUTORS

W. A. L. BLYTH, M.A., M.ED., PH.D., Professor of Education, University of Liverpool.

H. J. BUTCHER, B.A., PH.D., Professor of Higher Education, University of Manchester.

A. CASHDAN, M.A., B.ED., Lecturer in the Education of Handicapped Children, University of Manchester.

A. D. B. CLARKE, B.A., PH.D., Professor of Psychology, University of Hull.

D. H. HARGREAVES, M.A., Lecturer in Education, University of Manchester.

E . A. LUNZER, M.A., PH.D., Professor designate, Department of Education, University of Nottingham.

J. F. MORRIS, B.SC.(ECON.), PH.D., Senior Lecturer in Psychology, Manchester Business School, University of Manchester.

D. H. STOTT, M.A., PH.D., Professor and Head of the Department of Psychology, University of Guelph, Ontario, Canada.

F. W. WARBURTON, M.A., PH.D., Professor of Experimental Education, University of Manchester.

PART ONE

Individual Differences
in the Learner

1

Intelligence[1]

A. D. B. CLARKE

I. THE MEASUREMENT OF INTELLIGENCE: ITS VALIDITY AND RELIABILITY

1. *Introduction*

IT IS worth pointing out that intelligence is an inference from behaviour; it can be inferred in a variety of ways, the size of a person's vocabulary, his ability to solve problems in the abstract or in practical and concrete situations – all these are clearly 'intelligent' in varying degrees. There can be no measure of 'pure intelligence', even though the early workers thought that this was possible, simply because all actions recognized as intelligent are expressed via certain attainments such as speech, motor co-ordination, writing and so forth. No doubt these attainments are based on the efficient working of the central nervous system, but we cannot tell to what extent they are thus dependent. Let us take vocabulary as an example, for it often forms part of intelligence tests and indeed of subjective assessment. Knowledge of word meanings is certainly dependent on the nervous system but clearly does not blossom *in vacuo*; to varying extents it is related to the background, reading, schooling, and cultural level stimulating the child. It is thus partly a function of opportunity.

It should be clear from the foregoing that intelligence is highly complex, so much so that writers such as Hebb (1949) and others have distinguished two main concepts: Intelligence A or 'pure intelligence', and Intelligence B or intelligence as expressed in everyday life or as understood by the man-in-the-street. Vernon (1955a) adds to this scheme Intelligence C, or that which is measured by an intelligence test.

[1] This Chapter has been reprinted with minor modification from *Mental Deficiency: the Changing Outlook*, Edited by A. M. Clarke and A. D. B. Clarke, 2nd Edition, 1965, London: Methuen, and New York: Free Press, by permission of the publishers and editors.

Intelligence C should be a good and representative sample of B, but there is no way of knowing how far B is also a measure of A, which can only be inferred. Indeed A in this argument becomes a philosophical abstraction of use only in theoretical discussion.

Further problems, however, remain that are pertinent to the interpretation of intelligence test scores. These problems are concerned with the statistical validity of a given test, the reliability of the measuring device in view of errors of measurement, chance fluctuations, and genuine change of intellectual status; and, arising from a discussion of these factors and the influence of maturational and social factors, the prognostic value of intelligence test data (see Section II).

2. *Validity*

Validity can be defined as the degree to which the test measures what it purports to measure. The main difficulty which confronts validation is the problem of criteria, which is, of course, not confined to the validation of psychological tests, for it exists in many other scientific fields. One can find either arbitrary criteria or empirical ones; one can say that a new test seems to involve abstract thinking, and that therefore 'intelligence is what the test measures', or one can compare results with other intelligence tests which, by a sort of apostolic succession, have been correlated with earlier versions of the Binet test. Yet this, too, is ultimately a subjective technique. If, on the other hand, intelligence tests are validated against success in life situations such as academic work, once again one is confronted with an imperfect criterion. It is obvious that success in academic work involves other personality factors as well as intelligence, and, further, the degree of a person's achievement is itself not an objective uncontaminated criterion, since examination results or teachers' ratings are themselves to some extent subjective.[1] Yet satisfactory validation coefficients can be obtained in spite of these drawbacks.

While validation of tests apparently rests upon insecure foundations, these are perhaps not so inadequate as at first sight they may seem. Adverting to the undisputed fact that all mental activities which can be termed intellectual, even if only remotely so, correlate together positively, the problem at once becomes that of selection of adequate samples of those activities with the lowest possible intercorrelation and the highest possible correlation with the total score gained from them

[1] For an enlightening discussion of some of the factors involved, see Bull, G. M., (An examination of the final examination in medicine), *Lancet*, 1956, ii, 368–72.

all. In general, the lower the intercorrelations of the test items, the wider the spectrum of intellectual activity they will cover; and hence the better the test of general intellectual ability. These features will be found in reputable tests, and it is no accident that the latter also possess reasonable coefficients of external validity.

3. *Reliability*

The reliability of an intelligence test can be defined in terms of the degree to which it measures the same thing in the same way at different times, and this is somewhat easier to establish. There are, of course, three main methods of assessing reliability: the 'split-half' method, which measures internal consistency (itself implying reliability); the use of a parallel version (such as Stanford–Binet Form M compared with Form L) and finally by retest. The latter is probably the most useful method.

Sometimes the words 'test reliability' have been misunderstood because they relate to at least two variables; firstly, does the test measure the same thing in the same way on different occasions, and secondly, does the quality measured itself alter? As we shall see, both variables tend to overlap. Nevertheless we will be concerned with what might reasonably be termed 'reliability of measurement' and 'reliability of persons tested' (that is, their ability to change) both under the general heading of test reliability.

Later discussion will make it clear that in any retest coefficient both variables play a part. 'Reliability of measurement' can best be assessed by immediate retest. If a group of persons are tested and then retested on the following day with the same scale, various factors combine to reduce perfect reliability from + 1·0 to an actual 0·9 (Thorndike, 1933). These in all cases represent personal fluctuations; the examiner may make minor errors in scoring, or in giving instructions, or in the establishment of rapport, while in the subject, alterations in mood, in physical condition, fatigue, boredom, anxiety, changes in incentive, practice effects and misunderstanding of instructions may be relevant. Combined, these errors of measurement certainly reduce the value of test results, and should always be taken into account.

It will be seen that over longer time-intervals retest coefficients tend to decrease steadily, and that since errors like those discussed above are unlikely to be cumulative, this must reflect a real change in the qualities tested, that is, 'unreliability of persons'. This is a point which results in considerable confusion; it is by no means uncommon for the following apparently tautological argument to be advanced: 'over several years test scores change, owing to imperfect correlation'. It is further implied that such changes are statistical and have no psychological significance. It is difficult to see why it should be assumed that it is more likely that the expressed statistical relationship should cause alterations in individual test performance, rather than vice versa, that the quality measured itself may undergo a certain degree of progressive change, which is inevitably reflected in a decreasing coefficient of correlation. It should be unnecessary to labour this point, but the distinction is frequently overlooked in otherwise sophisticated literature.

Much of the remainder of this chapter will in fact be concerned implicitly with the validity and reliability of intelligence tests.

II. SOME GENERAL ASSUMPTIONS UNDERLYING INTELLIGENCE TESTING

1. *'Intelligence can be measured'*

It has long been recognized that people vary in their capacity to deal effectively with their surroundings, and everyday life provides countless natural intelligence tests. The most significant fact in the whole field is that all cognitive activities, including those which might only remotely be termed intellectual, correlate together positively. This indicates that from the assessment of the level of cognitive ability in any one sphere, better than chance predictions of the level of the other abilities are possible. Theoretically, several alternative but equally valid explanations of these findings may be made. One may, for example, account for them by postulating a fundamental or master ability that is to varying degrees present in all cognitive activities, that is to say, involving differential amounts of general cognitive ability or of a general 'factor' of intelligence. In addition, specific abilities, different for different activities, may be postulated to account for the findings that a person may be much better or much worse at some tasks than at others. Alternatively, it may be held that cognitive activities may be grouped according to their functional similarity. Group abilities or group 'factors' may then be postulated to account for the high correlations between the activities within a certain group. Or again, the sampling theory accounts for the intercorrelation of cognitive activities by postulating the existence of numerous independent abilities. These, though each limited in scope, each enter into a great many activities, and the correlation between tests will depend on the number of abilities these have in common. A good intelligence test attempts to be an effective small sample of cognitive processes, which like all good samples carries within it a microcosm of the whole. It ensures this, as mentioned earlier, by choosing items with relatively low intercorrelations yet each of which correlates well with the total score derived from them all. Clearly, the lower the intercorrelations, the wider the spread of activities sampled.

In theory, therefore, it is clear that a relatively short test can be produced with implications wider than the individual test items themselves, and in practice this can be demonstrated by the correlation between some real-life intellectual activity and the intelligence test result. There is thus no doubt that the first proposition 'intelligence can be measured' is largely correct.

2. *'Intelligence is normally distributed'*

From the early days of intelligence testing the assumption has been made that the majority of persons are of medium or near average intelligence, with relatively few of very superior or very inferior ability, and that mental qualities are akin to some physical factors such as height or weight in forming a Gaussian curve of distribution. This assumption can be neither proved nor disproved in detail since its criterion, the test, is arranged precisely to meet the requirement of normal distribution. Arguments about it are thus circular. While this reservation must be made, it is nevertheless not an unreasonable assumption in terms of everyday experience.

Similarly, arguments about the precise shape of average mental growth curves tend to be unprofitable, for arrangement or rearrangement of test items are bound to influence such curves. In fact, a mental growth curve is the result of complex interaction between the persons tested and the test items, and it is thus only possible to relate a given curve both to the specific test and to the specific standardization sample. It is illegitimate to argue that because mental growth on the Binet test gives a curve of such-and-such a shape that therefore mental growth in general proceeds in this form.

3. *'The IQ is constant'*

This proposition was made very early in the history of the mental testing movement, indeed so early that it had to be an untested assumption simply because insufficient time had elapsed since the invention of intelligence tests. It is noteworthy that Binet himself (quoted by Skeels and Dye, 1939) commented that

Some recent philosophers appear to have given their moral support to the deplorable verdict that the intelligence of an individual is a fixed quantity, a quantity which cannot be augmented. We must protest and act against this brutal pessimism. We shall endeavour to show that it has no foundation whatsoever. . . . A child's mind is like a field for which an expert farmer has advised a change in the method of cultivating, with the result that in place of desert land we now have a harvest. It is in this particular sense, the only one that is significant, that we say that the intelligence of children may be increased. One increases that which constitutes the intelligence of a school child; namely the capacity to learn, to improve with instruction.

Binet's use of the words 'Some recent philosophers . . .' is surely significant. The theory of I Q constancy was a philosophical one congruent with the somewhat mechanistic attitude to man current fifty years ago, and thus the majority view simply accepted that a child's relative status was fixed and unalterable.

As data began to accumulate over the years, one or two experts had doubts about I Q constancy. Thus Burt (1921), discussing retests over periods of several years, notes that I Q constancy 'is but imperfectly realized'. Mental growth curves appearing in the textbooks, however, implicitly supported the theory. Such curves, while true of *averages*, neglect individual variability which is the rule rather than the exception. For example, the late developer is one in whom mental growth does not proceed by uniform increments as the curve suggests. Indeed, if individual mental growth were a uniform process, then this would represent the one form of biological growth not characterized by 'fits and starts'.

Two papers by Nemzek (1933) and Thorndike (1940) summarize in all 359 studies carried out before 1940; Clarke and Clarke (1953) point out that these researches show consistently that: (*a*) the predictive value of the I Q (as measured by test–retest correlation) decreases as the interval between the tests lengthens; and, as a corollary, (*b*) although the group or population average may not alter greatly, there will be considerable change of status of some individuals within that group (subsequent retests showing that to varying extents some subjects increase in I Q, some decrease, some fluctuate, and some remain constant); while (*c*) mental tests given to children during the pre-school years have usually little predictive value, and assessments during infancy have no relationship with later status (except, of course, in cases of severe mental deficiency, the early diagnosis of which is discussed in Chapter 5). It should, moreover, be noted that mental tests designed for early childhood are really tests of sensori-motor development, and their failure to relate to later status may be due either to the fact that different personal qualities are being measured at different times, or to the fact that the period of infancy and the pre-school years is one of maximum variability in growth, or both.[1]

To illustrate conclusions (*a*) and (*b*), the practical implications of commonly observed test–retest correlations may be considered. Reviews by Nemzek (1933), Thorndike (1933), and Thorndike (1940) have shown that retest correlations are rarely as high as 0·95, and that on *immediate* retest the most probable value is 0·90. Shapiro (1951) demonstrates the implication of this latter as follows:

> Let us assume that we have a test with a test–retest correlation of 0·9 and a standard deviation of 16. These data mean that, out of every three children obtaining an average score of 100, one would obtain a retest score above 107 or below 93. On the basis of the same data, out of every 10 children obtaining an average score on the first test, one child would obtain a score above 112 or below 88 on the second test. (These illustrations assume that no learning has taken place.)

Over time-intervals of several years, test–retest correlations are usually much lower than 0·9. Honzik, Macfarlane, and Allen (1948) found a retest correlation of about 0·6 for a time-interval of 12 years, after following up a representative sample of urban children from infancy to the age of 18 years. They tested over 150 children at the ages of 6 and 18, and found that the IQs of 58 per cent changed 15 or more points; the IQs of 35 per cent changed 20 or more points; and the IQs of 9 per cent changed 30 or more points. In only 15 per cent of cases was the change 9 points or less. Individual IQ constancy over this period was thus exceptional. The group averages, on the other hand, showed a maximum shift in IQ over this time of only 5 points. The maximum individual IQ change was 50 points.

---

[1] The work of Maurer (1946) provides a notable exception to conclusion (*c*). It was found that, on a long-term follow-up, certain non-verbal items on the Minnesota Pre-School Scale yielded significant correlations with later status. Much more research is, however, needed on pre-school tests before their commonly poor predictive validity can be fully explained.

Both some supporters and some opponents of these findings have, however, been misled by their somewhat vague use of the word 'change'. It seems clear from examination of the text (*op. cit.*, p. 312) and of the graphed mental test performance of their case 967 (*op. cit.*, p. 320), that by change they mean maximum variation between any two tests during a given period of time. Consequently, the above figures have sometimes been wrongly interpreted as indicating the change in IQ between test results at age 6 and the test results at age 18, whereas they represent *maximal variations for individuals during the whole time period.* Recognition of this ambiguity would seem to go a long way towards reconciling Vernon's (1955a) criticism that IQs are more stable than some writers deduce from this and other researches. In another paper (1955b), implying that the reported changes are greater than would seem possible from the correlation coefficient, he points out that Honzik *et al.* obtained a median variation of about 16 points over the 6–18 year age range. 'This is exaggerated because the group was superior in ability and because it was tested mainly with Terman–Merrill, which has a large standard deviation.' His first point, that IQs are more variable towards the higher end of the scale, is naturally common to all other studies of persons of high ability, but the second point seems to be incorrect, since at age 6 the subjects were tested with the 1916 revision of the Stanford–Binet which Hilden (1949) estimates from Terman's data (in the absence of published material) has a standard deviation of 13 points. At age 18 the subjects were retested with the Wechsler, which has a standard deviation of 14·5 points. If the writer's interpretation is correct, the 'median variation of about 16 points' mentioned above is really the 'median maximal variation' for all subjects. There would then be no discrepancy with Vernon's calculation (personal communication) that the true median variation of scores between the 6 and 18 year tests is about 8 points, corresponding to the obtained correlation of 0·61. Thus, half the group changed within plus and minus 8 points, and half altered more than this, some by very much larger amounts. With these provisos in mind this study appears to be a very important one.

Similarly, Hilden (1949), studied the intellectual growth of 100 children, and has reported findings on 30 of these examined from early childhood to late adolescence. In this small sample, too, individual variability in IQ was often found: the mean variation was 0·42 SD points (6·8 IQ points) and the mean maximum variation (mean of the two most discrepant scores for each individual) was 27·0 points.

Dearborn and Rothney (1941) have reported findings from the important Harvard Growth Study in which both mental and physical development in children were investigated over many years; their book gives results from many different researches on several hundred children. They conclude that

'prediction of growth at various ages is extremely hazardous, but is particularly so during the period of adolescence . . . marked variability in individual growth curves appears throughout the course of the growth period. . . . The principle of individual variability goes right to the root of such problems as constancy of the IQ. . . . We have established the fact that variability rather than consistency of growth is the rule, that prediction except for average of groups is extremely hazardous. . . .'

It has commonly been accepted that in adult life the IQ tends to be much more constant than in childhood or adolescence. This may in general well be true, but until recently there has been a dearth of longitudinal research in this field. A number of such studies of rather special groups have, however, come to fruition in more recent years. Owens (1953), for example, carried out a careful thirty-year follow-up of 127 males to whom Army Alpha, Form 6, had been administered as an entrance test at the Iowa State College during 1919. On most sub-tests there was a significant increase in scores, and for the total group on all sub-tests the increment averaged half a sigma. It was not possible to be certain whether these increases had occurred during college life and had not been maintained, or whether there had been small and slow improvement during the whole period. Moreover, these tests only measured verbal abilities. Nevertheless, these findings are of great importance.

Bayley and Oden (1955) and Bayley (1955) have also challenged the belief that intellectual growth necessarily ceases in adolescence. This investigation of the adult intelligence of the subjects of the Terman Study of Gifted Children showed that scores on the difficult Concept Mastery test increased over a twelve-year period by about half a sigma. The age range of the thousand subjects varied from 20 to about 50 years. When grouped into five-year age intervals, the increments were found at all ages and with curves of very similar slope.

Similarly, Nisbet (1957) retested after twenty-four years a group of 141 graduates who had first taken a shortened version of the Simplex Group Test at the age of 22. The average increment over this period was estimated to amount to 0·7 or 0·8 sigma. Nisbet quotes a further five American studies with similar implications.

Bradway and Thompson (1962) have reported an interesting twenty-five year study in which pre-school and adolescent IQs were compared with adult Stanford–Binet and WAIS IQs. The Stanford–Binet IQ showed a mean increment of 11 points from adolescence to adulthood, the averages for the subjects in 1931 being 113; in 1941, 112; and in 1956, 123, with similar sigmas of 15–16 points throughout.

Much more work is needed on the natural history of adult intellectual growth and decline, particularly in relation to environmental factors. It is already clear, however, that the view that intellectual growth necessarily ceases in adolescence is no longer tenable so far as verbal abilities are concerned, and, as will be pointed out in Part II, studies of some types of subnormal persons show increment in tested intelligence as age increases.

To illustrate conclusion (*c*), namely, that mental tests in the pre-school years have little predictive value, Honzik *et al.* can again be cited. Tests at 21 months correlate less than 0·1 with the results at the age of 18 years. Similarly, Bayley (1940) found that mental scores derived from tests at 7, 8, and 9 months, while correlating highly with scores a few months later, had a relationship in the region of zero with all measurements after the age of 30 months. Indeed, in at least three researches quoted by Jones (1946) small negative correlations were found between intelligence scores in infancy and test scores in later life. As age increases, however, so does the correlation with later intellectual status. Thus, Bayley (1949) found that for 27 children tested from infancy onwards, the correlations with the test score at the age of 18 years became positive at the age of 2, and by the age of 4 had become 0·52.

From the wealth of available data it is clear that, in the general population, the concept of a rigidly constant IQ is contradicted by the facts; IQ constancy over long periods of time during the years of mental growth is the exception rather than the rule. It should be remembered, however, that IQ constancy is a relative concept, and that radical changes (over 25 points in either direction) are rare.[1] In the

---

[1] Vernon (1955a) suggests the following formula for the calculation of the median variation of IQ changes: $0·674\sigma \sqrt{1-r^2}$ for a single retest, and $1·349\sigma \sqrt{1-\bar{r}}$ for repeated retests. Thus, with the standard deviation of 15, and a retest correlation of 0·7 over a five-year period during childhood, a median variation of 7 points is obtained; that is, 50 per cent of the sample change within ± 7 points, and 50 per cent by more than this (17 per cent may rise or fall 15 or more points and nearly 1 per

literature, however, a few most unusual and apparently authentic cases have been reported where over many years IQ variations of 50 or so points have occurred.

III. CAUSES OF IQ CHANGE

The causes of IQ variability can be subsumed under four headings, the first three of which do not represent real change at all:

1. *Errors of measurement*

The IQ may vary because of alterations in mood of the person tested, or due to misunderstanding of the instructions, to the cultural bias of the questions, or to errors of scoring. Similarly the IQ may vary from one test to another simply because of differences in the standardization of the two tests. Thus, an IQ of 80 on a test with a standard deviation of 15 points does not mean the same thing as an identical IQ on a test with a standard deviation of 20 points. In fact, it would be equivalent to an IQ of 73 on the second. On the 1937 Stanford revision of the Binet, for example, the scatter of scores varies at different ages, and unless corrections are made, the IQ of a child will vary over the years for reasons of standardization alone; and the further the IQ from the mean the greater the variation.

Statistical regression to the mean is another concept used to explain IQ changes, especially at the extremes of high or low intelligence. Where errors of measurement on the same or different tests are concerned, or where different tests have a low initial correlation, regression of extreme scores is inevitable and of little psychological significance. The whole concept of statistical regression is far less simple than it might sound, however, and has been responsible for considerable confusion in discussions of IQ changes. It is not difficult to appreciate, for example, that on a test such as the Progressive Matrices a person who makes a very low score, say 8/60, is more likely to score higher on

---

cent may vary as much as 30 points either way). Vernon states that with repeated retesting, fluctuations are about half as wide again. This formula, however, while it appears to be a useful way of deducing the amount of change in normal groups in which increment and decrement are balanced, nevertheless underestimates the amount of variability in admittedly rare groups where there is a strong tendency for most members to increase or to decrease in IQ. In such cases the test–retest correlation will be higher than in a normal group, because the changes are unidirectional.

retest (test practice of course adds to this possibility) simply because 'chance' tends to be normally distributed and there are more possible changes in the positive than in the negative direction. The opposite argument holds good for scores near the maximum. But it is difficult to see how these factors would influence I Qs in the 80's or 90's to any extent.

McNemar (1940) has discussed the whole problem in detail but there remain a number of dubious points in his argument which neglects to attempt explanation of the phenomenon. He gives two main examples. First he suggests that a group of 8-year-old boys of Swedish extraction will have a mean height half a sigma above the American average for that age. If these same boys are measured again at the age of 16, the correlation between the two sets of measures will not be high, that is, there will have been considerable change of relative status in height. The group will still be half a sigma above the American mean (presumably for genetic reasons) and there will have been no general regression. We would expect regression within the group, however; the extremes of 8-year-old tallness or shortness would be relatively less extreme at the age of 16, while others less deviant at age 8 would have become more deviant later.

In contrast, McNemar gives a second example. If, on the basis of measurement, a group of boys had been chosen as above average, a general tendency would occur for the group mean to be nearer the universe mean upon later measurement. It will be seen, therefore, that regression to the general mean in McNemar's view is dependent upon initial selection on the basis of test score. 'In other words, an inferior or superior group will not move towards the general mean on a retest unless they have been selected as inferior or superior on the basis of an initial test' (*op. cit.*, p. 89). Now statistical regression is usually stated to be due to measurement errors; in the examples given, however, it is likely that measurement errors would be negligible, so other factors must be relevant. What these may be McNemar does not say, although he admits that the concept is descriptive rather than explanatory.

Clarke, Clarke and Brown (1959) have given examples of the confused way in which writers have used regression as an explanatory device, and have suggested two different mechanisms. The first involves errors of measurement of two different kinds, which are far less simple than they sound, and the second, the tendency for growth to be a non-linear process (see sub-section 4). There seems to be a tendency for groups selected on the basis of extreme test score to include members whose position at the time of selection is either partly the result of 'chance' or of an unusual growth fluctuation. At points later in time, neither is likely to operate to the same extent, either because 'chance' tends not to favour or disfavour the same person twice, or because of the cyclic nature of individual growth, or indeed, a combination of both.

Thus regression is likely to be due both to 'chance' and 'real' factors. In both events, it will tend to be balanced in the general population by others moving outwards from the average.

2. *Test practice*

Increments in I Q tend to occur as a result of having taken a particular test on more than one occasion. Practice effects are, however, rather small, averaging 4 or 5 points. Where deliberate 'coaching' takes place, on the other hand, then the increment may be very large and as much as an average of 15 points with intelligent persons (see Vernon, 1954).

3. *Incorrect testing*

One factor which has tended to bring the IQ into disrepute is incorrect testing by persons inadequately qualified in psychometrics. The main errors are as follows:

(*a*) A very short test is given. Generally speaking it should take at least an hour to obtain a valid I Q on an individual test.

(*b*) No new test is given, but a previous result is quoted as indicating present status. This might not be unreasonable if the individual were adult, and if the I Q remained rigidly constant; but this latter is unlikely with the majority of children.

(*c*) The wrong test is given. For example, a person with many years of institutionalization cannot be accurately assessed on tests demanding a good degree of general knowledge. Or again, a purely verbal test for a deaf person will obviously tend to reflect mainly his restricted verbal experiences. Similarly, the administration of the Binet to adults is quite incorrect owing to lack of standardization.

(*d*) The test is given in a traumatic situation which disturbs the person so much that he cannot do himself justice.

(*e*) Abbreviations of a standard test are given, yet the results are based on the norms for the full test. This is analogous with a medical examination which is limited to testing the condition of the central nervous system.

These five forms of incorrect testing almost inevitably result in underestimation of the IQ.

4. *Variations in the rate of intellectual growth*

Perhaps the most important single fact in this field is that test–retest correlations decrease as the interval between the tests lengthens. On immediate retest the inter-test correlation is usually about 0·9, but as Eysenck (1953) has pointed out, the correlation on the average steadily decreases by about 0·04 per year (for large groups), so that, for example, the most likely value after seven years would be 0·62. This indicates relative and progressive change of status by members of the group under study; some increase, some decrease, some fluctuate about a given point, and some remain constant. Since there is no reason to suppose that errors of measurement are cumulative, this must be a *reflection of real change in intellectual level due to different rates of development*. Intellectual growth is thus comparable with physical growth in proceeding at different rates at different times. Clarke, Clarke, and Brown (1959) give examples of both types of growth curve for individuals and show their essential similarity.

Various authorities cite internal or external factors as being separately or jointly responsible for variations in the rate of mental growth, but research is only now beginning to clarify aspects of the old nature–nurture controversy. It is very likely, however, that the search for a precise formula for their relative importance is founded on the same sort of misconception as the belief in IQ constancy. Much will depend on the bio-social background of the particular sample under study. Thus a group of persons suffering from phenylketonuria may owe their condition almost entirely to hereditary factors, while a group from extraordinarily adverse social circumstances may be affected in the main by their nurture.

To sum up, therefore, we can say that in general the IQ, if properly applied and interpreted, gives a most valuable indication of a person's *present* status on the functions tested, and relates him to others of similar age. For predictive purposes, however, although undoubtedly useful (particularly in a constant environment), it is fallible and the longer the time for which prediction is made, the greater the possibility of change. In addition, the IQ is an invaluable tool for research. Much of the current criticism of the IQ is related to its misuse. For example, it has been used in a somewhat rigid way for educational selection, and Vernon (1955b) has pointed out that a relatively inflexible system cannot do full justice to relatively flexible children. The attack by teachers and others has been directed rather more to the *method* of selection than to selection as such; there is little doubt, however, that if one is forced to select, then use of the IQ will improve the process, which will nevertheless continue to result in error to varying extents. The alternative methods, mainly subjective, such as teachers' opinions or clinical judgement are susceptible to rather greater errors due to 'halo' and other effects.

Nowadays psychologists are increasingly critical of the global nature of the IQ. Moreover, early attempts by such persons as Wechsler to seek test patterns as diagnostic instruments have largely failed. Recent work by Kirk and McCarthy (1961) and Kirk (1962), however, has revived the hope of a measuring instrument which will reveal intellectual strengths and weaknesses, which will have a real meaning in suggesting therapeutic methods for those with learning difficulties, and which will allow the effects of such procedures to be evaluated. Kirk and McCarthy have produced the Illinois Test of Psycholinguistic Abilities based upon Osgood's model of the communication processes. The model involves two channels of communication: (1) auditory and visual inputs and (2) vocal and motor outputs. It involves two levels of organization, a representational or meaning level and an automatic sequential level. It also involves three processes; decoding, association and encoding. From this nine discrete tests have been constructed, each of which taps a level or process through one of the channels of communication. The resulting cognitive profile for the subject identifies his particular strengths and weaknesses. This approach may well prove to be extremely valuable for research, and the results of further investigations using this instrument are awaited with greatest interest (see Bateman 1965).

IV. UNITS OF MEASUREMENTS

We turn now to a consideration of the ways in which first results are expressed.

1. *Mental age and the I Q*

The term mental age was coined by Binet and has played an important part in the mental test movement. As many have indicated, the phrase is nothing more than a test score – its reality is entirely dependent on the items in the test and on its standardization.

Greene (1941) has summarized some of the main disadvantages as follows: (1) *inequality of steps*. Since increments in ability during the years of mental growth become progressively less, clearly a mental age year in early childhood has a greater weight than in early adolescence.

(2) *Changes in meaning of mental ages above adult level.* Greene points out that the Stanford investigators have arbitrarily extrapolated mental age scales into the adult range, but that obviously, with increments in average test score ceasing in mid-adolescence,[1] a mental age of, say, 20 years is far from being what the majority of 20-year-olds achieve, and thus possesses an entirely different meaning from, say, a mental age of 10. As will be seen, Wechsler (1937) has also given a detailed and critical case against the term mental age.

(3) *Different processes measured at different ages.* Binet-type scales show a definite change from performance to more abstract verbal skills with increase in mental age. Thus different sorts of ability may be sampled at different mental ages.

(4) *Components of equal mental ages.* The question has often been raised whether the same mental age at different chronological ages means the same thing, and it is generally agreed that in fact there may be considerable differences in meaning. One can go further than Greene in pointing out the same mental age at the same chronological age may not have the same meaning for different persons, since after all an MA represents the sum of various component successes, and the same sum can obviously be achieved with widely differing components. This applies, perhaps, particularly to the mentally deficient, who in the higher grades characteristically show a wide scatter of subtest scores.

The intelligence quotient or IQ has already been discussed, but it remains to detail criticisms of it as a unit of measurement. Since the original equation leading to the estimation of the IQ uses MA as the numerator, the above criticisms of mental age must in part apply to the IQ (except as estimated by Wechsler's method, see below).

It is necessary in comparing IQs on different tests to ensure that means and standard deviations are similar, and also within a given test that the same holds true at different ages. In the 1937 revision of the Stanford–Binet, for example, the adjusted means vary from 104·1 at age 3 to 99·8 at age 6. The standard deviations, however, show serious and considerable variability, ranging from a standard deviation at 6 of 12 points and at age 12 of 20 points. It was not until five years after the publication of this scale that a table of corrections was published by

---

[1] As will be seen in Section V, this is only true on the average; a number of studies of both subnormals and persons of high ability have shown that intellectual growth may continue well into adult life under special circumstances.

McNemar (1942), and unfortunately to this day many who use the Stanford–Binet test are unaware of the necessity to correct their I Qs at certain ages, and that failure to do this will result in individual I Q changes for reasons of test standardization alone. The 1960 revision, however, makes allowances for this type of error by inserting corrections in the tables.

The calculation of the I Q is, of course, affected by the artificiality of mental ages used for adults. Terman tried to solve the problem by retaining CA at 15 in the equation for all those whose real age exceeded that amount. The phenomenon of deterioration in ability with increase of age raises an additional difficulty for his solution.

Wechsler (1937) has critically reviewed the whole field and done much to overcome confusion by calculating the I Q in a novel way. He points out that: (*a*) although means tend to remain very similar, this does not imply that scores well above or below the mean will not be variable due to varying standard deviations at different ages, and (*b*) that intellectual growth does not proceed by equal amounts throughout its development. Thus, any method assuming a linear relationship between M A and C A, as in the Binet test, cannot give constant values for any considerable proportion of the growth period. This latter has three consequences: (i) for the average individual the mean value of the I Q will change from age to age; (ii) numerators used in the I Q equation increase more slowly than do the denominators, and this difference is considered to be most marked in cases of low ability. This is believed to be an effect of the particular logarithmic relationship that connects mental with physical age; and (iii) the ultimate arrest of mental growth in mid-adolescence has absurd results, as already indicated, in the calculation of adult I Qs. Wechsler concludes that such I Qs are not I Qs at all.

Wechsler proposed to overcome these difficulties by expressing raw scores in terms of standard deviation units. For historical reasons the mean was set at 100. He used the Probable Error (0·6745 times the standard deviation) and defined I Q 90 as one P E below the mean (the P E was chosen as the appropriate unit because plus and minus one P E from the mean embraces 50 per cent of the general population, taken to represent the average person). I Q 90 is normally regarded as the lower limit of average ability, and from this zero point the calculation of all other I Qs becomes a matter of simple arithmetic; having obtained the mean and standard deviation of the distribution, a table of 'z-scores' is prepared, and for each actual score simple substitution gives a corresponding I Q.

Wechsler considers that this method has the advantages of (1) dispensing with all assumptions about the precise relations between intellectual and chronological ratings at birth; (2) relieving us of the need for committing ourselves to any fixed adult mental age; (3) enabling us to calculate IQs with the same meaning at all other ages; and (4) retaining the original and only important meaning of the IQ as an index of relative brightness.

While Wechsler's method has a decisive advantage over earlier ones, it is only fair to point out that his IQs, to use his own words referring to the work of others, 'are not IQs at all'. As Mursell (1949) indicates, the method is really a variant of standard deviation scoring.

2. *Standard deviation scores and standard scores*

Standard deviation scores are obtained by dividing the difference between the test score and the mean of the distribution by the standard deviation. Thus, if a person's IQ is 90 on a test, with a mean of 100 and a standard deviation of 15 points, the equation becomes $\frac{90-100}{15} = -0.67$. Such a method is very useful in comparing the subject's status on tests with differing standard deviations (see p. 13), since it gives a common unit of measurement independent of differing test distributions.

Standard scores eliminate decimal points and minus signs. The mean is arbitrarily set at 50 and the standard deviation given the value of 10 points. The formula $\frac{(X-M)10}{\sigma} + 50$ is used for calculating standard scores; thus the example quoted above would yield a standard score of 43.

The particular advantage of standard scores, apart from the fact that they give a common unit for test results, is that the units are equal throughout their range of 20–80. Hence they can be added or subtracted without any resulting distortion due to inequality of the scale.

It will be appreciated that although, following Greene (1941), a distinction has been made between standard deviation and standard scores, these are in fact variants of the same procedure and indeed are sometimes both given the same generic name, 'standard' or 'z-score'.

Percentiles

The use of percentiles as units into which raw scores can be transformed has been quite popular. This method has the advantage of being particularly easily understood; thus someone scoring on the 40th percentile achieves a position higher than the lowest 39 per cent of the population, and lower than the top 60 per cent. There are, however, considerable disadvantages. Owing to the bunching of scores in the middle of the distributions, the scale is not one of equal steps. Thus at the two extremes of a distribution, a difference of, say, five percentiles is far greater than a similar amount at the centre. Therefore it is not legitimate to add and subtract percentile scores for a person from a number of tests.

SUMMARY OF SECTIONS I–IV.

Provided intelligence tests are properly standardized and carefully administered, they provide an objective and valid measure of a person's present intellectual status. This is achieved by comparing the individual score with the relevant norms for the particular age group of the general population. All activities of a cognitive nature correlate together positively, and a good intelligence test will represent an effective and valid sample of such processes, and will correlate well with those activities in life which are commonly recognized as depending on intelligence.

For prediction of future status, intelligence tests are less reliable (although still valuable) not so much because of unreliability of the *test* but because within limits people alter in relative standing. During childhood and adolescence, mental (like physical) growth does not proceed at a uniform rate and the individual's position with respect to others in his age group thus tends to vary from year to year, this being reflected in changes in IQ. Granted normal and relatively unchanging material and cultural opportunities, however, the IQ tends to be constant within broad limits (e.g. while under normal conditions a change in IQ in a child from 80 to 140 would be exceedingly unlikely to occur, a change from 80 to 95, or 118 to 110, would be a not uncommon finding after a period of several years from the first test). If, however, during childhood, a change occurs from or to an environment *markedly* inferior to the population average, then there is likely to be considerably greater variation in intellectual status during an individual life-span, and the same may of course occur to victims of diseases of the nervous system.

V. GENETIC AND ENVIRONMENTAL STUDIES OF INTELLIGENCE[1]

1. *Introduction*

In the previous section the strengths and weaknesses of intelligence testing have been outlined; we now turn to the age-old problem of the effects of nature and nurture upon intelligence. The literature on this subject is immense and to review it fully would require a separate book; the present contribution will therefore present a selection of the most relevant investigations, but the references given should enable the interested reader to obtain most of the basic material. It is proposed to consider (*a*) the rationale and (*b*) the peculiar difficulties of each main method of investigation before discussion of results. In addition, it should be borne in mind that general statements about the relative importance of heredity and environment may be, like all averages, misleading when applied to an individual case or group. Thus, the intellectual condition of a person suffering from phenylketonuria is likely to be due entirely to hereditary factors; on the other hand, a person brought up in an exceptionally bad social environment may be impaired largely because of his adverse experiences. We need, therefore, always to inquire about the specific genetic and cultural factors which might be operative in any particular sample studied, and to be cautious of generalizing the findings to other and different populations. It is probable that lack of caution in this respect has been at least partly responsible for apparently contradictory findings by investigators of this field.

The word environmental needs definition for the purposes of this chapter. It is perfectly correct to regard brain damage due to trauma or resulting from the effects of maternal rubella in early pregnancy as environmental in origin, and there is seldom any controversy over these or allied conditions. The present section, however, will be concerned only with the rather less obvious and much more controversial effects

---

[1] Much of the emphasis in this section concerns mildly subnormal persons; this is legitimate in a general text for two interacting reasons. First, most of the better-controlled studies in this field have been carried out on this type of population, and second, it is commonly agreed that with certain forms of subnormality, environmental effects are 'writ large'.

of social environments; thus in this section, environmental is used as a synonym for cultural.

In the past the problems to be outlined here have been the subject of heated and often bitter controversy, but the dust raised by the protagonists of nature or nurture served largely to obscure the issues. It is apparent that extremists on both sides overstated their case; the geneticists believed that heredity was the only potent factor while the environmentalists postulated a naïve and mechanical behaviourism. It is significant that in the past a section such as this might have been headed 'Nature *versus* Nurture', with the implication that only one of these was relevant; nowadays it is better realized that nature and nurture reciprocally interact and cannot be conceived of apart. This remains, however, a central issue in psychology for both theoretical and practical reasons and is obviously of particular relevance to the causation and treatment of mild subnormality and deprivation. It is to be hoped that, with passions cooling a little, the way is now clear for the undertaking of crucial experiments which will help to settle the many outstanding problems.

The data to be presented mainly concern the mentally deficient of high grade but in each context one or more researches will be mentioned in which normal persons have been involved.

2. *Studies of Families*

Rationale. This is the oldest method of investigating the genetics of intelligence, having been employed by Galton and Goddard. The assumption was that if certain qualities such as genius or mental deficiency appeared in a given family generation after generation, then that quality must be inherited.

Difficulties. The study of families is the classic method in animal genetics where breeding is rapid, life-span short, and where the environment can be rigidly controlled. In man, however, the converse is true; thus investigations have to be retrospective, and material relating to persons more than a generation or two in the past tends to be fragmentary, anecdotal, and hence of low reliability. The second problem is the difficulty of separating out the relative effects of heredity and environment. Thus while it is true that some families have been distinguished and powerful for many generations, it is difficult to establish how far this may have been due to native ability, or to the exceptional environment and privileged position provided by each generation for the next. On the other hand, it might be expected that if environmental factors were prepotent then among the monarchies a high rate of outstanding intellect would be found, and this is manifestly incorrect. In summary, the difficulties presented by this method of investigation render the material thus gained of no more than general interest, and interpretation of it far from crucial.

It is common knowledge that in England such families as the Cecils, Wedgwoods, Darwins and Galtons, have produced an unusually high proportion of persons of outstanding ability for many generations. The best known study of the mentally deficient was carried out by Goddard (1912), who described in detail the two families stemming from the same father, Martin Kallikak. This man joined one of the many military companies that were formed at the time of the American Revolution, and while on service formed an association with a feeble-minded girl whom he had met in a tavern. He had an illegitimate son by this girl who gave the child his father's name in full. At the time of the study, there were 480 descendants, of whom 143 were known to have been feeble-minded, while only 46 were considered normal. The rest were unknown or their status doubtful. These persons married others of similar type and Goddard had on record 1,146 individuals: 'of this large group we have discovered that two hundred and sixty-two were feeble-minded, while one hundred and ninety-seven are considered normal, the remaining five hundred and eighty-one being still undetermined . . .'

The first Martin Kallikak provided for posterity a control group by marrying later a respectable girl of good family by whom he had further children. At the time of the investigation these numbered 496 in direct descent, none of whom were mentally deficient, although three were said to be 'somewhat degenerate'. In general, these descendants had a superior social and economic status, married into the best families in their state, produced a larger number of professional people, 'in short, respectable citizens, men and women prominent in every phase of social life'.

The record of the Juke family described by Dugdale (1910) through five generations, has been used to show familial incidence of criminality, destitution and mental subnormality. The original finding was that of 709 descendants of one morbid couple, a small proportion were socially competent, while the vast majority were in the criminal and social problem group.

As already stated, the main difficulty in studying such families as these is that the basic data are of unknown validity, and that genetic and environmental factors cannot be assessed separately. Thus, little is really known about the girl who gave birth to Kallikak's illegitimate son; if she was feeble-minded it would have been important to know something about the cause of her condition but in retrospective research this was clearly impossible. Further, the state of squalor in which she lived, together with her own mental subnormality, regardless of genetics, would seem likely to have had a profoundly adverse effect upon her son, and as is well known, a vicious circle is often initiated in such circumstances.

For genetic research, the study of family histories is, of course, essential and much more fruitful where conditions are involved which sharply distinguish affected from unaffected persons (e.g. defect due to the action of recessive genes). Penrose (1949) gives an excellent account of such investigations.

3. *Studies of Twins*

Rationale. Identical twins result from the splitting of one fertilized ovum, and therefore possess identical heredity; fraternal twins, on the other hand, arise from two ova, separately fertilized, and, in terms of probability, their hereditary similarity need be no greater than for ordinary siblings. Thus comparison of identical with fraternal twins, and with siblings, may be expected to yield information on both genetic and environmental influences. Particularly valuable information may be expected to emerge from a study of identical twins brought up together, and similar pairs reared apart, especially if in the latter case environmental differences have been great and separation from an early age. This method of study in human genetics can theoretically be regarded as crucial.

Difficulties. Unfortunately several practical difficulties have so far limited the usefulness of the theoretically best method for evaluating the contribution of nature and nurture (and their interaction) to the development of intelligence; they are summarized as follows:

(1) The differentiation of identical from fraternal twins is not perhaps as straightforward as it might seem, and if not checked at birth by examination of the placenta is often a matter of inference some years later. Identical twins must of course be of like sex and are commonly physically very similar; fingerprints, iris pigmentation, presence or absence of mid-digital hair, scapular shape, and a number of other

factors are commonly used for establishing identity (cf. Eysenck, 1952).

(2) There is reason to believe that the environment, both pre- and post-natal, of identical twins is more similar for each pair than for fraternals, and for fraternals more similar than for siblings. Thus identical heredity may be accompanied by a more nearly identical environment than is found in children reared together. (On the other hand, however, it is known that multiple births are more hazardous than single-births, and not infrequently one twin may be injured or even still-born.)

(3) So far as the crucial study of identical twins reared apart is concerned, very few such pairs have been discovered and studied and of these even fewer were found to have been reared in widely differing socio-cultural conditions. Thus, with heredity 'held constant', the variable 'environment' has not been fully accessible. For full information on the effects of environment on intelligence, a group of about 30 pairs of identical twins would be needed, one half of which were brought up in adverse circumstances and the other half in the best and most stimulating environment.

The correlation between the IQs of randomly selected pairs of un-related children is zero; of cousins about 0·25; of siblings brought up together about 0·5; of fraternal twins reared together about 0·7; of identicals reared together 0·9. This progressive increase of correlation associated with a progressively closer genetic relationship, has been interpreted as indicating that heredity plays the dominant part in determining intelligence. (It must be remembered that a correlation of 0·9 between two sets of persons is as high as can be gained by retesting the same set of persons on two occasions separated by a short time-interval and using the same test.) That such an interpretation is at least over-simplified is obvious for two main reasons; firstly, if environment had little relevance one would expect that correlations between fraternal twins and between siblings would be similar and about 0·5, because both fraternals and untwinned siblings arise as separate fertilized ova. The discrepancy between 0·7 and 0·5 provides a rough measure of environmental difference in groups which usually have fairly similar conditions of upbringing, and it is by no means negligible. Using the technique of squaring the correlation coefficient as a rough measure of 'the contribution of one variance to the other', we can estimate the environmental effect at about 24 per cent. Adding to this an error variance of at least 19 per cent, the remaining variance, namely 57 per cent, could be ascribed to heredity, a figure rather similar to that proposed by Penrose

(1949) on rather different grounds. And it has already been stressed that heredity will be seen as important in the case of subjects whose environmental experiences are fairly similar. Thus it could be argued that such an estimate would reflect a maximal influence of genetical factors, and that where conditions were less uniform then environmental factors would increase in importance. Moreover, compared with normals, the high-grade mentally deficient come in the main from markedly inferior conditions and it might therefore be assumed that such factors would play a considerable part in the aetiology of intellectual defect.

There are no general studies of mentally deficient twins, although a number of interesting investigations of pathological defect occurring in one or both of a given twin pair can be found in the literature. A most important study of normal twins is that reported by Newman, Freeman and Holzinger (1937), whose sample included 50 pairs of fraternals, 50 pairs of identicals, and 19 pairs of identical twins reared apart. These latter had been separated in most cases at a very early age and for a long period of time and they were studied in adult life.

The Binet IQ correlations for the three groups were as follows: identicals, 0·910, fraternals, 0·640, and separated identicals 0·670. The mean IQ difference for the latter was 8·2 with a range from 0 to 24 points. In a highly critical review, McNemar (1938) suggests that the correlations should be corrected for age and range when they become 0·888, 0·631, and 0·767, respectively. He goes on to challenge the statement of Newman *et al.* that 'the correlation for the separated cases are ... much lower than the corresponding values for unseparated identical twins'. After such correction, McNemar believes that it cannot be claimed that there is a significant difference between the resemblances of unseparated and separated twins. There follows a highly technical argument which in Holzinger's (1938) view was without much point, but he does admit to some minor errors and to some 'clumsiness' in analysis. Such criticism, however, did not in general show the study of Newman *et al.* to be vulnerable. McNemar's cautious conclusion is nevertheless worth quoting:

> It appears that the only evidence which approaches decisiveness is that for separated twins, and this rests ultimately upon the fact that four pairs reared in really different environments were undoubtedly different in intelligence. This fact can neither be ignored by the naturite nor deemed crucial by the nurturite.

An examination of these 19 pairs of identical twins reared apart shows, as Thorpe (1946) points out, that the significant differences between them were always in the same direction as differences in educational opportunity. Marked differences in mental ability, as indeed McNemar conceded, were in every case associated with similarly marked differences in educational and other opportunity. Thus, although it is obvious that this study has controversial features which make interpretation also equivocal, it appears that environment can have a marked effect upon development. To illustrate these points, a brief account of two twin pairs reared apart can be given. Twins A and O, studied by Newman (1929), were separated at the age of 18 months, one being brought up in a crowded middle-class part of London during the First World War, with an interrupted elementary education. The other was brought up in an adoptive home by a socially superior family in Canada; she received an uninterrupted academic education. In the end, both became secretaries, having had nine years of schooling, but O scored 12 points higher on the Stanford–Binet than her twin who had been brought up in London. Another pair, studied by Newman *et al.* (1937), differed in educational and cultural opportunities, one never getting beyond elementary school due to frequent moves on the part of her family, while the other, though reared in a modest home, completed a college education. The former became a saleswoman and later an office worker, while the latter became a teacher of history and English. They were studied at the age of 35, when the social and intellectual superiority (24 IQ points) of the twin who had had the better opportunities was apparent. These environmental differences are the most marked occurring in the cases studied by Newman and his colleagues; but it is apparent that even within Western cultures much wider social and cultural differences exist; for example, the difference between the environment of a child in a 'breakdown' family in a London slum in contrast to the opportunities of a child with professional parents is much greater than in the cases studied by Newman. It would be assumed, therefore, that environmental influences would be more potent if twins were separated into vastly different homes such as these.

This same point, as the author indicates, applies to the much more ambitious investigation recently reported by Shields (1962). Forty-four pairs of monozygotic separated twins were studied on physical measures, intelligence, extraversion, neuroticism and other factors. A control group of non-separated monozygotic twins was also used. The separated twins showed very close resemblance on many measures; on a combined intelligence score, for example, the correlations for non-separated and separated identical twins were + 0·76 and + 0·77 respectively. These correlations were substantially higher than those for dizygotic twins reared together, and certainly point to the strong influence of genetic factors. Nevertheless, it seems probable that the influence of environment was masked by the cultural similarity of the homes in which the children lived. In two-thirds of the separated twin pairs, for example, one twin was brought up by relatives, and Shields notes that 'the degrees of social and cultural differences between the families . . . were as a rule not remarkable. . . .' Although this is an excellent and careful study, it cannot reveal the full role of environment although it certainly demonstrates the strength of hereditary forces.

Burt's (1966) study included 53 pairs of monozygotic twins reared apart. Only 10% were brought up with relatives and considerable differences in enviroment were claimed. Differences in attainment were related to these differences but there remained a very high correlation for intelligence which appeared to be independent of environment.

4. *Studies of Children in Foster Homes*

Rationale. If children are separated for any reason from their true parents, a comparison of their intellectual and social status (*a*) with their true parents, and (*b*) with their foster parents, should give an estimate of the relative parts played by heredity and environment. In their simplest form, the following propositions may be made: if heredity were prepotent, it would be expected that whatever the new environment of the foster home, the child would approximate to the true parental level. If, on the other hand, environment were prepotent one would expect the converse, namely that whatever the level of the parents, the child would approximate to the level of the foster parents, and further, the longer the time spent in the foster home, the closer this correlation would be.

Difficulties. There are certain drawbacks to this method which may be summarized as follows:

(1) Adoption and fostering of children usually take place when they are very young, and sometimes when they are new-born. Except for obvious and gross mental deficiency, it is impossible to predict future status from tests or clinical observation at this age. Such tests rely very

largely on measures of sensori-motor development which have little in common with later intelligence tests, and which intercorrelate rather poorly with themselves. Thus the basis (*a*) for equating groups, and (*b*) for follow-up study tends to be unsatisfactory.

(2) Selective placement of the potentially or actually brighter children in better homes, and duller in homes of lower status, has in fact be-devilled much of the experimental work in this field. Thus when later evaluations reveal the superiority of children in the better foster homes this could result from either their better genetic potential, or the better environment, or a combination of both.

(3) Once again, a full range of environmental possibilities is for obvious reasons not employed in the placement of homeless children, and the levels of foster homes are likely to be more homogeneous than for the general population.

As Jones (1954) points out, we are particularly in need of experi-mental placement, planned randomly, to overcome such factors, thus avoiding retrospective research which may often fail to reveal biases of this kind.

A pioneer study of Freeman, Holzinger, and Mitchell (1928) contrasted mental test variations of children placed in superior foster homes with those shown by children in more average homes. Those in the former gained 10 points in IQ on the average over about four years, while the latter gained only 5 points. In general, the earlier the placement, the greater the gain. A study of correlations between foster children reared together and siblings reared apart also indicated environmental effects, and correlations between IQs of foster children and their foster parents increased from 0·34 to 0·52 over four years. This early study has been criticized on the usual grounds that the results may be due to selective placement, which undoubtedly must have occurred (note the initial correlation of 0·34 between children's and foster parents' IQ).

Burks (1928) studied the development of over 200 foster children, as well as a control group of over 100 children living with their own parents in similar socio-economic conditions. At the end of the study, foster children's IQ correlated to the extent of 0·42 with a combination of fathers' mental age, vocabulary, mother's vocabulary, and the family income. On the same variables the control children's IQs correlated to the extent of 0·61. Differential increments had occurred, favouring the control children, due in Burks' view to innate differences in ability, and she concluded that home environment contributes only about 17 per cent of the variance in IQ. The interpretations by Freeman *et al.* and Burks of somewhat similar findings are very different, and, according to Thorpe (1946), who reviews them excellently, this divergence is due to the strongly hereditarian outlook of Burks; Freeman, on the other hand, seems to appreciate the evidence for hereditary forces, but is willing to explore the influence of superior homes and educational facilities on the social and intellectual development of children. In his view, the results indicated the importance of such facilities, and of early placement. A detailed review of these and other general studies is to be found in Jones (1954).

Skeels and Harms (1948) have studied the mental development of children with inferior social histories who had been placed in adoptive homes. They pointed out that a research of this nature would be likely to have important implications almost whatever the results; thus, if children failed to benefit from placement in superior homes, then it would seem that selective placement would be desirable. If, however, data relating to social background and parentage have little predictive value, then the emphasis shifts to the quality of the foster homes. Their study concerned children selected on the basis of inferior social history and who were placed in adoptive homes in infancy or under 2 years of age.

There were three groups. Group I consisted of 107 children whose mothers had been classified as mentally retarded with IQs of 75 or less. All were committed to an orphanage at less than 6 months of age, and placed in adoptive homes when less than 2 years old. Approximately 80 per cent were illegitimate, and all but 20 had been tested at the close of the study. These 20 appeared to be not very different from the remainder, as judged on the basis of the histories of the true parents. In contrast to the homes of the true parents, the foster homes were selected in general for their adequate adjustment in the community; foster parents were regarded as intelligent, dependable and stable. The occupational level was higher than that of the true fathers, and was above that of the population as a whole. Mean age at the time of placement was 5·3 months (range: 8 days to 23 months), and two-thirds of the group were fostered under 6 months of age. The mean IQ of the 87 children at an average age of $5\frac{1}{2}$ was 105·5 with a standard deviation of 16·7, and a range of from 55 to 141. These results were in some cases gained on the Kuhlmann–Binet, in others on the 1916 Stanford–Binet, and in others on the 1937 Stanford–Binet. Children's intelligence showed a small but significant correlation with the intelligence of true mothers, the results on the Kuhlmann–Binet being largely responsible for the correlation of the whole group.

Group II was composed of children whose fathers had low occupational status; a reasonable inference was that on the average their intellectual level would also tend to be low. The mothers of these children seemed also likely to be in the lower ranges but this was. not so marked or uniform as in Group I. The foster homes for the children were markedly superior to those from which the children issued and somewhat superior to those in Group I. The children, 111 in number, were placed in foster homes at a mean age of 5 months, with a range from 8 days to 21 months. The average age at the time of assessment was a little over 5 years, and the mean IQ (Kuhlmann–Binet, 1916 Stanford–Binet, and 1937 Stanford–Binet) was 110, standard deviation of 15, and a range from 55 to 154. Where the IQs of both the child and the true mother were known (75 cases) the correlation between them was on the borderline of significance at the 5 per cent level. There was some evidence of selective placement when true mothers' IQ was considered in relation to occupational level of the foster home.

Group III was composed of 31 children whose mothers were known to have IQs below 75 and whose fathers were unskilled or slightly skilled labourers, hence very probably of low IQ. Occupationally the foster homes were markedly above that of the population from which such children were drawn, and slightly above the general population as a whole. The mean IQ of the true mothers was 62·6, standard deviation of 8·6, and a range from 40 to 75. All but seven of the true fathers were in the lowest occupational classification.

The children were tested at a mean age of 5 years 4 months, ranging from 1 year 1 month (a totally unreliable age for predictive assessment) to 10 years 6 months. On the same tests as previously the children averaged 104 with a standard deviation of nearly 16 points. Correlations with true mothers' IQ and with the educational level of the foster mothers were not significant. There was no evidence of selective placement in terms of true mother education in relation to foster mother education, nor between true mother IQ and foster mother education. But there was a tendency for children of duller mothers to be placed in homes which were occupationally lower; the difference (5·6 IQ points) did not, however, reach statistical significance.

These studies are of considerable interest and appear to be free from many of the weaknesses of some of the earlier work from the University of Iowa. At the very least they indicate that children from poor or adverse backgrounds tend to do better than might be expected if early in life they are given the advantage of average or above average foster homes. The genetic implications are, however, less clear. We do not know, for example, whether any of the true mothers may have been mentally deficient for 'organic' reasons (e.g. because of disease or injury); such persons are as likely as any to be genetically normal, and the same might be said for true fathers. The fact that some mothers were as low as I Q 40 is suggestive of organic factors in their cases. The authors, however, are careful not to draw any genetic conclusions, which would clearly be unwarranted so far as Groups I and II are concerned, and very doubtful in the case of Group III. Ideally, a study such as this should have a group of fathers and mothers of known low I Q, and in whom an organic aetiology had been excluded. Even this would be insufficient for genetic research if these persons had functioned well below their potential because of poor environmental conditions. In fact, genetic and environmental influences in groups such as these are almost inextricably mingled, but it is none the less important to show that children from such poor backgrounds at these ages appear to have a normal chance of superior, average or subnormal intelligence, because far too often an over-simplified genetical viewpoint has resulted in such persons being given no alternative to institutional upbringing, with all that this implies.

At the same time it should be recognized that a clear indication of the presence of forces other than environmental ones (presumably genetic) also emerges from the data, and the authors fail to draw the reader's attention to this. If environment alone were responsible for the status of the children we would expect only a small scatter of IQs in the moderately homogeneous foster homes in which they were placed. Yet we find a fairly normal distribution of ability with a considerable proportion below average while enjoying the advantages of above average environments. This study is important in demonstrating that people are not born equal nor do they respond or change uniformly when introduced to similar conditions.

Skodak and Skeels (1949) summarize their earlier studies (Skeels, 1938; Skodak, 1939; and Skodak and Skeels, 1945) on a group of foster children followed up from infancy until adolescence. While there exist a large number of cross-sectional studies of children in foster homes, repeated evaluations of the same children into adolescence or adulthood have been rare. Their earlier reports provoked intense

C

controversy (see McNemar, 1940; and Wellman, Skeels, and Skodak, 1940), but in this final paper the authors feel that the intensity of such discussion had dissipated in the previous decade as evidence accrued showing that modifiability of intelligence was not an unusual phenomenon.

The foster homes in these studies were above the average of their community in economic security and in educational and cultural status. The primary factors in the matching of the infants to prospective homes were, owing to meagreness of information about the child's family background, the stipulations of the foster parents regarding religion, sex and hair colour, in that order. This method of placement of children from relatively inferior socio-economic backgrounds into substantial homes thus provided the setting for these studies, and, as the authors say, it did not seem possible that children with such meagre potentials, as predicted from the intellectual, academic and occupational attainments of the true parents, could measure up to the demands of cultured, educated foster parents.

Skodak and Skeels indicate that children committed to public agency care have parents whose general social, vocational and adjustment levels are substantially below that of children who become wards of private agencies or who are adopted through private channels. The criteria used for inclusion of children in these studies were (*a*) the child was placed in an adoptive home under the age of 6 months; (*b*) the child had been given an intelligence test prior to November 1936, and after one year's residence in the adoptive home; (*c*) some information, though of variable amount and reliability, existed concerning the natural and adoptive parents; (*d*) the child was white, and of north European background. This group was representative of the available children, because there was no systematic withholding of children because of poor histories, nor was there a group excluded because of low intelligence test scores.

In the first follow-up report (Skodak, 1939), out of a total of 180 children it was possible to retest 152 during 1937–38. On the third examination (Skodak and Skeels, 1945) 139 children were reassessed. The fourth and final visit in 1946 resulted in the present sample of 100. It was concluded that this final group was representative of the original total group.

Table 1 shows the main results, and it will be noted that the mean IQ for this group had remained above average throughout early childhood, school age and into adolescence. The Kuhlmann–Binet was used for all children under 3 years, and at later ages the 1916 Stanford–Binet. At the time of final examination, the 1937 Stanford–Binet was also given.

TABLE 1. *Longitudinal data on 100 adopted children*
(after Skodak and Skeels, 1949)

Test	Age	Mean IQ	SD	Range
I	2 yrs. 2 mo.	117	13·6	80–154
II	4 yrs. 3 mo.	112	13·8	85–149
III	7 yrs. 0 mo.	115	13·2	80–149
IV (1916)	13 yrs. 6 mo.	107	14·4	65–144
IV (1937)	13 yrs. 6 mo.	117	15·5	70–154

Rather wide fluctuations in IQ between tests were found throughout the entire period. The general trend was towards losses when the first infant test was taken as a standard for comparison. But by and large, such fluctuations tend to occur normally and the children did not greatly change their positions relative to the general population as a whole. Where marked changes did occur, there were related factors which could usually be identified in the individual case.

If a comparison was made of the occupational status of 73 of the true and the 100 foster fathers, it became apparent that not only were the foster fathers above the average of the population as a whole, but they were conspicuously above the mean for true fathers, who were well below the population mean. Thus the children of parents at one occupational extreme were placed in homes the occupational level of which was at the other. Similarly, the educational status of the true parents was significantly below that of the foster parents, and the mean of the whole population. There was no significant relationship at any period between foster parents' education and the foster children's IQs, but, of course, the range of both variables was somewhat limited. Intelligence test results were available for 63 true mothers, 59 of which were based on the 1916 Stanford–Binet, 1 on the Terman Group Test,

2 on Otis, and 1 on Wechsler–Bellevue. Tests were given by trained examiners under ordinary conditions, usually after the mother had decided to release the baby for adoption. The mean IQ of these true mothers was 85·7 points with a standard deviation of 15·8. The mean IQ of the children at the age of 13½ on the same test was 106 with a standard deviation of 15·1 points. This 20-point difference between the two means is highly significant and of considerable social consequence. It should be noted that there was no difference between the mean IQs of children whose mothers had been examined and those whose mothers' IQs were unknown.

Some of the most controversial data emerge from the correlations between true mother and child IQs at different stages in the child's development. Thus, at test I, the relationship was zero; at test II, the correlation was 0·28; at test III, 0·35; at test IV (1916), 0·38; at test IV (1937), 0·44. It appeared, therefore, that test scores during the first two years of life bore no relationship to the scores of mothers, nor did they show a very high relationship to the children's own later scores (the correlation was 0·35). By 7 years of age a substantial correlation with true mothers' IQ was reached, which remained of the same magnitude in adolescence provided the 1916 Stanford–Binet was used with both children and mothers; it was further increased if the 1937 revision was used. The authors agree that many reasons can be advanced for the low correlations between infant and later measures, and state that there is considerable evidence for the belief that as a group these children received maximal stimulation in infancy with optimum security and affection following placement at an average of 3 months of age. The quality and amount of such stimulation seemed to have little relation to the foster family's educational and cultural status. Available data such as occupational status and formal education are not in the authors' view sufficiently sensitive to be useful in measuring these less tangible differences in child-rearing practices, an attitude also advanced most cogently in the more recent monograph by Wittenborn (1956). The correlational findings can be interpreted in two ways; if the genetic interpretation is favoured, then the mother's mental level at the time of her examination is considered to reflect her fundamental genetic constitution and ignores the effects of whatever environmental deprivations or advantages may have influenced her own mental development. Thus it would be assumed that children of the brighter mothers would turn out to be brighter regardless of the type of foster home into which they were placed. The increasing correlation might support this view, since the occupational differences between foster parents are not large. Both biological regression to the mean, and the role of the unknown fathers, complicate the picture, however, even though the mean IQ of the children is so much higher than that of the true mothers. If, on the other hand, the environmental interpretation is favoured, then the question is raised whether the increasing correlation between true mother and child reflects the tendency to selective placement, with the influence of the foster home having a greater effect as the child grows older. In fact, it is clear that there was a small tendency towards selective placement, probably particularly prevalent at the extremes. The authors conclude, therefore, that the 'increasing correlation . . . cannot be attributed to genetic determinants alone'.

The relationship between the educational status of 92 of the true mothers and the children's IQ was also assessed; correlations were zero at test I, but thereafter varied between 0·31 and 0·37 during the four remaining tests. Jones (1954) quotes some interesting unpublished data by Honzik, in which she showed a close similarity between these correlations and those obtained on a sample of about 200 children living with their own parents. This similarity in Jones's view provides added evidence as to the relatively small weight of environmental factors in producing parent–child resemblances in the variables studied. On the other hand, selective placement may again complicate the issue, but the correlations between foster parent education and child IQ were approximately zero at all age levels.

It will be apparent that a longitudinal research of this nature, while in many ways superior to cross-sectional studies, leaves many questions unanswered or unclear. This is partly the result of it having been originally begun as a service project rather than as a planned research which might have overcome methodological defects and informational lacunae. The use of relatively crude indices is a further limiting factor, and there is little doubt that future work of this nature must study in far greater detail the dynamics of the foster home situation. Nevertheless, a relatively conservative general conclusion would be that these children on the whole showed a marked difference from their natural parents, particularly from their mothers. Once again, it is clear that the children show a very different picture from what might have been expected in view of their background; but the mechanisms at work in producing such a difference are somewhat unclear.

Wittenborn's (1956) monograph, is mentioned here because its results indicate a way in which some environmental effects, in spite of selective placement, can be measured. It also shows the need for a more intensive study of home conditions and child-rearing practices. Wittenborn pointed out that heredity can be suspected as 'a confronting third variable' in correlations between developmental criteria and environmental measurements when the particular aspect was usually considered to have an hereditary component (e.g. intelligence). Such correlations would be a likely effect of selective placement. Where, however, developmental aspects not considered to have an hereditary basis were shown to relate to conditions of child rearing in the foster home, there would be some reason to believe that these were not due to selective placement but emerged as a response to these particular practices. For example, it was shown in the younger sample of foster children that there was a correlation of 0·33 between phobic reactions and unsympathetic child-rearing practices (operationally defined). Such relationships were not particularly strong, and if, as the author and his collaborators suspect, many are an expression of the formative role of the environmental differences, they should not be taken as indications of the possible maximal importance of such differences; their importance may be much greater than indicated. It seems likely, they conclude, that inharmonious, incompatible and rejective adoptive parents may tend to produce children who are aggressive and fearful. Such findings as these help us little to answer questions concerning the relative importance of nature and nurture in producing *intellectual differences*, but do indicate a method of approach to the study of home conditions and foster parental attitudes which might be useful with the question of intelligence and overcome the crudity of earlier work.

5. *Studies of the Effects on Intelligence of Special Environments and of Environmental Change*

Rationale. This method either measures the intelligence of children before and after some major environmental change, or compares the level of functioning of individuals in special circumstances with those of similar age and type in the population as a whole. The assumption is that if cultural differences affect intellectual development, then poor environments will on the whole produce lower test scores than good environments; and further, that removal from one cultural milieu into a very different one will produce increments or decrements in IQ according to the nature of the environmental change.

Difficulties. One of the main difficulties of this method is the establishment of proper experimental controls. Bias may result from equating groups at early ages before mental tests give reliable prognostic estimates; from various selection factors, and from failure to take into account normal variability and maturation. Other shortcomings of this technique will be mentioned in the text in connexion with individual researches.

Probably the most satisfactory study of the effects of special environments on normals is that by Husén (1951) quoted by Vernon (1955a and 1955b). Husén showed that adults who obtain full secondary and university education have a 12-point increment on the average over others of the same initial IQ who left school at the age of 15. Similarly, Vernon's demonstration that there is a differential decline in mental test performance such that those in non-intellectual jobs decline more rapidly than those in intellectual work is another indicator of environmental effects. Moreover, Honzik *et al.* (1948) considered that children whose mental test scores showed the most marked fluctuations had life histories which showed unusual variations with respect to disturbing and stabilizing factors. Nevertheless, there were other children whose scores remained constant despite highly disturbing experiences.

An interesting study by Skeels and Dye (1939) investigated the effects of differential stimulation on mentally retarded children. The initial observation was accidental. Two children under 18 months old, in residence at a state orphanage, gave unmistakable evidence of marked mental retardation. Kuhlmann–Binet intelligence tests were given to both, the results on one (at 13 months) being IQ 46, and on the second (aged 16 months) IQ 35. Qualitative and behavioural assessments supported these results. There was no indication of organic defects.

These two children were recommended for transfer to a state school for the mentally deficient but the prognosis was at the time regarded as poor. After transfer, they were placed in a ward of older girls whose ages ranged from 18 to 50 years and in mental age from 5 to 9 years. Six months later the psychologist visiting the wards of this institution was surprised to notice the apparently remarkable development of these children. They were accordingly re-examined on the same test as before, this time gaining IQs of 77 and 87 respectively. A year later their IQs had risen to 100 and 88. At the age of about $3\frac{1}{2}$ the two children's scores were 95 and 93.

The hypothesis to explain these results was that the ward attendants had taken a particular fancy to these two babies who were the only pre-school children in their care. They were given outings and special play materials. Similarly, the older and brighter inmates of the ward were particularly attached to the children and would play with them during most of their waking hours; for these two it was clearly a stimulating environment. It was considered that a further change would be desirable if the intellectual alteration was to be maintained, and accordingly they were placed in rather average adoptive homes at the age of $3\frac{1}{2}$. After about fifteen months in these homes re-examination, this time with the Stanford–Binet, resulted in IQs of 94 and 93 respectively. These unexpected findings raised a number of important questions. Observation suggested that similar children left in an orphanage nursery made no such gains in the rate of mental growth. Adult contacts were at a minimum and limited largely to physical care. Adoptive placement was clearly inappropriate, owing to the lack of certainty that progress would occur. The most reasonable solution would seem to lie in a repetition of the 'accidental experiment' but this time in a planned and controlled manner. Thus research was started involving an experimental group of 13 children whose ages ranged from 7 to 30 months, and Kuhlmann–Binet IQs from 35 to 89. Mean age at the time of transfer to the state school was 19 months and mean IQ was 64. Once again, clinical observation supported the IQ classification; for example, a 7-month-old child in the group could scarcely hold his head up without support, while another at 30 months could not stand alone and required support while sitting in a chair. After the close of the experimental period it was decided to study a control group of children remaining in the orphanage. This group consisted of 12 children, whose ages ranged from 11 to 21 months, and IQs from 50 to 103. Mean age at the time of the first test was 16 months, with a mean IQ of 86. No marked differences in the birth histories of the two groups were observed, nor in their medical histories. Family histories indicated that the majority came from homes of low socio-economic levels with parents of low intellect, and there were no important differences between them.

The members of the experimental group in general repeated the experiences of the first two children and also attended the school kindergarten just as soon as they could walk. In the case of almost every child, some adult, either older girl or attendant, would become particularly attached to him or her and would figuratively 'adopt' him. This probably constituted an important aspect of the change. Members of the control group, however, had environments rather typical of the average orphanage. The outstanding feature was the profound lack of mental stimulation or experiences usually associated with the life of the young child in an ordinary home. Up to the age of 2 years, the children were in the nursery of the hospital. They had good physical care but little beyond this; few play materials were available and they were seldom out of the nursery room except for short walks or periods of exercise. At the age of 2, they graduated to cottages where overcrowding was characteristic. Thirty to thirty-six children of the same sex under 6 years of age were under the care of one matron and three or four untrained and reluctant teenage girls. The matron's duties were so arduous that a necessary regimentation of the children resulted. No child had any personal property. The contrast between these two environments is obvious (cf. Bowlby, 1951).

During the course of the experiment the average increase in IQ of the experimental group was 27·5 points, the final IQs at the conclusion having a mean of 91·8. The difference was highly significant, the 't' value being 6·3. Gains ranged from 7 to 58 points; three made increments of 45 points or more, and all but two increased by more than 15 points. The length of the experimental period depended in an individual case upon the child's progress, varying from 5·7 months to 52·1, with a mean of 18·9 months.

The development of the children in the control group was almost precisely the opposite from those in the experimental group. The average IQ at the beginning was 86·7 and at the end was 60·5, an average loss of 26·2 points. The 't' value of 6·1 showed the clear significance of the findings. Apart from one child who gained 2 points, all showed losses varying from 8 to 45 points. Ten of the twelve children lost 15 or more points. The average length of the experimental period was 30·7 months.

Table 2 summarizes the main findings, and the implications are, on the face of it, clear. Children brought up in psychologically poor environments show relative deterioration, while those brought up in environments more nearly similar to the normal will advance to varying extents, and both types will faithfully tend to follow in the direction of the environmental shift. The writers tell us that subsequent to this and other experiments, orphanage conditions have been considerably improved.

There are several criticisms which must nevertheless be made of this study. First, the testing of the infants in both groups was done at ages when these are anyway unreliable from a long-term point of view;

thus their level at the commencement would normally give little clue about subsequent development, although admittedly gross developmental anomalies (particularly motor) seemed to have been present. Second, the groups were by no means matched even for IQ. The experimental group had a lower mean initial IQ than the control; this raises the possibility of unknown selection factors. The experimental periods for both groups was markedly different; the experimental group had a shorter time on the average in better conditions, while the control group had a longer period under extremely poor conditions (30 months versus 18 months). A straightforward comparison of the effects of the two environments cannot therefore legitimately be made. Third, the inclusion of a control group was apparently an afterthought at the conclusion of the main experiment. Clearly, proper planning would have involved a control group from the outset. In a sense there

TABLE 2. *Mental test results, mainly Kuhlmann–Binet*

| | Experimental group | | Control group | |
	Before transfer	*After transfer*	*First test*	*Last test*
Mean	64·3	91·8	86·7	60·5
SD	16·4	11·5	14·3	9·7
N	13	13	12	12

was some sort of control, although it was not as efficient as it could have been; it is of interest that in both groups the initial IQs at these early ages gave little prediction of a relatively short-term outcome. The fourth point is that although members of both groups had apparently the same early experiences in the orphanage, they were not identically impaired at the commencement of the experiment. Thus, the initial differences between them were clearly due to factors other than environmental ones in infancy. Later, however, environmental factors apparently reversed the relationship. This must mean that unknown selection factors were operating, although, in fairness, it must be added that the initial superiority of the control group should have aided rather than penalized it. This, then, is an extremely interesting study, which however, is not free from criticism. The results are strongly suggestive, and more recent work seems to have supported the findings. In addition, Skeels and Skodak have recently completed a follow-up of the two groups first studied in the late 1930s. It has been shown that the marked disparity between them has been maintained in adult life (Skeels, 1966). and the publication of this challenging research is awaited with interest.

The work reported by Bernardine Schmidt (1946) is probably the most controversial in the literature. She studied 322 children between the ages of 12 and 14 who had been placed because of low intelligence in special schools. Three such schools were experimental using intensive methods, while the remaining two were regarded as controls, in which the traditional approach to such children was maintained. The mean IQs of the experimental groups ranged between 49 (SD 10) and 56 (SD 10), while the two control means were 61 (SD 2·3) and 63 (SD 2·1). The special programme for the first three groups was directed not only to assisting them while at school but at preparing them for community adjustment later. There were six specific goals: (1) development of desirable personal behaviour, (2) improvement of basic educational skills, (3) the development of the manipulative arts, (4) improvement in work and study habits, (5) learning of occupational and related vocational information, and (6) pre-employment experience. This programme lasted for three years, and every eighteen months the Stanford–Binet, Bernreuter Personality Inventory, and Vineland Social Maturity Scale were given, and there was a follow up for a period of five years after the end of the school programme. The control groups showed a slight decrease in average IQ after five years but the experimental groups made very large increments, from a mean of 52 to a mean of 89. Similar striking gains were reported in other spheres. Sarason (1949) wonders whether some of the controversy that has been raised by Schmidt's data is not due to differences in the various concepts of mental deficiency, pointing out that if incurability is regarded as a necessary criterion, then on that view these subjects were not mental defectives. However, this suggestion is overshadowed by Kirk's (1948) trenchant challenge which cast considerable doubt on the validity of the data. When investigating these findings, he was unable to gain access to the original data, and found discrepancies in the class records with the data published by Schmidt. He pointed out that the author did not explain how retarded semi-literate children could have been given the Bernreuter Personality Inventory, with its necessary high level of comprehension. Her reply (1948) can scarcely be considered impressive, and does not attempt to deal with each of Kirk's points one by one. There is thus some doubt about the whole study; nevertheless, as will be seen, several researches since then may indicate that some at least of her findings were correct, even if the interpretation she gave may not have been entirely so.

Two papers by Guertin (1949 and 1950) discuss the characteristics of 25 patients whom he regarded as pseudo-feeble-minded; that is, persons who had shown large increments of IQ and who had advanced towards intellectual normality. A control group of patients was selected on the basis of matched pairs, all relevant variables being held constant; this group increased in IQ by only 3·2 points (range of changes: −38 to +13). The experimental group, however, had altered from a mean of 59 points to a mean of 83 (range of changes +6 to +43 points) and these gains had occurred until nearly the age of 30. The subjects were of course selected on the basis of having made large increments, so were not typical of the general mentally deficient population with which Guertin was working; no doubt some of the increase was spurious because different tests were used at different times for the assessments.

Guertin indicated that it had yet to be demonstrated that there were true differences in cross-sectional clinical data between those who are truly feeble-minded (by which he meant permanently so) and those who show deferred maturation. Pre- and post-admission data were extracted from the case histories under twelve different headings (e.g. age of walking, adjustment while on parole, family background, etc.). Four professional and experienced persons were asked to judge which of each pair (experimental and control) was the more likely to have made large IQ changes. All judges scored better than chance (50 per cent), ranging from 64 per cent to 74 per cent correct. The most useful criteria for assessing the likelihood of later improvement appeared to be a history of inadequate home care, and the absence of a familial history of mental deficiency. Guertin pointed out that there were stable trends occurring in the longitudinal data, and that therefore these changes could not be due to errors of measurement. The best explanation, he believed, was that delayed maturation stemmed from environmental understimulation. Those who showed marked increases did so after the age of 16, and tended to come from less adequate home environments.

Clarke and Clarke (1954b) have described a study of cognitive changes in the feeble-minded which was undertaken as a result of observing that in a small group of high-grade patients there had occurred in some cases quite large changes in IQ, ranging from a decrease of five points to an increase of 25 points on the Wechsler–Bellevue Test, Form I, over a time interval of about 18 months. A control group was matched for initial IQ and age and retested after a short time-interval to find the maximal effects of test practice, errors of measurement, and underestimation at the time of the first test. It was found that the increases in the first group were significantly greater and could not be accounted for by these factors. It was further noted that several writers such as Burt (1947), McKay (1942), Roberts (1945), Spaulding (1946) and Guertin (1949) had noted such changes, and in some cases had suggested hypotheses to explain them. Seldom, however, were such hypotheses submitted to experimental verification.

In order to ascertain how often such changes were likely to occur a representative sample of 59 patients were retested with the same test, and Table 3 shows the main results.

TABLE 3. *Results of test and retest on Wechsler, Form I, for 59 patients retested after an average interval of 27 months*

	Original full scale IQ	Retest full scale IQ	Difference scores
Mean	66·2	72·7	6·5
SD	14·0	13·4	6·2
N	59	59	59

t (correlated means) = 8·074, significant beyond 0·1 per cent level
IQ range at original test: 35 to 98
IQ range at retest: 40 to 97
Age range at retest: 14 to 50 years,[1] mean 23·5, SD 8·1
Period between test and retest: mean 27 months, SD 6 months
Range of IQ changes: −7 to + 25 IQ points

Almost half these patients showed gains of 8 points or more, and it was obvious that for the majority of such persons the increments occurring over this relatively short interval did not represent the total change which the individual had already made or would make in the future. The picture presented by the data showed a considerable

[1] Only nine patients were over 30 years of age.

proportion of the certified feeble-minded advancing towards or into intellectual normality.

Several hypotheses were examined to explain the results; control group data disposed of the possibility of test practice or initial under-estimation due to nervousness affecting to any extent the data. There was a small but significant tendency for those of lower IQ to make the larger changes ($r = -0.311$), but no other relevant relationships emerged except for one. This final hypothesis was that those whose history included early adverse environmental circumstances would be those who made the larger increases. Twelve criteria such as 'neglect', 'N.S.P.C.C. intervention', 'cruelty', etc., were formulated, and an independent investigator, who knew neither the patients nor their test scores, applied them to the 59 case histories, separating them into two groups, those from very bad homes and the remainder (many of whom came from fairly bad homes). The former showed a mean increment of 9·7, SD 6·3, and the latter a mean of 4·1, SD 4·9, very similar to control group data. Table 4 shows the distribution of these changes.

TABLE 4. *Distribution of IQ changes*

Change	Very bad homes	Remainder	Controls[1]
−7 to 0 IQ points	1/25 = 4%	8/34 = 24%	4/29 = 14%
+1 to +7 IQ points	6/25 = 24%	17/34 = 50%	19/29 = 65%
+8 IQ points or more	18/25 = 72%	9/34 = 26%	6/29 = 21%
+10 IQ points or more	12/25 = 48%	5/34 = 15%	1/29 = 3%
+15 IQ points or more	7/25 = 28%	0	0
+25 IQ points	1/25 = 4%	0	0

(The first three rows in each of the three groups are braced together; Controls braced to = 100%.)

[1] The control group consisted of patients retested after a time-interval averaging 3 months, in order to establish the maximal effects of test practice, errors of measurement, and underestimation.

The difference between the gains made by the two groups was significant at the 0·1 per cent level, and confirmed the hypothesis that a record of early adverse experiences was related to IQ improvement, often many years later. This suggests that such experiences tend to retard mental development for many years, after which the effects begin to fade, IQ increments thus occurring. It was concluded that the increments seemed to be more the effect of being removed from a very adverse environment rather than of entry into a relatively better one, since there was no correlation with length of institutionalization, nor with particular type of treatment and training. These changes were related to IQ variability in normals, being different only in three respects: first, they tended to be unidirectional; second, they were relatively large in relation to the fairly short time-interval; and third, they took place at ages when mental growth is normally assumed to have ceased. It was suggested that further research might show how such relatively spontaneous changes could be both accelerated and improved.

Marchand (1956) studied changes in psychometric test results in a group of patients who had had outside employment experience after institutional training; 123 patients were investigated and the interval between initial test and final retest averaged about 11 years. Before placement, their IQs ranged from 40 to 91, with a mean of 58·8, while the final range was from 36 to 99, with a mean of 68, the average rise being 9·2 IQ points. It was found that 88 per cent attained higher IQs after having had outside employment experiences, 50 per cent rising by from 1 to 9 points, and 38 per cent increasing by from 10 to 31 points. A control group of 20 patients who were of similar IQ range, but lower average (52·9), and whose members had not been in employment outside the institution over a period of about 9 years, showed a slight average decrease of 1·4 IQ points. It was considered that there had occurred consistent differences in the drives and attitudes of those who had shown significant IQ changes.

Marchand is at pains to point out that this was a retrospective study, using very loose criteria which cannot be considered as scientific research but merely as a survey suggesting possible future work. He does not consider that it has proven that outside employment for mental defectives has been the sole cause of general IQ rises, but does believe that when institutions offer enriching and satisfying experiences, one of which may be outside employment, the individual patient has a better chance of responding nearer to maximal functioning. Clearly there may well have been selection factors involved originally when the particular patients were chosen for outside placement, and a similar bias presumably operated in the fact that the members of the control group were not so chosen. A further difficulty is that apparently some of the tests were different, such that an initial assessment may have been on the Stanford–Binet and a final one on the Wechsler. This would in itself perhaps account for some of the variability. Further, we are not told whether the Stanford–Binet IQs for the younger patients were corrected for variability of standard deviation at different ages, where relevant, and this might again result in some spurious changes. Nevertheless, provided these results are looked at with some caution, as the author wishes, the study is suggestive and interesting.

Clarke, Clarke and Reiman (1958) have followed up the earlier

TABLE 5(*a*). *Test–retest data, Wechsler, Form I, over six years Group from very bad homes*

	1949 FS IQ	1952 FS IQ	1955 FS IQ	Diff. '49/'52	Diff. '52/'55	Diff. '49/'55
Mean	59·6 (66·4)	70·7 (76·1)	75·8	11·1 (9·7)	5·1	16·2
SD	9·7 (14·1)	11·4 (13·4)	10·3	4·2 (6·3)	5·0	6·1
N	9 (25)	9 (25)	9	9 (25)	9	9
t (1-tail test)				7·929 sig. 0·1% level	3·059 sig. 1% level	7·969 sig. 0·1% level

IQ range: 1949   47–72
        1952   58–86
        1955   64–91

Age at final retest: Mean 26·4, SD 5·5 yrs.
Period between first and final test: Mean 70·9 mos., SD 2·5 mos.
Range of IQ changes: +3 to +22 points. (10 points and above: 8/9 = 89 per cent; 15 points and above: 7/9 = 78 per cent.)

TABLE 5(*b*). *Group from less adverse homes*

	1949 FS IQ	1952 FS IQ	1955 FS IQ	Diff. '49/'52	Diff. '52/'55	Diff. '49/'55
Mean	62·3 (66·1)	66·8 (70·1)	72·5	4·5 (4·1)	5·7	10·2
SD	13·4 (14·1)	13·0 (13·1)	13·3	4·4 (4·9)	5·1	6·6
N	19 (34)	19 (34)	19	19 (34)	19	19
t (1-tail test)				4·460 sig. 0·1% level	4·872 sig. 0·1% level	6·737 sig. 0·1% level

IQ range: 1949   35–87
          1952   40–89
          1955   48–100

Age at final retest: Mean 27·9, SD 9·5 yrs.
Period between first and final test: Mean 74·2 mos., SD 5·3 mos.
Range of IQ changes: −2 to +21 IQ points. (10 points and above: 10/19 = 53 per cent; 15 points and above: 5/19 = 26 per cent.)

   t (between Group from very bad homes and Group from less adverse homes) = 2·403 (sig. above 2·5 per cent level, 1-tail test).

   The figures in brackets show the data for the original group of which the present subjects formed a part.

work of the first two authors, and have reported the results of three further studies of cognitive and social changes in the feeble-minded. Their first new study followed up those persons who were still available in 1955–56 from the 1954 research. Nine patients from the original group of 25 patients from very bad homes were still accessible, and 19 of the original 34 from not such bad homes were also accessible. A large proportion of the remaining 31 had been discharged, so that those who remained were likely to be the less satisfactory members of the samples; hence estimates of IQ change over nearly six years would probably be minimal for the whole of the original group. The differential availability of the members of the two groups is in itself of social note. The fact that relatively fewer of those from very bad homes were still available, once again underlined the better prognosis of those from the worst social conditions. Further, of the 9 from very bad homes, 8 were already working in the community whereas only 4 of the 19 from not such bad homes were so placed.

The previous Table 5 shows the main results.

It will be noted that the members of the very bad home group had increased by about 16 points over six years (significant at the 0·1 per cent level), while those from the less adverse homes had improved by about 10 points (significant at the 0·1 per cent level) over a similar period. Particularly the former group now showed a substantially different cognitive picture than originally, and the authors considered that the results confirmed the earlier study; those with the greater damage due to deprivation in early life made a greater recovery. It was unlikely that the IQ increments *caused* the better social adaptation noted earlier; rather the increase must be regarded as one facet of more or less total personality development, as Marchand (1956) suggested, which may well be associated with the same general causation.

The second study (1958) involved the retesting of those who remained from the high-grade patients admitted to the hospital about four years previously. The main question for investigation was whether IQ changes in this type of person were a function of time-interval between tests, as is sometimes implied for normals. The present time-interval was roughly double that of the 1954 research. Thirty-two of an original 60 were still available, and once again it appeared that these were the less satisfactory members of the original sample. An independent investigator, knowing neither the patients nor their test scores, applied the twelve criteria to the case notes, and once again divided the sample into two groups, those from the very bad homes, and those from the not such bad homes. Subsequently retesting was carried out by a psychologist who knew neither the patients nor their histories nor their earlier test scores. The mean increment of the very bad home group was 11·5 points, with a standard deviation of 6·3 points, while the increase of the remainder was an average of 7·2 points, with a standard deviation of 6·6 points. In the former, the increment over the doubled time-interval was not so very much larger than the one found in the 1954 research (11·6 versus 9·7). Clearly, therefore, increment is not a direct function of length of the period between test and retest for this group. This supports a subsidiary result of the first (1958) study, where it was found that such persons made their maximum change in the earlier period and thereafter changed more slowly. The group from the less adverse homes made an increment much more nearly double that of the similar group in the 1954 research (7·2 points versus 4·1), which again links with a finding in the first (1958) study that IQs on the average increased steadily throughout the six-year period for those patients whose early histories had been less adverse.

The third (1958) study was devoted to a special problem; the original (1954) research had suggested that IQ increments in this population resulted more as an effect of removal from adverse conditions rather than of entry into relatively better ones. It was important to determine whether a special environment would stimulate and accelerate IQ increments in this age range and population.

The subjects selected for the testing of this hypothesis were a group of 21 who had received intensive training followed by placement in industrial work in the community. This was in all cases expected to lead to discharge of these patients from care, and success rates of this and similar groups had already indicated the superiority of this over traditional methods of training and placement. Once again home conditions were independently assessed and followed by independent retesting. It was found that those from the worst homes had increased by 14 points on the average, while those from less adverse conditions had gained an average of 10 points. These were not very different from results of the second study (1958) over a similar time-interval and indicated only very small effects of the difference in environments. Thus, while early *negative* environmental influence had profoundly adverse effects, *positive* stimulation in adolescence or later exerted little influence upon the IQ. It seemed that entry into any non-adverse environment would allow intellectual damage to fade to varying extents.[1] Socially, however, these special conditions had resulted in profound changes in the subjects. Clarke and Clarke (1959) have further considered the implications of their studies, and summarized the results in graphical form as in fig. 1 below. They draw attention to the almost linear increase, over six years, in the proportion of persons in the groups

---

[1] These authors draw attention to some remarkably similar findings (Widdowson and McCance, 1954) in an entirely different field of deprivation. Following malnutrition, German war-time orphanage children showed increased physical growth rates, and difference in diets did not result in differential increases; rather the children grew equally well and more rapidly than normal on all diets.

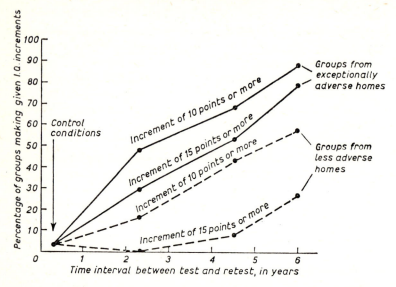

Fig. 1. Cognitive recovery from deprivation. This shows the increasing proportion of different but comparable groups of feeble-minded patients exhibiting increments in IQ of 10 and 15 points with increase in time-interval between test and retest. Increments of 20 points or more are not shown, but for the 6-year interval 33 per cent of the group from exceptionally adverse homes and 5 per cent of those from less adverse homes made gains of this order.

drawn from very bad homes, making given increments in IQ. Using comparable criteria and similar populations, the findings of the Clarkes have been independently confirmed by Roswell Harris (1959).

Mundy (1955) carried out both a pilot and main study of environmental influences upon the IQ. In the latter she used an experimental and control group, each consisting of 28 adult females certified as feeble-minded, and considered that the two were initially equated on a number of important variables, the only difference being that one had had employment experiences while the other had not. These groups were tested and then retested after two years, during which the controls remained in the institution, while members of the experimental group enjoyed normal life experiences, mostly in residential wage-earning employment. The Wechsler and Progressive Matrices tests were used, and on retest, the controls showed an average Wechsler increment of

2·25 points, and on the Matrices, 3·46 points. The experimental group, however, gained an average of 11 and 9·82 points respectively. Mundy believed that these results indicated that present environmental differences induced differential gains, but the validity of this conclusion clearly rests upon whether control and experimental groups were in fact initially equal in all respects. We are told, however, that there was no clinical selection by the hospital for outside employment, and that 'any able-bodied patient who wished for outside work was found suitable employment as soon as this was feasible'. This suggests that members of the experimental group had, through drive, ambition and initiative, asked for outside employment and hence gained it, while for several years at least the members of the control had been content to remain within a good institution; there was thus a difference between the groups in terms of 'self-selection'. It should be added, however, that in a personal communication the author has stated that some cases were originally transferred to employment for administrative reasons; this would reduce the amount of 'self-selection', but it might be an indication of selection by the hospital. A further reason for believing that the control group contained atypical patients was the extraordinary stability of their test scores over the two-year period; 25 out of the 28 remained within O and plus 4 IQ points of their original Wechsler result, and no patient increased by more than 6 points. This would imply a higher test–retest correlation than has been reported elsewhere in the literature. Because of these two factors, namely self-selection or selection in the experimental group, and very unusual IQ constancy in the control group, Mundy's conclusion is open to some doubt, and in view of the findings of Clarke, Clarke and Reiman (1958) on a similar population, it may well be that the IQ change would have occurred differentially in any reasonable environment. Where these two researches agree, however, is that early very adverse experiences played a part in retarding intellectual and general development.

Kirk (1958) has reported the results of a very carefully controlled experiment on the effects of pre-school education on the intellectual and social development of mentally retarded children. The investigation was designed to provide factual data for or against the general contention that special educational provision early in life could alter the children's rate of development.

Eighty-one defective children, aged between 3 and 6, were identified and studied for between three and five years. Twenty-eight formed the Community Experimental Group, attending a pre-school in the community and being followed up for between one and four years after leaving. Fifteen children were members of the Institution Experimental Group, attending an institution pre-school, and being followed up in the same way as in the first group. Twenty-six children constituted the Community Contrast Group and a further twelve, in a different institution from the second experimental group, constituted the Institution Contrast Group.

The IQs of the subjects ranged from 45 to 80. They were examined at the beginning of the experiment, during the pre-school period and again on follow-up after leaving the pre-school. The results were analysed both by case studies of the children in the experimental groups, and by the more conventional type of statistical comparisons. For the former, each child was placed in one of seven developmental levels, ranging from 'uneducable' to 'average'. It was found that 30 of the 43 children who had received pre-school stimulation showed an acceleration in growth rates during the experimental period and retained that level subsequently. They had raised their developmental classification from between one and three levels.

Analysis of test scores showed differential increase on the Binet, Kuhlmann and Vineland scales, all significant at less than the 0·05 level. On the Binet, for example, the range of IQ changes from the beginning to the end of the study for the Institution Experimental Group varied between a loss of 17 points and a gain of 33. The average increment was 10 points. For the Institution Contrast Group, however, there was an average decrement of 6½ points, with a range of from −19 to +10. The Community Experimental Group showed a total average Binet increment of nearly 12 points, while the Community Contrast Group showed a 7-point increment. The difference between the two Contrast Groups is interesting, and obviously has a bearing upon interpretation of the effects of some kinds of institutional upbringing. In brief, it was clear that pre-school education whether in the community or the institution had positive and, within the time limits of the study, lasting effects on intellectual and social development. Nevertheless, as Kirk indicates, group comparisons may well mask intra-group differences. It became apparent that it was much more difficult to displace the growth rates of those children with definite organic aetiologies. This finding is in accord with the Clarkes' work on IQ changes reported earlier. The results also suggested two further conclusions; first, that 'within limits the greater the changes that are made in the environment, the greater are the changes in the rate of

growth'; and second, that holding the home factor constant by studying
siblings from the same family one of whom did, and the other who did
not attend pre-school, it was clear that the pre-school had provided
compensation for inadequate home environment.

An unexpected finding by Kirk was that the Community Contrast
Group after a year in school showed an upward trend in IQs and
SQs, thus narrowing the gap between its members and those who
had had the advantage of pre-school stimulation. Kirk notes that 'this
could mean that pre-schools for mentally-handicapped children are not
necessary, since the children will accelerate their rate of development
after entering school at the usual age of six'. A further study of the
Community Contrast Group, however, suggested that children from
adequate homes tend to accelerate their growth rates during later
school experience, while those from inadequate homes did not. This
difference was, however, not significant statistically, no doubt partly
because of the small number (8 out of 26) in this group who came from
inadequate homes.

The general inference from the study, then, is that both pre-school
and early school education have beneficial intellectual and social
effects. Pre-school stimulation, however, seems to be particularly
important for those from inadequate homes. Kirk's investigation is
likely to prove a fruitful stimulus to later ones. It is one of the few in
the whole literature which cannot be criticized on methodological
grounds. It has thus shown, among other things, that the complex
problems studied can be brought under experimental control.

The work reviewed by Bowlby (1951) is too well known to need
summary; it is highly relevant to some of the findings already quoted
on the effects of early adverse environment in childhood which have
played some part in producing mental deficiency. His review is, however, almost entirely concerned with deprived children rather than with
adolescents or adults, a point which he notes with care. Bowlby is
pessimistic about the recovery of children from early psychological
damage, particularly if they do not receive full psychotherapy. Yet
some of the subjects in the researches quoted here could scarcely have
had worse early environmental influences, and many in adult life had
done better than might have been expected from either Bowlby's thesis
or the traditional viewpoint. Part of this greater success was naturally
due to improved economic conditions, but a substantial part also to
individual change. Yet few subjects received psychotherapy. Similarly,
some of the social studies of defectives from adverse conditions,

particularly the exemplary monograph by Charles (1953), have shown that they tend not to develop according to a rigid stereotype, and that many eventually function at a dull-normal or normal level. Two very important questions arise; first, to what extent is human resilience an important variable, and what in fact is it? Does it depend upon the basic resources of the nervous system, genetically determined, or upon early learning experiences or both; why is it that some children succumb while others do not; why are some utterly overwhelmed by such experiences while others emerge apparently unscathed? Second, is it possible that when other deprived children are studied in adolescence or later from Bowlby's point of view, it will be found that initial psychological damage, as in many high-grade defectives, tends steadily to be repaired? This is the view of Clarke and Clarke (1959) who have briefly reviewed the whole field of deprivation, concluding that to varying extents there exists a tendency towards spontaneous recovery from the effects of early adversity.

VI. THE MECHANISMS OF ENVIRONMENTAL INFLUENCE

All too little is understood about the mechanisms of environmental influence, although the correlates of subcultural deficiency have been well known since Burt's pioneer surveys. The conclusions then advanced were that poverty, bad housing conditions, and lack of stimulation were contributory but not prime causal agents. The main cause, writes Burt, was 'unquestionably heredity'.

There is no doubt that a proportion of those with IQs between 50 and 75 do in fact owe their condition almost entirely to genetic factors. With a correlation of only about 0·5 between parents and their children, it is to be expected that for parents with average IQs of, say, 90, some of their children will fall well below this figure and some well above. Nevertheless, from the recovery of many of the most deprived and neglected high-grade defectives, many of whom ultimately achieve borderline- or dull-normality in IQ, it seems reasonable to suppose that their condition is quite largely environmental in origin. That is to say, various factors combine to prevent the subcultural defective from reaching his genetic potential. In brief, then, we can identify three sub-populations which make up the group we know as high-grade or educable defectives; first, the genetic cases; second, the subcultural, who under the best child-raising conditions would seldom be average members of the population, but whose present condition is largely environmental in origin; and third, those with minor neurological or biochemical anomalies of development.

A brief summary may now be given of what is known of environmental agencies which prevent the development of intelligence to its full potential.

1. *Lack of childhood stimulation*

In its most extreme, and fortunately, very rare form, there is little doubt that social isolation can even cause low-grade deficiency. One of the two cases described by Davis (1947) of illegitimate children secreted in attics for the first five or six years of life, made a dramatic recovery from imbecility and speechlessness. This girl, reared by a deaf-mute mother in conditions of semi-darkness and silence, eventually attained intellectual normality after rescue from these conditions and special skilled treatment. One or two other cases of this type seem to owe their deficiency primarily to such isolation.

The damaging effects of bad institutions upon young children have already been mentioned. A number of careful studies have underlined the virtual impossibility of permanent attachments to adults (Rheingold, 1956, 1960) as well as the relative lack of adult contacts. While the popular insistence upon maternal–child interaction is probably partly a cultural value judgement, studies of kibbutzim children also emphasize the importance of *permanence* in adult–child relationships, as well as of generous staff–child ratios.

In the institution, the child's main learning model is other children rather than adults, and this would seem to be a potent reason for retardation of development. Kellmer Pringle and Tanner (1958), for example, showed that at the age of 4 years, a group of residential nursery children living in excellent material conditions were retarded in speech to the extent of 10 months, in comparison with a group of day nursery children of similar background, who lived in poor conditions with their mothers.

Large numbers of careful studies have revealed the correlates of low social and economic class (e.g. Douglas, 1964). These include poor material and often, though not invariably, poor psychological conditions. There can be little doubt that both have a direct effect in preventing children from reaching their full potential. Where the environment is actively adverse (e.g. cruelty or neglect) these effects are more profound in all areas of psychological development.

2. *Speech and cognitive development*

It is increasingly recognized that language is of immense importance in development. Until recently the view was held that for the young child speech had two functions; first, and obvious, the need to communicate and understand; and, second, the role of egocentric commentary, proposed by Piaget. Luria (1961), however, has revived interest in the relation between speech and thought. In a series of brilliant experiments with young pre-school children, he has shown that speech is also externalized thinking, essential to problem-solving. It is a means whereby behaviour is regulated and integrated. This being so, speech retardation due to environmental influence is likely to weaken the earlier stages of cognitive development And since each stage depends upon the integrity of previous stages, this situation tends to be perpetuated.

Approaching this problem from a new sociological angle, Bernstein has suggested the existence of two very different speech codes. The first, termed 'restricted', is to be found in the lower socio-economic groupings of the population. It is characterized by non-analytical, here-and-now statements, tends to be direct and concrete, using, for example, 'heavy-duty' verbs. In contrast, the middle and upper classes also possess an 'elaborated' speech code. This is analytical and explanatory, with many qualifications and precision of vocabulary. Bernstein gives evidence which underlines the penalty paid by children reared under public speech as compared with those with formal. He argues that education necessarily employs formal speech and concepts, so that it must more and more tend to become a foreign language for many working-class children.

In one experiment, for example, Bernstein (1960) compared a group of 61 working-class messenger boys with a group of 45 subjects matched for age and sex, drawn from one of Britain's well-known public schools. These two groups were given the Progressive Matrices, a non-verbal test, the difference between them averaging 8–10 IQ points. For Mill Hill vocabulary, however, the differences reflected 23–24 IQ points superiority by the non-working-class group. Later work (1962a and b) has revealed more clearly the nature of linguistic differences between social classes.

Large-scale social and psychological surveys also yield findings of relevance to the nature–nurture problem. The Scottish Survey of 1947, for example, confirmed the significance of the inverse relationship between family size and verbal intelligence, irrespective of social class. Nisbet's (1953) interpretation that, in effect, dilution of parental care in larger families is responsible seems far the most plausible explanation. Maxwell (1961) points out that although high scorers are to be found in all social categories, their respective proportions differ. Moreover, in the upper strata (where in general one assumes nature and nurture to be excellent) the proportion of low scorers is very small indeed.

Research upon concept formation and concept attainment (e.g. Furth, 1964) lends support to the view that the relationship between speech and intelligence is probably even more complex than is perhaps implied above. A useful start has, however, been made, and one can expect this field of investigation to prove rewarding.

VII. CONCLUSIONS

Let us attempt to outline some general conclusions which emerge from this review.

It may be assumed that heredity plays an essential part in determining the limits of intellectual development, but these limits are considerably wider than was formerly thought. With moderate uniformity of environment, individual differences result largely from genetic variations. The feeble-minded, however, more than any other group in western culture, have been reared in most adverse circumstances, followed in many cases by further lengthy periods in residential schools and institutions, with all that this implies. Thus the feeble-minded in such conditions seem likely to be functioning towards the lower end of their spectrum of potentialities, while normals under ordinary conditions of life approximate more closely to their upper limits. Thus it is worth while to consider in detail the data on this extreme group.

It is possible to assess in a cautious and conservative manner the extent to which the observed cognitive deficiency of institutionalized subnormal patients results from their conditions of nurture. This estimate can be made from the data on IQ increments among typical high-grade patients considered in detail earlier, and is based on the *assumption that the amount of measured recovery is equivalent to the degree of original psychological damage.* Such a procedure, is, however, likely to *underestimate* the effect of adverse nurture for three reasons:

(1) A very long follow-up would be needed to measure the total process of recovery, and this has only been carried out systematically

on social aspects of high-grade mental deficiency (Charles, 1953), with results, incidentally, consistent with those on IQ increments. Thus assessments based on a six-year period between test and retest in the decade and a half (age 15 to about 30) in which increments are most common, are likely to be minimal.

(2) It is possible that the range of potential development already referred to is itself narrowed by adverse experiences and there is indeed some evidence from other research that this may be so. Thus the amount of measured recovery (i.e. of increment) is again likely to underestimate the degree of intellectual damage induced by adverse nurture in this group.

(3) The data obtained in these researches were based on persons still available for retesting, and strong evidence existed that these were the less promising members of the original samples; thus, once more, minimal assessments are probable.

Nevertheless, bearing all these limitations and provisos in mind, and using measured recovery over six of the crucial years as the criterion, it is evident that the most adverse conditions, characterized by cruelty and neglect in childhood (representative of about 40 per cent of sub-normals in institutions), retard intellectual development by *at least* an average of 16 points (SD 6). Similarly, unsatisfactory social conditions, or life-long institutional upbringing but not involving such a severe degree of deprivation (characteristic of something like 40–50 per cent of subnormal parents), retard intellectual development by *at least* an average of 10 points (SD 6). It may well be, however, that the total effect is considerably greater and research will eventually establish more accurate figures. It is indeed likely that a much higher proportion of such persons will make large changes than occurs in the normal population.

It seems very probable that findings such as these represent one of the factors accounting for Penrose's (1949) demonstration that the incidence of high-grade mental deficiency declines markedly from the age of 15 onwards. Thus, from these two entirely different approaches, a similar picture emerges.

It is also evident that environmental deprivation does not operate in a rigid and mechanical way; a wide variation in individual suscepti-bility to psychological damage and resilience thereafter is maintained, and the individual outcome is immensely varied. What these factors of susceptibility and resilience are based upon is an obvious field for research.

The main conclusion is that for children or young adolescents, with IQs in the 50's, 60's, or 70's, a necessarily bad outcome cannot be predicted if they have also been reared in adverse conditions either in their own homes or in institutions. This clearly has implications both for theory and practice. These findings fit well the general thesis that, contrary to psychoanalytical theory, non-reinforced early experiences tend to have effects which in man usually fade or at least show a shift in severity as time increases (Clarke, 1968).

Finally, the methodological imperfections so characteristic of much research in this field are nowadays well understood; it is to be hoped, therefore, that future investigations will be planned in such a way as to avoid these weaknesses. The work and theories of Piaget, Hebb and Harlow seem likely to provide the impetus to new research upon the fundamental problems of human development.

If we consider the nature–nurture problem generally, it is already clear that reliable evidence is being accumulated. The search for precise formulae for the importance of either factor is being abandoned in favour of isolating particular effects of particular conditions. If it be true, as we have stated, that extreme social isolation can cause imbecility, or that crowded and inadequate institutions can cause gross motor retardation, among other things (Dennis and Najarian, 1957; Dennis, 1960) then it is obvious that nurture is all-important. It is equally obvious that nature falls into precisely the same category.

Put very simply, it is self-evident that concept formation must ultimately depend upon informational input from the environment. Where such input is lacking, concept development must also be lacking. What is not yet clear is to what extent later environmental enrichment will compensate for earlier impoverishment. It seems that while with man we cannot speak of critical periods of learning, there are nevertheless optimal periods for different functions.

Accepting, therefore, an interaction theory of nature and nurture we can reach the rough equation that where environment is adequate the observed differences between children must be largely genetic in origin, and where it is adverse, the environmental effects (masked in the earlier case) are superimposed upon genetic differences. This being so, it is at once apparent that large sections of the population are underfunctioning to varying degrees. This problem has recently been considered by Hunt (1961) in a scholarly book. He writes that:

> The hope of increasing the average level of intelligence by proper manipulation of children's developmental encounters with their

environments provides a challenge of the first order. In this challenge the theory of man's nature and the fact of his welfare are obviously intertwined.

Hunt's view is completely in accord with that advanced in this chapter. And while we remain in comparative ignorance of some of the mechanisms which retard development, we already know enough to be able to say that some forms of higher-grade mental deficiency can be alleviated or perhaps even prevented by appropriate environmental manipulation. Within the field of normality, too, there is evidence that intellectual growth rates can be accelerated, and that, after maturity, the rate of intellectual decline can be affected by environmental influences. The way is now open for some exciting experiments and in these, a sophisticated use of the IQ will have much to offer. Indeed, progress is already being made with early intervention programmes in the United States (e.g. Gray and Klaus, 1965. Heber 1968). In these programmes, infants from problem families are given special stimulation and educational enrichment. Results of carefully controlled studies look promising but if long-term effects are to be achieved long-term enrichment will be required.

REFERENCES

BATEMAN, B. (1965). *The Illinois Test of Psycholinguistic Abilities in Current Research.* Urbana, Illinois: Institute for Research on Exceptional Children.

BAYLEY, N. (1940). Mental growth in young children. *Yearb. Nat. Soc. Stud. Educ.* **39,** 11–47, quoted by Jones in Carmichael (1954).

BAYLEY, N. (1955). On the growth of intelligence. *Amer. Psychol.* **10,** 805–818.

BAYLEY, N., and ODEN, M. H. (1955). The maintenance of intellectual ability in gifted adults. *J. Gerontol.* **10,** 91–107.

BERNSTEIN, B. (1960). Language and social class. *Brit. J. Sociol.* **11,** 271–276.

BERNSTEIN, B. (1962a). Linguistic codes, hesitation phenomena, and intelligence. *Language and Speech* **5,** 31–46.

BERNSTEIN, B. (1962b). Social class, linguistic codes and grammatical errors. *Language and Speech* **5,** 221–240.

BOWLBY, J. (1951). *Maternal Care and Mental Health.* Geneva: W.H.O.

BRADWAY, U. P., and THOMPSON, C. W. (1962). Intelligence at adult-hood: a twenty-five year follow-up. *J. educ. Psychol.* **53**, 1–14.

BURKS, B. S. (1928). The relative influence of nature and nurture upon mental development: a comparative study of foster parent–foster child resemblance and true parent–true child resemblance. *Yearb. Nat. Soc. Stud. Educ.* **27**, 219–316.

BURT, C. (1921). *Mental and Scholastic Tests* (second edn.). London: Staples Press.

BURT, C. (1966). The genetic determination of differences in intelligence: a study of monozygotic twins reared apart. *Brit. J. Psychol.* **57**, 137–153.

CARMICHAEL, L. (1954). *Manual of Child Psychology*. New York: Wiley.

CHARLES, D. C. (1953). Ability and accomplishment of persons earlier judged mentally deficient. *Genet. Psychol. Monogr.* **47**, 3–71.

CLARKE, A. D. B. (1967). Problems in Assessing the Later Effects of Early Experience. In Miller E. (ed.), *Foundations of Child Psychiatry*. London: Pergamon.

CLARKE, A. D. B. (1968). Learning and human development. The 42nd Maudsley Lecture. *Brit. J. Psychiat.*, **114**, 1061–1077.

CLARKE, A. D. B., and CLARKE, A. M. (1953). How constant is the I Q? *Lancet* **ii**, 877–880.

CLARKE, A. D. B., and CLARKE, A. M. (1954b). Cognitive changes in the feeble-minded. *Brit. J. Psychol.* **45**, 173–179.

CLARKE, A. D. B., and CLARKE, A. M. (1959). Recovery from the effects of deprivation. *Acta Psychol.* **16**, 137–144.

CLARKE, A. D. B., CLARKE, A. M., and BROWN, R. I. (1959). Regression to the mean: a confused concept! *Brit. J. Psychol.* **51**, 105–117.

CLARKE, A. D. B., CLARKE, A. M., and REIMAN, S. (1958). Cognitive and social changes in the feeble-minded – three further studies. *Brit. J. Psychol.* **49**, 144–157.

DAVIS, K. (1947). Final note on a case of extreme isolation. *Amer. J. Sociol.* **52**, 432–437.

DEARBORN, W. F., and ROTHNEY, J. W. M. (1941). *Predicting the Child's Development*. Cambridge, Mass.: Sci.-Art. Publ.

DENNIS, W. (1960). Causes of retardation among institutional children. *J. Genet. Psychol.* **96**, 47–59.

DOUGLAS, J. W. B. (1964). *The Home and the School*. London: Mac-Gibbon & Kee.

DUGDALE, R. L. (1910). *The Jukes*. New York: Putnam.

EYSENCK, H. J. (1952). *The Scientific Study of Personality*. London: Routledge and Kegan Paul.

EYSENCK, H. J. (1953). *Uses and Abuses of Psychology*. Harmondsworth: Penguin Books.

FREEMAN, F. N., HOLZINGER, K. J., and MITCHELL, B. C. (1928). The influence of environment on the intelligence, school achievement, and the conduct of foster children. *Yearb. Nat. Soc. Stud. Educ.* **27,** 103–217.

FURTH, H. G. (1964). Research with the deaf: implications for language and cognition. *Psychol. Bull.* **62,** 145–164.

GODDARD, H. H. (1912). *The Kallikak Family*. New York: Macmillan.

GRAY, S. W. and KLAUS, R. A. (1965). An experimental preschool programme for critically deprived children. *Child Development.* **36,** 887–898.

GREENE, E. B. (1941). *Measurements of Human Behaviour*. New York: Odyssey Press.

GUERTIN, W. H. (1949). Mental growth in pseudo-feeblemindedness. *J. clin. Psychol.* **5,** 414–418.

GUERTIN, W. H. (1950). Differential characteristics of the pseudo-feebleminded. *Amer. J. Ment. Defic.* **54,** 394–398.

HEBB, D. O. (1949). *The Organization of Behaviour*. London: Chapman and Hall.

HEBER, R. (1968). The role of environmental variables in the etiology of cultural-familial mental retardation. *Proc. First Congr. Internat. Assoc. scient. Stud. mental Defic.* 456–468.

HILDEN, A. H. (1949). A longitudinal study of intellectual development. *J. Psychol.* **28,** 187–214.

HOLZINGER, K. J. (1938). Reply to special review of 'Twins'. *Psychol. Bull.* **35,** 436–444.

HONZIK, M. P., MACFARLANE, J. W., and ALLEN, C. (1948). The stability of mental test performance between two and eighteen years. *J. Exp. Educ.* **17,** 309–324.

HUNT, J. McV. (1961). *Intelligence and Experience*. New York: The Ronald Press.

HUSEN, T. (1951). The influence of schooling upon IQ. *Theoria* **17,** 61–88.

JONES, H. E. (1954). Environmental influences on mental development. *In* Carmichael L. (ed.). *Manual of Child Psychology*. New York: Wiley, 631–696.

KELLMER PRINGLE, M. L., and TANNER, M. (1958). The effects of early deprivation on speech development: a comparative study of four year olds in a nursery school and in residential nurseries. *Language and Speech* **1**, 269–287.

KIRK, S. A. (1948). An evaluation of the study by Bernadine G. Schmidt. *Psychol. Bull.* **45**, 321–333.

KIRK, S. A. (1958). *Early Education of the Mentally Retarded.* Urbana, Ill.: Univ. Illinois Press.

KIRK, S. A. (1962). The effects of educational procedures on the development of retarded children. *Proc. Lond. Conf. scient. Stud. ment. Defic.*, 1960. **2**, 419–428.

KIRK, S. A., and MCCARTHY, J. J. (1961). The Illinois Test of Psycholinguistic Abilities – an approach to differential diagnosis. *Amer. J. ment. Defic.* **66**, 399–412

LURIA, A. R. (1961). *The Role of Speech in the Regulation of Normal and Abnormal Behaviour.* J. Tizard (ed.). London: Pergamon Press.

MARCHAND, J. G. (1956). Changes of psychometric test results in mental defective employment care patients. *Amer. J. ment. Defic.* **60**, 852–859.

MAURER, J. M. (1946). *Intellectual Status at Maturity as a Criterion for Selecting Items in Pre-School Tests.* Minneapolis Press.

MAXWELL, J. (1961). *The Level and Trend of National Intelligence.* (Scottish Council for Research in Education, **46**.) London: Univ. London Press.

MCKAY, B. E. (1942). A study of IQ changes in a group of girls paroled from a state school for mental defectives. *Amer. J. ment. Defic.* **46**, 496–500.

MCNEMAR, Q. (1938). Newman, Freeman and Holzinger's 'Twins: a study of heredity and environment'. *Psychol. Bull.* **35**, 237–249.

MCNEMAR, Q. (1940). A critical examination of the University of Iowa studies of environmental influence upon the IQ. *Psychol. Bull.* **37**, 63–92.

MUNDY, L. (1955). Environmental influences in intellectual function as measured by intelligence tests. Univ. London Unpubl. M.Sc. Thesis.

MURSELL, J. L. (1949). *Psychological Testing.* London: Longmans, Green & Co.

NEMZEK, C. L. (1933). The constancy of the IQ. *Psychol Bull.* **30**, 143–168.

NEWMAN, H. H. (1929). Mental and physical traits of identical twins reared apart. *J. Hered.* **20**, 49–64, 97–104, 153–166.

D

NEWMAN, H. H., FREEMAN, F. N., and HOLZINGER, K. J. (1937). *Twins: a Study of Heredity and Environment*. Chicago: Univ. Chicago Press.

NISBET, J. D. (1953). *Family Environment: a Direct Effect of Family Size on Intelligence*. Occasional Papers on Eugenics. No. 8. London: Cassell.

NISBET, J. D. (1957). Contribution to intelligence testing and the theory of intelligence. IV. Intelligence and age: retesting with twenty-four years interval. *Brit. J. educ. Psychol.* **27**, 190–199.

OWENS, W. A. (1953). Age and mental abilities: a longitudinal study. *Genet. Psychol. Monogr.* **48**, 3–54.

PENROSE, L. S. (1949). *The Biology of Mental Defect*. London: Sidgwick and Jackson (revised edn. 1954).

RHEINGOLD, H. L. (1956). The modification of social responsiveness in institutional babies. *Monogr. Soc. Res. Child Developm.* **21**, 1–48.

RHEINGOLD, H. L. (1960). The measurement of maternal care. *Child Developm.* **31**, 565–575.

ROBERTS, A. D. (1945b). Some IQ changes on the Stanford-Binet, Form L. *Amer. J. ment. Defic.* **50**, 134–136.

ROSWELL HARRIS, D. (1958). Some aspects of cognitive and personality test changes in a group of 100 feebleminded young men. Univ. Reading, Unpubl. M.A. Thesis.

SARASON, S. B. (1949). *Psychological Problems in Mental Deficiency* (second edn. 1953). New York: Harper.

SCHMIDT, B. G. (1946). Changes in personal, social and intellectual behaviour of children originally classified as feebleminded. *Psychol. Monogr.* **60**, 5, 1–144.

SCHMIDT, B. G. (1948). A reply. *Psychol. Bull.* **45**, 334–343.

SHAPIRO, M. B. (1951). An experimental approach to diagnostic testing. *J. ment. Sci.* **97**, 90–110.

SHIELDS, J. (1962). *Monozygotic Twins*. London: O.U.P.

SKEELS, H. M. (1938). Mental development of children in foster homes. *J. consult. Psychol.* **2**, 33–43.

SKEELS, H. M., and DYE, H. B. (1939). A study of the effects of differential stimulation on mentally retarded children. *Proc. Amer. Assoc. ment. Defic.* **44**, 114–136.

SKEELS, H. M. (1966). Adult status of children with contrasting early life experiences: a follow-up study. *Monogr. Soc. Res. Child Developm.* **31**, 3 (Whole No. 105).

SKEELS, H. M., and HARMS, I. (1948). Children with inferior social histories: their mental development in adoptive homes. *J. genet. Psychol.* **72**, 283–294.

SKODAK, M. (1939). Children in foster homes. *Univ. Iowa Stud. Child Welf.* **16**, 1–156.

SKODAK, H. M., and SKEELS, H. M. (1945). A follow-up study of children in adoptive homes. *J. Genet. Psychol.* **66**, 21–58.

SKODAK, H. M., and SKEELS, H. M. (1949). A final follow-up study of one hundred adopted children. *J. Genet. Psychol.* **75**, 85–125.

SPAULDING, P. J. (1946). Retest results on the Stanford-Binet. Form L, with mental defectives. *Amer. J. ment. Defic.* **51**, 35–42.

THORNDIKE, R. L. (1933). The effect of the interval between test and retest on the constancy of the IQ. *J. educ. Psychol.* **24**, 543–549.

THORNDIKE, R. L. (1940). 'Constancy' of the I.Q. *Psychol. Bull.* **37**, 167–186.

THORPE, L. P. (1946). *Child Psychology and Development.* New York: The Ronald Press.

VERNON, P. E. (1954). Symposium on the effects of coaching and practice in intelligence tests. V–Conclusions. *Brit. J. educ. Psychol.* **24**, 57–63.

VERNON, P. E. (1955a). Presidential address: the psychology of intelligence and *g. Bull. Brit. Psychol. Soc.* **26**, 1–14.

VERNON, P. E. (1955b). The assessment of children. In *Studies of Education.* Univ. London Inst. Educ. **7**.

WECHSLER, D. (1944). *The Measurement of Adult Intelligence* (first edn. 1937, second edn. 1941, third edn. 1944). Baltimore: Williams and Wilkens.

WELLMAN, B. L., SKEELS, H. M., and SKODAK, M. (1940). Review of McNemar's critical examination of Iowa studies. *Psychol. Bull.* **37**, 93–111.

WIDDOWSON, E. M., and MCCANCE, R. A. (1954). Studies on the nutritive value of bread and on the effect of variations in the extraction rate of flour on undernourished children. *Sp. Rep. Ser., Med. Res. Counc.* No. 287. London: H.M.S.O.

WITTENBORN, J. R. (1956). A study of adoptive children. *Psychol. Monogr.* **70**, 1–115.

2

Human Abilities and their Assessment

H. J. BUTCHER

I. THE HIERARCHICAL STRUCTURE OF ABILITIES

1. *Discussion of terminology*

THE USE of such terms as intelligence, ability, aptitude, achievement, attainment, creativity, is often inconsistent and confusing. A preliminary word about how they are to be treated in this chapter will not be amiss.

General intelligence and its status as an administrative tool and as a theoretical model have been discussed in Chapter 1. Definitions of intelligence have been notoriously manifold, but have had three main aspects, emphasizing either adaptation of the individual to his total environment, ability to learn, or ability to carry on abstract thinking (Freeman, 1962). From the point of view of distinguishing intelligence from other terms, the salient feature of all such definitions is that they imply either a unitary or a hierarchical theory of the structure of abilities. In other words, *all* cognitive functioning and all the kinds of behaviour we describe as intelligent are implied to be directed by a single kind of controlling faculty or very high-level skill. We talk of abilities and aptitudes but not of intelligences, and even if we talk of different kinds or aspects of intelligence, we are implicitly subscribing to a hierarchical theory.

There is an apparent exception in Hebb's idea of intelligence A and intelligence B and in Vernon's extension of this idea (already discussed in Chapter 1), but the exception is more apparent than real, since these separate 'intelligences' are not thought of as differing primarily in function, but rather as modifications of one another, or as phenotype and genotype. Furthermore, it is not suggested that intelligence A and intelligence B can be entirely separated or assessed without contamination from each other. The nearest true exception to the general

68

usage both among psychologists and laymen that 'intelligence' refers to one dominating, high-level function is Cattell's distinction between 'fluid' and 'crystallized' intelligence, which, when originally formulated, appeared very similar to Hebb's distinction between intelligence A and intelligence B, and was in fact put forward independently at about the same time. Like Hebb's also, this distinction seemed to be aimed at conceptual classification rather than at empirical separation. But more recently Cattell (1963), partly anticipated by Renshaw (1952), has produced evidence for two general intelligence factors by empirical research, demonstrating that different kinds of task have higher loadings on one or the other. Even if one accepts this theory, however, the two general factors still represent what is essentially one basic function, either modified or relatively unmodified by cultural and environmental effects. To sum up this short discussion, the use of the term 'intelligence' appears necessarily to indicate support for the view that a basic unity of function exists, dominating or organizing the multitude of performance in which learning and thinking are involved.

'Ability' carries no such implication. One certainly *can* speak of general ability, but equally of a large number of distinct abilities. In the U.S.A., in particular, many, perhaps the majority, of psychologists prefer to speak of abilities to avoid apparently subscribing to a hierarchical theory of intelligence. These alternative conceptions, their advantages and disadvantages, the weight of empirical evidence and the possibility of synthesis will be discussed in section 2. The concept of 'ability', along with that of 'intelligence', implies capacity or potentiality, possibly innate, relatively uninfluenced by experience, training and cultural conditions.

'Aptitudes', by contrast, suggest potentiality in a particular direction with no special implication that previous experience or training should be discounted. But, as the term is often used, there is a considerable overlap between aptitudes and abilities. In Cronbach's (1960) standard textbook, for instance, the first two batteries of tests discussed in the chapter 'Differential Abilities in Guidance' are the 'Differential Aptitudes Tests' and 'The General Aptitude Test Battery'. The two terms are thus commonly accepted as virtually interchangeable, but when they are distinguished, aptitudes are usually thought of as rather more specific, more dependent on training, and perhaps more directly related to vocational guidance.

Achievement and attainment differ from all the terms so far considered in that they refer to what someone has successfully done or learned rather than what he is capable of doing in the future. The idea of predicting future behaviour is not at all inherent in their definition, as it is to a large degree in the qualities previously mentioned. This distinction is a very familiar one, and requires no enlargement.

'Creativity' is a vague but useful word. To some extent it bridges the ideas of potentiality and achievement, since the 'creative' people studied are usually those who exercise their creative talents. Or, to put the same point in another way, productivity is taken into account as well as originality, although this may be partly due to the difficulty of finding other criteria in what is a new field of systematic research. It also bridges the separate fields of research into cognitive and temperamental qualities, although again this is more a matter of empirical than of theoretical necessity. The subject has attracted great and justified interest in recent years, and because systematic research is all much more recent and less generally familiar than the corresponding work on abilities and attainment, a considerable and otherwise disproportionate amount of space in this chapter will be concerned with it.

2. *How many kinds of ability?*

The tendency to talk sometimes of one general intelligence factor and sometimes of manifold abilities is so old (dating back at least to Plato) that one must suspect on *a priori* grounds that both are useful ways of describing human behaviour. An examination of research results leads to the same conclusion.

As is well known, Charles Spearman, the principal pioneer of factor analysis, clung as long as possible to the belief that *all* mental processes involved in problem-solving or abstract thought could be accounted for by one universal general factor corresponding approximately to the popular idea of intelligence, and one factor uniquely specific to the particular mental task. During the twenties and thirties of this century, however, after a great deal of controversy, it gradually became clear that the general factor found by Spearman was not adequate to explain all the common variance if a representative selection of tasks was analysed. In other words, some group factors were needed to account for the correlations between tests which still remained significant even after the effects of the general factor had been removed, and Spearman's simple theory had to be revised. These group factors, demonstrated to be necessary by Burt (1939), El Koussy (1935) and others, were interpreted as abilities (e.g. verbal ability, numerical ability, spatial ability and so forth) lower in the hierarchy than general intelligence, and less important also in the sense that each of them, and sometimes all of them together, accounted for less variation in performance than did general intelligence by itself. Thus it gradually became clear that the findings of the British school of factor analysts lent some support to both the monists and the pluralists. They demonstrated firstly that a statistical factor could be isolated which corresponded fairly closely to the notion of general intelligence and which entered into very nearly all aspects of intelligent behaviour as assessed by tests, examinations or ratings, and secondly that this factor, although it accounted usually for a large proportion of the variation in performance, needed to be supplemented by some half-dozen further common factors interpretable as rather more specialized abilities.

At about the same time, however, Thurstone in Chicago was devising a means of analysing the structure of abilities in quite a different way. The technique of factor analysis, and this is a point which will be amplified later, does not in itself produce one unique set of factors but an infinite number of different sets, unless some particular criterion, either mathematical or psychological, is imposed. Thurstone took advantage of this fact and introduced a further innovation, the extraction of factors which were, or could be, correlated with each other, instead of being 'orthogonal' or independent, as the factors extracted by the British school always had been. He also introduced a criterion known as 'simple structure', which was intended to indicate a unique and logically satisfactory set of factors for each analysis.

Using these methods, Thurstone carried out several extensive and meticulous studies on both university students and secondary school (high school) children between 1935 and 1940, administering in each case some sixty cognitive tests designed to sample widely different kinds of thinking (see for example Thurstone, 1938; Thurstone 1941; Thurstone and Thurstone, 1941). He found six main (correlated) factors, which he interpreted as verbal meaning or comprehension, spatial thinking, reasoning, numerical ability, verbal fluency and memory. These six were believed by Thurstone to be the primary mental abilities, and were, so to speak, of equal status, not being subordinate to any 'general intelligence'.

The face value of these findings was to suggest that the concept of general intelligence was unnecessary, but this would be in fact a misinterpretation. Wherever a number of psychological tests or other variables are found to be significantly correlated, the possibility exists of performing a factor analysis and of thus isolating the common element or elements which are indicated by the fact of correlation. If one extracts independent, orthogonal factors, the process of simplification is at an end, and no higher-order analysis is possible. But by choosing to extract correlated factors, Thurstone in a sense left the analysis incomplete, since the fact of correlation between his factors implies the possibility of carrying out a higher-order analysis of the factors themselves to obtain a measure of their common elements. When a second-order factor analysis of this kind is performed on the 'primary mental abilities', the resulting supra-ordinate factor is the familiar one of general intelligence. What has happened in Thurstone's type of analysis is that his technique of extracting correlated factors with the criterion of simple structure has made it impossible for the general factor to emerge in the first instance.

As a result of extensive factorial work into abilities, we thus have two main alternative ways of looking at them. These are not contradictory, since they depend on two ways of analysing the same data. We may either adopt the British, hierarchical view and ascribe as much variation in performance as possible to variations in general intelligence, accounting for what remains by subsidiary group factors, or we may adopt Thurstone's view that the variation in performance is most satisfactorily accounted for by variation in five or six overlapping abilities, with the further option of making an assessment of general intelligence from the scores on tests of these 'primary mental abilities'. If one has obtained a fairly wide and varied set of test results, and if the time, labour and computational facilities are available, the two-stage analysis is likely to give the fullest and most useful information about the structure of abilities.

II. TECHNICAL REQUIREMENTS OF PSYCHOLOGICAL TESTS

The user of ability tests needs to know something of their efficiency and of the criteria by which this is judged. Traditionally, the two main criteria of this kind have been described as 'validity' and 'reliability'. These concepts are complex and deceptive, and test theory is still being actively developed. In the present section an attempt will be made firstly to summarize, as briefly and clearly as possible, the most important features of these criteria as they have generally been understood, and secondly to outline some recent thinking and new developments.

1. *Validity*

Validity is the more important and elusive property. A common-sense explanation is that a test is valid in proportion as it assesses the psychological trait or quality that it is designed to assess. This explanation is intuitively fairly clear and satisfactory to most people, but a little thought reveals that it is extremely difficult to find precise and scientifically satisfactory means of determining a test's validity and even of specifying accurately what is being determined. Clearly some operational verification is required over and above the general subjective impression that the test is producing the right result. This subjective appearance of validity ('face validity') has some use in motivating the subject and from a public relations aspect, but little more can be said in its favour. Rather similarly, 'content validity', or the extent to which a test contains obviously relevant material, is of considerable importance in judging tests of attainment and essay-type examinations, but of less importance in the case of abilities, and is again not easily susceptible to objective assessment or quantification.

The more important aspects of validity are summarized under two main heads, (*a*) construct or conceptual validity, i.e. the extent to which a test embodies and represents a psychological concept, and (*b*) predictive validity, the extent to which it successfully predicts some other behavioural performance. Construct validity comes close to our first, intuitive definition, and for this reason is difficult to establish other than by an elaborate chain of inferences. Predictive validity is desirable in that it provides an operational and quantifiable criterion – or criteria. Its disadvantage is indicated by the need to add 'or criteria' to the last sentence. There is no one validity, as judged in this way, but a multitude of possible different validities, according to the particular criterion chosen, and there will rarely be one that appears entirely unarbitrary. 'Concurrent validity' is sometimes distinguished from 'predictive validity' as the power of a test to predict some other behaviour immediately rather than in the future, but clearly this is simply a matter of degree, not of principle, and every intermediate gradation is possible.

Construct validity can rarely be expressed in numerical form. It can be inferred from the formulation and verification of hypotheses about the test or measure being validated. To assess the construct validity of a test designed to measure numerical ability, we should form the hypotheses that skilled mathematicians, other things being equal, would obtain higher scores than other people, that boys of thirteen might do slightly better than girls, that the test would correlate more highly with school performance in algebra than in French, and so forth. Construct validity thus depends on a whole network of inferences and is not in general quantifiable. But there is one exception. One may interpret construct validity as the loading of the test on a factor. If by the analysis of a carefully chosen battery, a factor of numerical ability is clearly isolated and interpreted, the loading of a test of numerical ability on the factor will give a quantitative measure of validity. This is probably the best approach to validity in theory, but a factor loading of this kind may not mean much in practice. Until greater agreement on the technique of factor analysis is reached, one would be much wiser to rely on the more indirect, inferential approach to construct validity already described. There are signs, however, that factor technique may become more standardized in the future. In Section I of this chapter, a sketch has been given of the alternative methods and interpretations that are possible, and clearly in this case, the adherents of these methods will reach different conclusions about the factorial validity of a particular test. Equally, however, some indication was given of means of reconciling alternative methods, and with the advent of electronic computers and 'analytical' or objective programmes of factor rotation, standardization of technique and interpretation is no longer a chimera. Even when this is achieved, there will still remain sampling problems, both of people and of variables, the latter being the more difficult, since the factorial approach to validity necessitates, implicitly or explicitly, the sampling of variables over the whole area of the construct.

From this brief account, it should be clear that, in the writer's view, construct validity is the fundamental type, both because it is closest to the intuitive idea which gradually evolved into the concept of validity and because it includes most of the other kinds of validity as sub-divisions. Thus, as we have shown, the commonest means of establishing construct validity is by the verification of hypotheses, and these hypotheses will often refer to the various predictive and concurrent validities – in other words, to the degree of correlation between the test and various future and present criteria.

In 1954, a committee of the American Psychological Association attempted to produce a definite account of test requirements and to standardize nomenclature. It recommended the recognition of four kinds of validity, all of which have been briefly discussed here, content, predictive, concurrent, construct. This is clearly a rather arbitrary and unsatisfactory classification with terms applying to different levels and different degrees of generality. Later in this section we shall discuss recent, alternative suggestions for the schematization of validity.

2. *Reliability*

The second test requirement, that of reliability, must be discussed equally briefly. Here again neither the basic concept nor the classifications of sub-divisions and types nor the methods of assessment rest upon an agreed, unequivocal theoretical basis.

Traditionally, reliability has been defined as covering two kinds of consistency, consistency over a period of time, and consistency from one part or one form of a psychological test to another, i.e. internal consistency. Although in practice a test that has high reliability in one of these two ways generally is also high in the other, this does not appear logically necessary. For this reason, suggestions have often been made that the two kinds of reliability should be given different names, e.g. consistency and stability.

Reliability over time (stability) is determined by the test–retest procedure. In so far as a test when re-administered places people in the same order as on the first administration, as shown by the correlation between the two sets of scores, it is reliable in this sense. Clearly, however, the resulting coefficient is a function of the people as well as of the test. Firstly, its interpretation will be affected by the sampling procedure (and this applies to all our discussion both of validity and reliability), and particularly by the range of ability in the sample; both validity and reliability will be reduced in a selected sample of people who do not cover the full range of ability. Secondly, the people may change in respect of the quality being tested between the two administrations, and such changes may be random or systematic and affected or unaffected by the first administration (e.g. memory, practice effects).

Internal-consistency reliability, on the other hand, largely excludes such intra-personal variations, being based on one administration of the test. As its name suggests, it is concerned with the consistency of separate parts of the test, and the best-known method of estimating this is called the 'split-half' method, in which each half of the test is scored and totalled separately and the subjects' scores on the two halves are correlated. If the halves of the test are formed by taking odd and even-numbered items respectively, the split-half method (with Spearman–Brown correction) usually gives an accurate enough idea of the internal consistency of the test for practical purposes, but a more refined estimate, under certain assumptions, can be obtained by using one of the Kuder–Richardson formulae. These can be found, with a discussion of the assumptions required, in Guilford (1965). Internal consistency is also sometimes estimated by analysis of variance, which should give similar results in appropriate circumstances to the Kuder–Richardson method, and is particularly useful for the case in which the internal consistency of scores can be analysed in terms of several clearly defined sources of variation. A typical example is the marking of English essays where there may be a choice of topic and several markers, and the effect of these factors on reliability can be separately assessed.

It will be clear even from this summary that reliability, and particularly internal-consistency reliability, is mainly a means to an end, whereas validity, and particularly construct validity, is an end in itself, as far as judging the test is concerned. An analogy may make this clearer. The user of an unreliable test may be compared with a tennis player whose racket is variable, so that the ball sometimes comes off it hard and true, and sometimes unexpectedly weakly. But if he finds himself playing tennis with a squash racket or even a baseball bat, this is like using a test of low validity. It may be an admirable instrument in itself for some purpose, but not for the game of tennis.

3. *Recent technical developments*

Recent developments in assessing the efficiency of tests have been directed towards rationalizing and generalizing the concepts already discussed. Only an outline of the general direction and scope of one or two of these developments can be given here.

Cronbach *et al.*, (1963) argue in favour of unifying the various kinds of test reliability by considering them all as indices of the extent to which we can generalize in various directions from a given set of results. They point out that the idea of parallel forms of a test, for instance, which has formed an important part of traditional reliability theory, is a vague one. Tests can be parallel in some respects and not in others. Cronbach and his co-authors demonstrate the vagueness of the concept of 'parallel' tests by invoking a hypothetical test with instructions 'Write down all the words you can think of that begin with the letter 't'. 'Parallel' tests might be constructed in many ways, e.g. substituting another letter for 't' or by asking for words ending in 't'. They therefore recommend a more specific definition of the universe of conditions of observation (e.g. different tests forms, different scorers, different

occasions) about which the psychologist wishes to make generalizations. Once this universe is clearly defined, and a sample drawn from it,
the appropriate coefficient can be chosen and the conclusions drawn
will have a pre-defined degree of generality.

Cattell (1963) also puts forward extensive new ideas which have
important implications for the future of ability testing, and which are
described in more detail by Cattell and Butcher (1968). Two of the main
ideas are proposals for *standardized* and for *second-order* indices of
test efficiency.

The following example will indicate what is meant by standardized
indices and will illustrate the possible gain in economy of conceptualization and in convenience for users of psychological tests. No experienced psychologist accepts reliability and validity coefficients at
their face value. When he sees the figures reported in journal articles or
in test handbooks, he necessarily makes implicit corrections to allow
for such factors as the range of ability sampled and the length of the
test. In the latter case, for example, he may choose for practical purposes a test of moderate length and moderately high validity rather
than one of inordinate length and only slightly higher validity. The
chances are, however, that he will make this choice by rough impression, and not by detailed estimate of the relative validities of the two
tests per unit of length. One of Cattell's proposals is that the reliability
and validity of tests should be determined and reported in the latter,
standardized form, or, better still, in terms of reliability and validity
per unit of testing time.

The proposals for second-order measures of test efficiency can also
be most simply illustrated by considering the problems of the applied
psychologist making a choice between available tests. One or two of
the ways in which a simple acceptance of the figures reported for
validity and reliability may be misleading have been mentioned in the
last paragraph, but there are many others. The predictive validity of an
intelligence test, for instance, will vary widely according to the external
criterion chosen, and this variation will be greater for some tests than
for others. Similarly, validity will vary if the test is administered to
different national groups, and the same is probably true of cultural
sub-groups within one country. Some of this variability will be ascrib-
able to the varying suitability of the test to the respective classes of
people irrespective of the range of ability within classes. Here again,
some tests will show less variability than others, and, other things being
equal, these will be the most flexible and useful measures. Cattell there-

fore suggests that tests should be evaluated not only by the simple validity and reliability figures, but also by the range of validities and reliabilities in different circumstances. Something of the kind has often been done roughly and intuitively, but not explicitly by coefficient and formula.

III. CREATIVE ABILITIES

1. *General introduction*

Since about 1950, American psychologists have been much concerned with the study of 'creativity'; some of the resulting work has been rather superficial, but the topic is undoubtedly an important one.

The general meaning of the concept is fairly self-evident. Cognitive tests as generally constructed and employed during the last fifty years have been quite limited and narrow in the kinds of ability they tap and in the sort of item they employ. This has been true both of general intelligence tests and of tests of special abilities and aptitudes. Both the kind of material employed and the usual multiple-choice type of item direct the subject's thinking along rather narrowly prescribed lines if he is to find the correct answer. If he *does* find an original and justifiable answer that the test constructor has not thought of, he will be penalized by being scored wrong. Admittedly this will be rare (though not impossible) in an adequately constructed test such as is normally used in selection procedures, but the point is that the design of the multiple-choice, objectively scored, test tends by its very nature to exclude original thinking.

There is a plausible common-sense case that originality and the power of achieving new, personal syntheses will never be detected, and may even be a handicap in tackling the conventional multiple-choice test. This is a case of course, that has very often been put forward by parents and teachers, but has usually been rejected by psychologists, partly on account of the considerable operational success achieved by tests of the conventional type, and partly because of the difficulty of assessing objectively such intangible and elusive qualities as originality or creativity. This quite reasonable distrust of the limitations of multiple-choice tests has also been the main reason for the retention of 'essay-type' rather than 'new-type' or objectively scored answers in examinations, but again this view has carried less weight with psychologists than with parents or teachers because of the frequently demonstrated subjectivity and unreliability typical of much examination marking

(Hartog, Rhodes and Burt, 1936).[1] Also of course, there is no guarantee that an 'essay-type' question will automatically give scope for originality and creative thinking. It may be phrased and marked so as to discourage or penalize them.

There would thus be a great gain and one would obtain the best of both worlds if 'creativity' could be assessed as objectively as 'intelligence', assuming for the moment (though it will be necessary to return to the question) that 'creativity' exists as something separate from 'intelligence'. This kind of phrase, about the existence or non-existence of psychological qualities, is obviously a kind of colloquial shorthand which has its dangers if one takes it too literally. But enough has already been said in an earlier section about the status and function of factors and similar abstractions for the reader to realize that the question is one of the useful and economical classification of patterns of performance rather than of the existence of faculties in any more profound sense.

There is a further attraction in the concept of creativity in that it bridges the two, usually distinct, psychological areas of ability and personality. The distinction between cognitive and temperamental traits is in many ways a useful one, but it is possible that the line has often been too rigidly drawn. R. B. Cattell has always made sure of including a measure of intelligence in his personality questionnaires both for adults and children. Conversely, Barron (1963) writes 'The vogue of the IQ is due to popular simplification. Intelligence is a complex set of interrelated aptitudes and abilities, some verging closely on the temperamental'.

It is therefore fairly widely agreed that it would be extremely useful to have reasonably objective psychological measures of creativity or originality. What is the present evidence that this is possible?

2. *The work of Getzels and Jackson*

One of the best-known studies is that by Getzels and Jackson (1962) who investigated a highly selected group of children (mean IQ about 130) in a private school near Chicago. Their general procedure was to discriminate by a battery of tests of 'creativity' between (*a*) children of exceptionally high IQ who were relatively uncreative and (*b*) children

---

[1] It is unfortunately necessary to quote a work written thirty years ago, since no more recent research into the reliability of examinations has been carried out on anything like the same scale. This is a remarkable and unfortunate fact, as Wiseman (1961) has pointed out. What little work of this kind has been done has been reviewed recently by Cox (1966).

who were exceptionally creative, but of relatively low IQ (but still well above the average of the general population), and by comparing these two contrasting groups to study some of the correlates and consequences of high creativity. The two contrasting groups were quite small, numbering 26 and 28 respectively, being selected from a total of 450 children tested. Five paper-and-pencil tests of creativity were used in the selection of the groups, and these tests 'involved the ability to deal inventively with verbal and numerical symbol systems and with object–space relations. What most of these tests had in common was that the score depended not on a single predetermined correct response as is most often the case with the common intelligence test, but on the number, novelty and variety of adaptive responses to a given stimulus task'. Some of these tests were adapted from those of Guilford and Cattell, some were specially constructed. All intercorrelations between the measures of creativity were positive, between 0·15 and 0·53, and rather higher than most of the correlations of these measures with IQ, so that there is some evidence of a unitary trait other than intelligence being assessed by the battery.

Interesting differences between the 'highly creative' and the 'highly intelligent' children were found. The 'highly creative' group, in spite of a mean IQ 23 points lower, were superior in scholastic achievement (as measured by, e.g. a Stanford Spelling test and an Iowa Arithmetic test). But, in spite of this apparent 'over-achievement', they were less popular with their teachers, apparently because they were less conforming or less success-oriented by conventional standards of adult success.

Getzels and Jackson provide many more examples of differences between their 'highly intelligent' and 'highly creative' groups. They found a stronger sense of humour and some evidence of a more permissive parental upbringing among the creative children. But the findings about general level of achievement and the attitude of teachers are perhaps the most important.

How well substantiated and how reliable are these findings? Getzels and Jackson's work has been widely reviewed, criticized and re-interpreted, by De Mille and Merrifield (1962), Thorndike (1963), Burt (1962), Marsh (1964) and Vernon (1964). De Mille and Merrifield severely criticized the whole study on methodological grounds, particularly stigmatizing the omission of data about the subjects who were high on measures both of creativity and intelligence. Thorndike (my knowledge of this paper is based on a summary by Milholland, 1964) and Marsh independently carried out factor analyses of Getzels and

Jackson's table of inter-correlations between creativity and intelligence measures and concluded that much of the variation on the supposed measures of creativity was accounted for by a factor of general intelligence. Burt similarly concluded that 'indeed, the new tests for "creativity" would form very satisfactory additions to any ordinary battery for testing the general factor of intelligence', but also that 'there can be no doubt whatever that these new tests have succeeded in eliciting supplementary activities that are rarely tapped by the usual brands of intelligence test'. The wisest conclusion about the status of Getzels and Jackson's findings would certainly seem to be the one reached by both Burt and Vernon which is that their research should be regarded as exploratory, as the authors themselves suggest, interesting and worthy of replication and extension, but not as revolutionary or as adding anything more than supplementary knowledge to the generally held views about intelligence and abilities.

3. *Guilford's work on creative abilities*

The work of J. P. Guilford of the University of Southern California has already been mentioned earlier in this chapter. Much of it is relevant to the cognitive aspects of 'creativity', and his tests have been widely used in a large number of researches, including, as we have seen, that of Getzels and Jackson. A brief account of Guilford's theoretical system will show how these tests have been derived and how they fit in with his conception of the structure of abilities.

Guilford has formulated a three-way classification of abilities according to (*a*) the type of operation performed – for example, remembering or making an evaluative judgement, (*b*) the material on which the operations are performed – for example, single words, diagrams, or complex concepts, (*c*) the resultant form into which the material or information is processed – for example, into classes, systems or relations.

In Guilford's model, each possible combination from the types of operation, types of product and types of content represents a different ability. This way of classifying cognitive processes puts into practice and anticipates Humphreys' (1962) theoretical suggestions for the analysis of abilities in terms of 'facets'. Thus his complete scheme envisages $5 \times 6 \times 4 = 120$ different varieties of ability corresponding to the 120 cells of the cube in Figure 1, and by the technique of factor analysis he expects to find, in general, one factor for each of the 120 cells in his three-dimensional figure.

Thus, for example, the kind of operation which he calls 'divergent

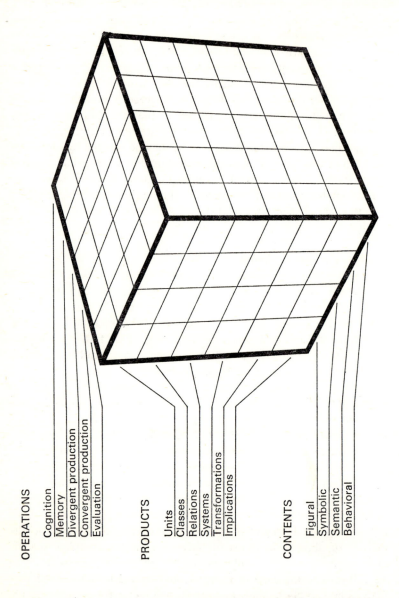

OPERATIONS

Cognition
Memory
Divergent production
Convergent production
Evaluation

PRODUCTS

Units
Classes
Relations
Systems
Transformations
Implications

CONTENTS

Figural
Symbolic
Semantic
Behavioral

Fig. 1. Three-way classification of abilities (from Guilford, 1956).

production', meaning primarily an open-ended type of task with no one right answer, when employed on symbolic material to produce units (rather than, e.g. classes or relations), result in the ability factor abbreviated as DSU (Table 1) and interpreted as word fluency. When the operation and the product remain unchanged in type, but the material or information to be processed is semantic rather than symbolic, i.e. involves meanings rather than simple signs, the ability required is called DMU and interpreted as ideational fluency.

Guilford and his associates have reported finding in empirical studies more than half of the 120 possible separate abilities needed to complete his model. Particular interest attaches in the present discussion to those which are grouped under the operation of divergent production, since many of these are seen by Guilford as components of creativity. Confining ourselves, therefore, to divergent production, we still have 24 possible abilities, which can be shown in a table with 4 columns (types of material or contents) and 6 rows (products).

Table 1, overleaf, is reproduced from Guilford and Hoepfner (1966). The last column, behavioural content, is composed of cells marked 'I' (under investigation) because this is still a hypothetical part of the system, lacking empirical support. But the idea is an interesting one, that a set of abilities might be identified which deal with the handling of information about human behaviour or, as Guilford and Hoepfner (1963) put it, 'information, essentially non-verbal, involved in human interactions where awareness of the attitudes, needs, desires, moods, intentions, perceptions, thought, etc., of other people and ourselves is important'. This corresponds with the views of Davitz and his associates, who in a study of the way emotional meaning is conveyed came to the conclusion (Davitz, 1964, p. 199) that 'it seems more reasonable to interpret emotional sensitivity itself as one kind of intelligence related to but in some respects different from other measures of verbal and non-verbal intelligence'. Although most of the sixty 'behavioural' cells in Guilford's cube are still vacant, he claims to have found tests and factors corresponding to a few of them, particularly in the 'cognition' type of operation. The first and second columns, dealing with figural and symbolic material respectively, are almost full and these full cells represent factors which Guilford considers to be rather solidly established. The last column, concerned with the divergent production of semantic material, i.e. meanings and ideas, is complete and contains most of the factors which Guilford interprets as components of or as related to creative thinking. In a complete account, however, of all aspects of

TABLE 1. *Divergent production factors*

	Figural	Symbolic	Semantic	Behavioral
Units	DFU	DSU	DMU	(I)
Classes	DFC	DSC	DMC	(I)
Relations		DSR	DMR	(I)
Systems	DFS	DSS	DMS	(I)
Transformations	DFT	(I)	DMT	(I)
Implications	DFI	DSI	DMI	(I)

Reproduced from Guilford and Hoepfner (1966)

creativity, the other columns would be involved. The 'figural' material in column 2, for example, would be expected to be related to various aspects of creativity in the visual arts, and perhaps also to other kinds of creativity, since 'figural' is used widely to cover other sense modalities besides the visual.

All this is rather abstract, and it may help to convey a better idea of Guilford's work if we list one or two of the tests corresponding to some of the ability factors, particularly to those in the 'divergent production' section:

DFU   'Add figural details to several replications of the same basic design to produce a variety of recognizable objects.'

DSU   'Write words containing a specified letter.'

DMU   'List consequences of a proposed unusual event, e.g. no babies born for one year.'

DSC   'Form as many different classes as possible from a given list of nonsense words.'

DFS   'Given three symbols, e.g. A, V and), invent a variety of monogram designs.'

These examples are all from Guilford and Hoepfner (1966), who provide the most recent progress report.

What are the advantages of this highly elaborate scheme, of which only a brief sketch has been given here? How important is it to the educational psychologist who wants to form a rational and useful picture of the nature of abilities?

Firstly, Guilford's account of the nature and structure of abilities is impressive simply because it can properly be described as a theory, in contrast to much research in the field of abilities which has rightly been criticized as blindly operational, or even as putting large numbers of tests into a kind of sausage-machine to obtain somewhat arbitrary ability factors. The three-fold classification of intelligent behaviour according to how it operates, what it operates on, and what is produced by the operation, forms a logical and useful frame of reference.

Secondly, and as an extension of this first point, Guilford's account of abilities is rather more easily related to the general body of psychological knowledge than are most factorial analyses. An attempt of this kind which discusses connexions or possible connexions between the theory of abilities and, among other topics, problem-solving and learning theory is made by Guilford (1961).

Thirdly, Guilford's theory, his analysis of many of the cognitive components in creative production, and the prolific flow of tests from his laboratory have all provided a good deal of stimulus to a new and more varied approach to high-level intellectual functions. Although general intelligence and the major group factors have proved highly useful and pervasive concepts and are nowhere near being generally superseded, few psychologists would claim that they account for all the variation in human ability that can be profitably studied. The ideas of Guilford, and of R. B. Cattell, as described earlier in this chapter, have injected new life into the subject.

On the debit side, the criticism that may be most strongly urged against Guilford's account of abilities, one that has been cogently put by Vernon (1964), is that his factors are too narrow and specific to have much predictive value except of narrow and specific criteria. Sultan (1962), for instance, as Vernon points out, found rather discouraging results when using a large battery of Guilford's tests with English grammar school pupils aged 13–14, being unable with this sample to find the expected factor structure in terms of such factors as Spontaneous Flexibility and Adaptive Flexibility. Similarly, little empirical evidence seems to be available about the actual predictive power of Guilford's creativity factors against real-life criteria, although one of his own associates (Schmadel, 1963) states that in her investigation, 'the proportion of variance contributed by the creative-thinking abilities to predicted grade-level achievement is approximately 0·18 for both Reading Vocabulary and Reading Comprehension, but only 0·06 for Arithmetic Fundamentals and 0·09 for Arithmetic Reasoning'. (The criteria referred to are parts of the California Achievement Test.) Hunt (1961) states flatly that 'in no situations are the minute, splinter-like factors of predictive significance' (p. 301). This is perhaps putting it too strongly, but undoubtedly Guilford goes to extreme lengths himself in extracting factors that are at the very opposite end of the scale from 'general intelligence' in terms of generality, and the consequence is that they are also at the opposite end of the scale in general predictive power. This is a necessary corollary of Guilford's policy of extracting a large number of very narrow, specific-like factors. Indeed it has been pointed out (Humphreys, 1962) that Thurstone (although himself a proponent of multiple abilities) supposed he had adequately sampled the whole area of abilities with less tests than Guilford has factors!

This discussion of Guilford's system has been something of a digression in a general examination of research on creativity, but it is relevant in that much of this research and the new wave of interest in the subject has been to quite a large degree led by Guilford, as in his Presidential address to the American Psychological Association (Guilford 1950), and much of it is based on tests constructed according to his theory. But one limitation of this approach is that, as earlier stated, the study of creativity properly bridges the fields of ability and personality, and all the work we have so far described has been concentrated on cognitive aspects.

IV. OTHER ASPECTS OF CREATIVITY

1. *Creativity and personality*

There is a considerable literature, however, from which we can only select a few illustrative examples, to show that the production of creative work in both the arts and sciences is associated with certain personality traits. So far the evidence is almost entirely correlational – there has been little possibility of controlled experiment or the disentanglement of cause and effect. On the whole, it is rather consistent, considering the recency of most such research.

Firstly, there is quite widespread agreement that creative scientists and most kinds of writers *do* need a generous endowment of conventional intelligence, but that this need not be exceptionally high. Anne Roe (1953), for instance, in one of her studies of eminent scientists, endorses Cox's remark that 'high, but not the highest intelligence, combined with the greatest degree of persistence, will achieve greater eminence than the highest degree of intelligence with somewhat less persistence'. Torrance (1964) further supports this view, suggesting that an IQ of about 120–130 is the minimum for most high-level creative performance.

Secondly there is a good deal of agreement about some of the other traits exhibited by creative people. One of Anne Roe's firmest findings about the eminent scientists she studied was that they displayed a marked degree of independence and self-sufficiency. 'More of these men than not, as boys, pursued rather independent paths, playing with one or a few close friends, instead of a gang.' And again, 'they are a very stubborn lot and cannot be pushed around. They do not seem to need to feel dominant with respect to other persons, but they definitely are not subservient'.

Rather similar results were found by Barron (1955) who used some of Guilford's tests and some projective techniques, and who found original or creative people to be more independent and dominant and to prefer complexity in their appreciation of works of art. Cattell and Drevdahl, also, who studied both scientists and writers of imaginative literature, using Cattell's 16 PF questionnaire, found independence or self-sufficiency a distinguishing trait among creative people. Cattell stresses that creativity is not exclusively cognitive, as Guilford's scheme may seem to imply, still less can it be equated with fluency or with two or three fluency factors. In one of their earlier studies, Cattell and Drevdahl (1955) studied 140 eminent research scientists in American universities (physicists, biologists and psychologists) and compared their mean scores on Cattell's 16 personality factors with the mean scores of the general population and also of university teachers and administrators. The profiles of the research scientists and of the university administrators and teachers showed a family resemblance, as one would expect, when compared with general population norms, but they also showed interesting differences from each other. Compared with their colleagues, the research scientists were significantly more 'schizothyme' (withdrawn, unsociable), less emotionally stable, more self-sufficient and more radical. The differences in schizothymia, self-sufficiency and radicalism were paralleled in Drevdahl's (1956) study of 'creative' and 'non-creative' students in science and arts subjects.

In another study Drevdahl and Cattell (1958) tested 153 writers of imaginative literature with the same questionnaire. Their average personality profile showed considerable general similarity to that of the research scientists, but interesting differences were also noticeable. Writers were found, as one might perhaps expect, to be higher on Cattell's factor I (emotional sensitivity or tender-mindedness) and on factor M ('Bohemianism' or unconcern, with an autistic tinge); also on factor Q4 (guilt proneness or 'ergic tension'), one of the components of anxiety in Cattell's system.

These results are interesting and plausible, suggesting that artistic creativity may be both more 'autistic' in nature than scientific creativity, in that the artist is less dominated by brutal, empirical fact, and that internal stresses and anxieties may be less antipathetic to artistic than to scientific production.

Taylor and Holland (1962) sum up what is known about the personality traits which are believed to be correlates of creativity as follows:

'There is some evidence that creative persons are more autonomous than others, more self-sufficient, more independent in judgement (they go against group opinion if they feel it is incorrect), more open to the irrational in themselves, more stable, more feminine in interests and characteristics (especially in awareness of their impulses), more dominant and self-assertive, more complex, more self-accepting, more resourceful and adventurous, more radical (Bohemian), more self-controlled, possibly more emotionally sensitive and more introverted but bold.'

2. *Creativity and environmental factors*

Even the most cursory survey must also include some account of what is known about environmental influences on creativity, its development and how it may best be fostered. Torrance (e.g. 1963, 1964) has written fairly extensively on this topic, which is a very live one at the moment among American educationists, and a short book by Bruner (1960) has been relevant and influential. The following account will be based in part on their conclusions.

Not very much is known about the effect of home influences and the effect of early training, although some indications found in the Getzels and Jackson research have already been mentioned. More work has been concentrated on the effects of schooling, and particularly on pressures and restraints both from teachers and from fellow-pupils. It is generally believed that the primary school years are crucial in the formation or non-formation of attitudes conducive to original and creative thinking, and Torrance (1964, p. 90) also claims that there are marked phases in which creativity waxes and wanes throughout the process of education.

'In the culture of the United States, one peak in development seems to be reached at age four-and-a-half. A drop, at age five, when the child enters kindergarten, is followed by increases in the first, second and third grades. At age nine, near the end of the third grade or at the beginning of the fourth, there is a rather severe decrement in almost all the creative thinking abilities. Then comes a period of recovery, especially for girls in the fifth grade. This recovery, however, is primarily in fluency and not in originality. The recovery in originality comes largely in the sixth grade. After this, there is another decrease between the sixth and seventh grades.

The shape of the development curve differs from culture to culture. Present indications are that, where there is a high degree of cultural continuity, development of these abilities is continuous. Drops in the curve appear to occur where cultural discontinuities coincide with discontinuities in development.'

In another paper, Torrance (1963) presents developmental curves of originality for children in Germany, Australia, India, and Samoa. One may suspect that the shapes of these curves are sometimes due to sampling artifacts, but his data for the U.S.A. are supported by other lines of evidence. Some of the causes ascribed for this waxing and waning of creative ability are of general importance, whether or not one accepts Torrance's account of the curve of development. They can be classified under three main heads, with some overlapping; teachers' attitudes, pressures from other pupils and school organization. Many of these points are 'obvious', some are controversial, others will infuriate teachers coping with difficult, over-large classes in dispiriting surroundings, but most have backing from empirical research (Torrance, 1964).

The teacher may prefer a conventional rote-learning approach, not only because it appears to be less trouble, but because he is disconcerted by original and unexpected solutions and is afraid of losing face. Similarly, he may feel a strong temptation to tell the original child 'what is best' in order to 'save time'.

Secondly, and this is a point that Bruner makes very effectively, teachers may disapprove in principle of 'guessing' and treat it as a kind of laziness. But, as Bruner points out, there may be kinds of guessing that require careful cultivation, and it may often be better for the student to guess intelligently than to give up or to plod along with the information he possesses. Obviously, the guessing is of different kinds, and even if done intelligently, should be supplemented by later verification, but to rule it out altogether as 'unscholarly' may lead to over-dependence on a rigid, uncreative way of thinking.

Another possible restrictive factor is a too narrow and traditional attitude to children's 'readiness' for particular topics and methods. This has often been particularly evident in the teaching of mathematics, where excessive emphasis has been placed on the mechanics of computation and particularly on 'accuracy'. Recent research has strongly suggested that many 'advanced' mathematical ideas can be grasped by ten-year old children who are not outstandingly gifted provided these ideas are divorced from their abstract mathematical expression and presented in terms with which the child is already familiar. An excellent introduction to many of the new topics that are increasingly being introduced into school mathematics teaching is provided by Fletcher (1964). Bruner quotes an experienced teacher of mathematics as saying, 'When I tell mathematicians that fourth-grade students can go a long way into "set theory", a few of them reply: "Of course". Most of them are startled. The latter are completely wrong in assuming that "set theory" is intrinsically difficult.'

Considerations of space preclude a systematic discussion of other factors which, it is strongly suspected, very often exercise a restrictive influence on children's creative thinking. Certainly as Torrance has shown, the peer-group can have this effect through harsh pressure towards conformity. This is probably particularly true of the U.S.A., but no doubt applies in other countries as well, though systematic evidence is lacking. Too wide a range of ability in a class may have a restrictive effect, and creativity may be stimulated in talented children by streaming. This is obviously a most controversial point, and beyond the scope of this account. Some of the available evidence, such as it is, is surveyed by Torrance.

Torrance also found that overemphasis or misplaced emphasis on sex roles exercised a restrictive influence, highly creative boys being likely to appear relatively effeminate and highly creative girls relatively masculine in their interests.

3. *Some recent developments*

Getzels and Jackson's study, as we saw in an earlier section, was one of the first major attempts to demonstrate a cognitive dimension in children that could be described as creativity and to distinguish it from general intelligence. The two main weaknesses of their pioneer work was firstly that the rather scanty details they provided in the way of statistical analysis supported their case only imperfectly, and secondly that they attempted to derive from the data too clear-cut a distinction between two types of children, the 'intelligent' and the 'creative'. Several subsequent researches (e.g. Edwards and Tyler, 1965; Hasan and Butcher, 1966) have suggested that the correlation between measures of 'creativity' and 'intelligence' is typically much higher than Getzels and Jackson found in their rather special sample, and that two different types of child such as they described can only be found by picking the extreme cases from a continuous distribution.

Very recently, Hudson (1966) has published an interesting book describing experiments with English schoolboys (in public schools and grammar schools) which are in many ways an adaptation and continuation of Getzels and Jackson's work. He clearly shares their distaste for elaborate statistical analysis and their conviction that two types or modes of thinking can be readily distinguished, and acknowledges a debt to them 'for the fresh air that they let in upon a world of musty, even foetid expertise' (p. 35). Hudson makes two main points, however, which have not emerged from the American research and which are worth further investigation. Firstly, he distrusts the common assumption that people who do better on tests of divergent thinking (nearly always 'open-ended' tests) are thereby shown to be more creative. Secondly, he finds a close correspondence between divergent thinkers and arts specialists, and between convergent thinkers and scientists. Much of his book is frankly speculative and polemical, but his arguments deserve consideration. The equivalence between 'divergent thinking' and 'creativity' *has* frequently been too lightly assumed, and it does appear at least plausible that one of the important differences between arts men (and women) and scientists coincides at least partially with the convergent–divergent distinction. Like Getzels and Jackson, however, Hudson concludes too readily that convergent and divergent thinkers are discrete, non-overlapping types. The truth must surely be that we are all both divergent and convergent thinkers according to situation, type of problem, conditions of administration, motivation and so on. Any statement to the contrary requires very solid and carefully derived evidence to support it.

Wallach and Kogan's (1965) book comes nearest to supplying such evidence. They begin by reviewing earlier reports of the distinction between creativity and intelligence, including the Getzels and Jackson book and papers by Cline, Richards and Needham (1963), Cline, Richards and Abe (1962), Flescher (1963), Torrance (1960), Yamamoto (1964a, 1964b, 1964c), and Guilford (1956, 1959, 1963). Their main conclusion from this survey is that no satisfactory demonstration has been provided of any separation of creativity from intelligence, and that the correlations between measures of 'creativity' are generally lower than those between a typical test of 'creativity' and one of 'intelligence' (pp. 12–13).

'In this section we have passed in review a considerable amount of evidence gathered by researchers concerned with the measurement of creativity. Our analysis of this evidence has pointed to the same general conclusion in all the instances considered. The measures that have been construed as indicators of creativity are not indicators of some single psychological dimension parallel to and distinct from the dimension of general intelligence defined by conventional intelligence test indices. On the basis of this evidence, then, there is questionable warrant for proposing the very conceptualization which most researchers have proposed: that creativity is not intelligence, and that individual differences in creativity possess the same degree of psychological pervasiveness as individual differences in general intelligence. This is a rather discouraging conclusion to have to draw. Two paths lie open to us at this point. One is to assert that no substantial cognitive dimension of individual differences exists in the creativity area which is independent of differences in general intelligence. Were this to have been our inference, the present research endeavor might have ended right here. The other path available to us, however, is to wonder if the measurement approach taken to the creativity domain in the studies we have reviewed is necessarily the correct one.'

Wallach and Kogan then describe a series of experiments which are designed, very successfully on the whole, to repair the methodological deficiencies of earlier work. They maintain that nearly all the previous attempts to assess creativity have been too narrowly confined within a psychometric, competitive frame of reference and that creative abilities are more likely to be displayed in less stressful circumstances. In their own experiments, therefore, they took great pains to ensure that close rapport was established with the 10–11 year-old-children who were to be the subjects and that all the psychological measures were obtained in game-like situations with 'test anxiety' at a minimum. Almost all the scores, moreover, were obtained from individual (not group-test) procedures. In these and other ways Wallach and Kogan's research is probably the most detailed and methodologically satisfactory attempt so far to obtain a meaningful and reliable overall assessment of children's creativity and of the extent to which it is distinguishable from intelligence.

Within the confines of this section it is possible only to mention very briefly a few of Wallach and Kogan's findings. The student with a special interest in abilities is strongly recommended to read their book. Firstly, they found that in their entire sample of 151 children, and also for boys and girls separately, their ten supposed measures of creativity proved to be highly intercorrelated, and that in contrast the correlations between 'creativity' measures and 'intelligence' measures were much

lower. The correlations of these two kinds averaged respectively about +0·4 and +0·1, and this result, the authors suggest, is a more effective demonstration of a dimension of creativity independent of intelligence than can be found in earlier work.

Wallach and Kogan also adopted the method used by Getzels and Jackson of forming contrasting groups of children high in creativity but relatively low in intelligence and vice versa, but (unlike Getzels and Jackson) reported results also from 'high-high' and 'low-low' groups. Extremely interesting results were obtained when the four groups were compared in terms of, for instance, self-confidence, attitudes to school work, social relationships, frequency of attention-seeking behaviour, anxiety level, and so on. A succinct summary of the main conclusions about these four groups is provided by the authors as follows:

'High creativity–high intelligence: These children can exercise within themselves both control and freedom, both adultlike and childlike kinds of behaviour.

'High creativity–low intelligence: These children are in angry conflict with themselves and with their school environment and are beset by feelings of unworthiness and inadequacy. In a stress-free context, however, they can blossom forth cognitively.

'Low creativity–high intelligence: These children can be described as "addicted" to school achievement. Academic failure would be perceived by them as catastrophic, so that they must continually strive for academic excellence in order to avoid the possibility of pain.

'Low creativity–low intelligence: Basically bewildered, these children engage in various defensive manoeuvres ranging from useful adaptations such as intensive social activity to regressions such as passivity or psychosomatic symptoms.

'Thus, our work progressed from the definition and operationalization of two types of cognitive activity to an investigation of their correlates in such areas as observable social and achievement-relevant behaviours, ways of forming concepts, physiognomic sensitivities, and self-described levels of general anxiety, test anxiety and defensiveness. From the findings obtained, it seems fair to conclude that the present definition of creativity denotes a mode of cognitive functioning that matters a great deal in the life of the child. Furthermore, consideration of the child's *joint* status with regard to the conventional concept of general intelligence and creativity as here defined is evidently of critical importance in the search for new knowledge concerning children's thinking.'

Wallach and Kogan (1965), p.303.

V. SUMMARY

In this chapter we have been concerned with human abilities and their assessment, with special reference to 'creativity'. We began with a brief discussion of the nature of intelligence, seeing it as a complex structure of abilities. How many distinguishable abilities are there? No clear answer can be given, because the statistical methods used by different investigators reveal abilities on diverse levels (from general to specific). It seems reasonable to suppose, however, that abilities can be grouped hierarchically.

The examination of this problem emphasized the importance of looking closely at the technical requirements of psychological tests of ability. The establishment of test reliability (self-consistency) proved to be quite difficult, but amenable to systematic improvement. The validity of a test (that is, the test's accuracy) was shown to be extremely hard to establish. Two aspects of validity were considered: 'construct validity' (the use of tests to reveal coherent psychological structures) and 'predictive validity' (the accuracy of tests in predicting future performance). Some recent attempts to sharpen the concept of validity were discussed, particularly the work of Cattell and his co-workers.

Finally, considerable attention was given to the relatively new field of research into creative abilities. One effect of this research has been to highlight the close relations that obtain between intellectual and temperamental factors. Measures of creativity are generally more bound up with factors of temperament than are conventional measures of intelligence. Nevertheless, they clearly tap areas of ability which are not adequately covered by the latter. Perhaps the principal difficulty in this type of research springs from the fact that it is not easy to arrive at measures which will clearly separate creativity and intelligence. The work of Guilford constitutes a noteworthy attempt to assay the several cognitive factors which may be relevant to performance of one kind or another. Intellectual functioning is seen as a product of a three-dimensional structure, for every performance supposes a specific kind of input, a specific mode of operation and a specific sort of output. Creativity appears within this model as a divergent mode of operation. Guilford's formulation is attractive in that it is clearly related to much current thinking in the field of learning theory. On the other hand it presupposes the existence of a large number of narrow 'abilities', nearly half of which lack any empirical support, while the predictive usefulness of the remainder is open to serious question.

Studies of creative persons bring out the importance of such temperamental factors as independence and persistence, indicating that Guilford's concept of creativity is too narrowly cognitive. Recent work also suggests the need for a closer examination of the facile dichotomy between convergent and divergent thinking and the easy assimilation: divergent = creative. Nevertheless, the work of Wallach and Kogan shows that, given a wider approach to the methodology of testing, it is possible to arrive at a battery of measures of creativity which are fairly well differentiated from measures of intelligence. Also, the combined use of the two yields a two-dimensional classification of pupils which may be of very considerable relevance to an understanding of the ways in which they react to the conditions of schooling.

REFERENCES

BARRON, F. (1955). The disposition toward originality. *J. Abnorm. Soc. Psychol.* **51,** 478–485.

BARRON, F. (1963). *Creativity and Psychological Health.* Princeton, N. J.: Van Nostrand.

BRUNER, J. S. (1960). *The Process of Education.* Cambridge, Mass.: Harvard Univ. Press.

BURT, C. (1939). The relations of educational abilities. *Brit. J. Educ. Psychol.* **9,** 45–71.

BURT, C. (1962). Critical Notice of *Creativity and Intelligence* by Getzels and Jackson, *Brit. J. Educ. Psychol.* **32,** 292–298.

CATTELL, R. B. (1963). Validity and reliability: a proposed more basic set of concepts. *J. Educ. Psychol.* **55,** 1–22.

CATTELL, R. B., and BUTCHER, H. J. (1968). *The Prediction of Achievement and Creativity.* Indianapolis, Indiana: Bobbs-Merrill.

CATTELL, R. B., and DREVDAHL, J. E. (1955). A comparison of the personality profile of eminent researchers with that of eminent teachers and administrators and of the general population. *Brit. J. Psychol.* **46,** 248–261.

CLINE, V. B., RICHARDS, J. M., and ABE, C. (1962). The validity of a battery of creativity tests in a high school sample. *Educ. Psychol. Measmt.* **22,** 781–784.

CLINE, V. B., RICHARDS, J. M., and NEEDHAM, W. E. (1963). Creativity tests and achievement in high school science. *J. Appl. Psychol.* **47**, 184–189.

COX, R. (1966). *Examinations and Higher Education.* (Duplicated). London: Society for Research into Higher Education.

CRONBACH, L. J. (1960). *Essentials of Psychological Testing.* New York: Harper.

CRONBACH, L. J., RAJARATNAM, N., and GLESER, G. C. (1963). Theory of generalizability: a liberalization of reliability theory. *Brit. J. Statist. Psychol.* **16**, 137–164.

DAVITZ, J. R. (1964). *The Communication of Emotional Meaning.* New York: McGraw-Hill.

DE MILLE, R., and MERRIFIELD, P. R. (1962). Review of 'Creativity and Intelligence' by Getzels and Jackson. *Educ. Psychol. Measmt.* **22**, 803–808.

DREVDAHL, J. E. (1956). Factors of importance for creativity. *J. Clin. Psychol.* **12**, 21–26.

DREVDAHL, J. E., and CATTELL, R. B. (1958). Personality and creativity in artists and writers. *J. Clin. Psychol.* **14**, 107–111.

EDWARDS, M. P., and TYLER, L. E. (1965). Intelligence, creativity and achievement in a non-selective public junior high school. *J. Educ. Psychol.* **56**, 96–99.

EL KOUSSY, A. A. H. (1935). The visual perception of space. *Brit. J. Psychol. Monogr. Suppl.* **20**.

FLESCHER, I. (1963). Anxiety and achievement of intellectually gifted and creatively gifted children. *J. Psychol.* **56**, 251–268.

FLETCHER, T. J. (ed.). (1964). *Some Lessons in Mathematics.* Cambridge: C.U.P.

FREEMAN, F. S. (1962). *Theory and Practice of Psychological Testing.* (Third edn). New York: Holt.

GERSHON, A., GUILFORD, J. P., and MERRIFIELD, P. R. (1963). Figural and symbolic divergent-production abilities in adolescent and adult population. *Reports from Psychol. Lab., Univ. of S. California, No. 29.*

GETZELS, J. W., and JACKSON, P. W. (1962). *Creativity and Intelligence.* New York: Wiley.

GUILFORD, J. P. (1950). Creativity. *Amer. Psychol.* **5**, 444–454.

GUILFORD, J. P. (1956). The structure of intellect. *Psychol. Bull.* **53**, 267–293.

GUILFORD, J. P. (1959). Three faces of intellect. *Amer. Psychologist.* **14**, 469–479.

E

GUILFORD, J. P. (1961). Factorial angles to psychology. *Psychol. Rev.* **68**, 1–20.

GUILFORD, J. P. (1963). Potentiality for creativity and its measurement in *Proceedings of the 1962 invitational conference on testing problems*. Princeton, N. J.: E.T.S.

GUILFORD, J. P. (1965). *Fundamental Statistics in Psychology and Education*. (fourth edn).

GUILFORD, J. P., and HOEPFNER, R. (1963). Current summary of structure-of-factors and suggested tests. *Reports from Psychol. Lab. Univ. of S. California.* **30**.

GUILFORD, J. P., and HOPFNER, R. (1966). Structure of intellect factors and their tests. *Reports from Psychol. Lab. Univ. of S. California.* **36.**

HARTOG, P., RHODES, E. C., and BURT, C. (1936). *The Marks of Examiners*. London: Macmillan.

HASAN, P. and BUTCHER, H. J. (1966). Creativity and intelligence: a partial replication with Scottish children of Getzels and Jackson's study. *Brit. J. Psychol.* **57**, 129–135.

HUDSON, L. (1966). *Contrary Imaginations*. London: Methuen.

HUMPHREYS, L. G. (1962). The organization of human abilities. *Amer. Psychol.* **17**, 475–483.

HUNT, J. MCV. (1961). *Intelligence and Experience*. New York: The Ronald Press.

MARSH, R. W. (1964). A statistical re-analysis of Getzels and Jackson's data. *Brit. J. Educ. Psychol.* **34**, 311–346.

MILHOLLAND, J. E. (1964). Theory and techniques of assessment. *Ann. Rev. Psychol.* **15**, 311–346.

RENSHAW, T. (1952). Factor rotation by the method of extended vectors. *Brit. J. Psychol. (Stat. Sect.).* **5**, 7–13.

ROE, ANNE (1953). A psychological study of eminent psychologists and anthropologists, and a comparison with biological and physical scientists. *Psychol. Monogr. Vol. 67.* **2.**

SCHMADEL, E. (1963). The relationship of creative-thinking abilities to school achievement. *Appendix A in Reports from the Psychol. Lab. Univ. of S. California.* **27.**

SULTAN, E. E. (1962). A factorial study in the domain of creative thinking. *Brit. J. Educ. Psychol.* **32**, 78–82.

TAYLOR, C. W., and HOLLAND, J. (1962). Development and application of tests creativity. *Rev. Educ. Res.* **32**, 91–102.

THORNDIKE, R. L. (1963). Some methodological issues in the study of creativity. *Proc. of 1962 Invitational Conference on testing problems.* 40–54. E.T.S. Princeton.

THURSTONE, L. L. (1938). Primary mental abilities. *Psychometr. Monogr.* **1**.

THURSTONE, L. L., and THURSTONE, T. G. (1941). Factorial studies of intelligence. *Psychometr. Monogr.* **2**.

THURSTONE, T. G. (1941). Primary mental abilities of children. *Educ. Psychol. Measmt.* **1**, 105–116.

TORRANCE, E. P. (1960). Educational achievement of the highly intelligent and the highly creative: eight partial replications of the Getzels-Jackson study. (*Research Memorandum BER–60–18*) *Bureau of Educ. Research, Univ. of Minnesota.*

TORRANCE, E. P. (1963). *Education and the Creative Potential.* Minneapolis: Univ. of Minnesota Press.

TORRANCE, E. P. (1964). Education and Creativity. Chapter 3 in C. W. Taylor (ed.) *Creativity: Progress and Potential.* New York: McGraw-Hill.

VERNON, P. E. (1964). Creativity and Intelligence. *Educ. Res.* **6**, 163–169.

WALLACH, M. A., and KOGAN, N. (1965). *Modes of Thinking in Young Children.* New York: Holt, Rinehart and Winston.

WISEMAN, S. (ed.). (1961). *Examinations and English Education.* Manchester: Manchester Univ. Press.

YAMAMOTO, K. (1964a). Role of creative thinking and intelligence in high school achievement. *Psychol. Rep.* **14**, 783–789.

YAMAMOTO, K. (1964b). Threshold of intelligence in academic achievement of highly creative students. *J. Exp. Educ.* **32**, 401–405.

YAMAMOTO, K. (1964c). A further analysis of the role of creative thinking in high-school achievement. *J. Psychol.* **58**, 277–283.

Since this chapter was written, the following publications have appeared which all, in different ways, amplify points made in the chapter.

BUTCHER, H. J. (1968). *Human Intelligence.* London: Methuen.

FREEMAN, J., BUTCHER, H. J., and CHRISTIE, T. (1968). *Creativity.* London: Society for Research into Higher Education, Monograph No. 5.

GUILDFORD, J. P. (1967). *The Nature of Human Intelligence.* New York: McGraw-Hill.

3

The Assessment of Personality Traits

F. W. WARBURTON

THE AUTHOR has previously made a brief general statement (Warburton (1961, 1962a, 1962b)), concerning personality assessment. The purpose of the present chapter is to recapitulate the main theme of these articles, to present some additional considerations, and, in particular, to outline more recent development, particularly the extensive work being carried out in the University of Illinois by R. B. Cattell, whose publications on the theory and practice of personality assessment and allied topics now extend to over 20 major books and some 270 articles.

I. IMPORTANCE OF THE TOPIC

Psychologists have explored human personality by many different methods, ranging from the murky depths of psychoanalysis at one end of the scale to the narrow precision of sensory perception at the other. The present article is confined to the study of personality *traits*, such as anxiety, sociability, sensitivity, dominance, and the like. Trait measurement is based on the psychometric techniques, notably factor analysis, which have been so successful in the analysis of intellectual ability, in which progress has been achieved by the thorough, although piecemeal, investigation of the whole field of ability, from mathematics and the classics to tactile discrimination, and the subsequent use of correlational and factorial methods to reduce hundreds of minor aptitudes to those few minor factors such as verbal reasoning, non-verbal intelligence and spatial ability, that account for most of the differences between individual ability. This is in striking contrast to the position in most fields of psychology in which investigators, in the absence of any reliable taxonomy, make up their own categories, in their own heads, i.e. undertake a task beyond the competence of their species

100

(programmed by God), although the task is within the scope of the electronic computer (programmed by Man). It is clearly worth-while for psychologists to investigate the application of these analytic methods to personality characteristics, despite the fact that the structure of personality is far more complex than that of ability. The compelling reason for studying personality traits is, of course, their importance in human history. The assessment of other people's 'personality', 'temperament', 'character', is perhaps the major preoccupation of the human race and certainly the most frequent topic of conversation. We could not survive socially for twenty-four hours without being trait psychologists and having some capacity to take people's wishes and feelings into account and to predict their reactions. Fortunately, it has proved possible to analyse human personality with some degree of success, as there is considerable consistency in people's social behaviour. Mr Brown isn't always Mr Brown, but he is as a rule, otherwise he wouldn't be himself. Without consistency (as well as flexibility) of personality social intercourse would become chaotic, and any form of personality assessment, such as interviewing or the writing of references, would be meaningless. Nor could people sensibly form friendships with one another and drama would become little but euphony. Despite its manifold difficulties, the study of the structure of personal characteristics is one of the most important tasks that awaits solution by quantitative psychology.

II. OBSERVATIONAL TECHNIQUES

The first obvious step in studying personality traits (or anything else) is to list them *in toto*, and the second to study their relationships in order to establish a workable taxonomy. Cattell, whose laboratory has carried out more work than any other in this field, began with Allport and Odbert's list of over 4,000 terms describing personal qualities, culled from the dictionary. At first sight, it might be imagined that the best procedure would then be to observe people's behaviour in everyday life. For example we might observe children in a playground, and count the number of times they behave in certain ways, e.g. how often they talk to one another (sociability), or hit one another (aggression). Such observational studies have occasionally been made both of children and of adults, but there are two major difficulties in this approach to the problem. Firstly, the environment cannot be controlled with any exactitude; for example, no two playgrounds produce identical social situations, nor the same situation on two separate occasions. The second difficulty is to obtain agreement between judges as to whether or not a person actually behaves in a certain way. Differences of opinion arise over such simple matters of fact as to whether one child spoke to another, and there are usually wide divergences in the interpretation of the individual acts claimed to show aggression, friendliness, etc. Thus the assessment of personality by observational methods differs basically from the assessment of ability, for which it is relatively easy to obtain standard situations, measures and interpretations.

III. MODES OF APPROACH TO PERSONALITY ASSESSMENT

Cattell attempted to study the whole domain of personality characteristics in three distinct stages. In chronological order, these were:

1. ratings of people's behaviour in everyday life, made by people well acquainted with them, e.g. by fellow students in a University Hall of Residence;
2. questionnaires concerning emotional and social reactions, e.g. Do you object more to (*a*) swearers or (*b*) gum chewers?;
3. objective tests, usually carried out under laboratory conditions, in which a person is set a task involving the personality, e.g. complex cancellation carried out under varying conditions of speed and difficulty, or playing shove-halfpenny.

Cattell decided to study ratings of everyday behaviour first, as they necessarily form the ultimate criterion of our personality which is basically shown by our behaviour in society, not how we claim to behave according to a questionnaire, or how we perform in laboratory tests.

1. *Ratings*

Ratings of persons under controlled conditions over long periods of three months or more, by teams of judges who know them very well, such as members of the same family, professional colleagues, or students living in the same hall of residence, give fairly reliable results.

The following precautions were taken. The personality traits to be rated, such as 'dominance', were clearly defined and exemplified by a list of 'critical incidents'. The assessors attended training courses in recognizing, distinguishing and recording the traits they were to assess. Each subject was rated by at least four, and sometimes twenty judges whose assessments were averaged. The reliability of ratings increased considerably with increase in the number of raters, since individual prejudices tend to cancel out when the ratings are summed. The rater lived with the subject, e.g. in a college, or was in constant social contact with him, and was consequently able to observe him for a long time and to see him in many roles and situations. The period of observation was at least two or three months and sometimes a year, so that the rater observed the subject in a number of emotional situations. There is some evidence that the reliability of ratings may decrease as the time of observation is increased from, say, a few hours to several days, but they rise again as the length of acquaintance is extended to periods of months and years. Typically the first fifty to a hundred hours of observation are spent in revising first impressions, and during this period the reliability tends to drop but high reliabilities of the order of 0·90 are sometimes found with judgements based on long periods of time.

One of the main difficulties in making ratings is that assessors are unduly influenced by stereotype and halo effects, i.e. they tend to rank the same person high or low in all traits. This can be partly avoided by taking the following steps:

(i) by having the traits rated one at a time, thus focussing attention on behaviour rather than on individuals. Assessments should be made on one trait only, using cards on which are written the names of the persons comprising the whole group. This method is less vulnerable to 'halo' effects than the assessment of one person at a time on a number of traits;

(ii) by having, in some traits, the 'undesirable' pole, e.g. suspiciousness', rated high and in others the 'desirable' pole, e.g. 'conscientiousness' rated high;

(iii) by allowing an interval of a day or two between single-trait ratings;

(iv) by discouraging the raters from discussing the subjects, since independent judgements are more valid and reliable than team decisions, which tend to reflect the opinions of the team's more dominant members;

(v) by giving verbal descriptions of the statistical range such as Grade A 'definitely above average', Grade B 'average' and Grade C 'definitely below average', and by giving psychological descriptions of individual traits such as extraversion;

(vi) by insisting that the whole scale be used. For example, on a 10 point scale some raters may completely avoid extreme grades such as '1' and '10', however many subjects they rate. It is advisable to tell these judges that they have been especially given extra pigeon-holes numbered 0 and 11, which must on no account be used.

2. *Questionnaires*

Questionnaires suffer chiefly from the drawback of being fakable, although this difficulty is not of the overriding importance that might at first be imagined. In practice the tendency of most subjects to give answers that are 'socially desirable' may be counteracted by various technical devices. Many questionnaires include an L-score (or lie scale) based on answers to a group of items that tend to place the subject in a good social and moral light, but are rarely practised in everyday life, e.g. 'I always keep secrets that I promise to keep', and 'I have always obeyed the law'. Also F-scores (face validity) can be used to spot the opposite type of person, one who undervalues himself, e.g. a person who thinks he is neurotic would probably answer 'true', to the items 'everything seems tasteless' and 'I have a headache most of the time', whereas in real life, neurotics are usually too worried about losing their sanity, their livelihood, their friends and their life to worry about little things like taste buds and headaches. Dodderers who cannot make up their own minds even about themselves can also be eliminated by the provision of 'can't say' or 'don't know' alternatives for each item, although little can be done about self-deceivers who give answers that bear little relationship to their everyday behaviour.

Alternatively, we may partial out the effects of social desirability (L-scores) by multiple regression techniques. This is rather complex statistically, and does not always give satisfactory results. Forced choice questions are sometimes used which ask subjects to choose between pairs of items previously shown to be similar in respect of social desirability (or undesirability) but which nevertheless act as discriminators of personality traits. Or the final version of a questionnaire can be confined to those items which subjects have found difficult to fake. In this method, the subjects first work under normal conditions, and then they retake the questionnaire after a long period of time under instructions to present themselves in as favourable a light as possible.

Differences between their responses on the two occasions are then analysed in order to spot the most fakable items. Faking is, of course, a personality characteristic itself, and a questionnaire may be used solely for the score it gives for this trait. Some industrial firms reject candidates for management training who have a high 'motivational distortion' score, on the grounds that high scores are either unprincipled or imperceptive, whereas other organizations prefer to take fakers, because this is thought to indicate a strong desire to succeed. Lie scales are, in fact, measures of anxiety and their efficiency as predictors of vocational success depends on whether anxiety is an advantage or disadvantage in the occupation concerned. It must be remembered, however, that blatant cheating is the exception, not the rule. And it must play a very small part in the responses of children or those who take tests anonymously for research purposes, or for people who ask for advice or help, as in a psychiatric or child guidance or marriage guidance clinic, where people may be given a personality questionnaire to fill out for diagnostic purposes. For instance, a husband and wife who are on bad terms might complete a questionnaire not only for themselves but for each other as well, so that points of misunderstanding can be highlighted. Similarly, a mother and father might answer a questionnaire as they think their child would answer it. Faking is likely to be a more serious problem in selection than in guidance, since the subject's main purpose in selection is to secure as high a score as possible, whereas in guidance, whether educational or psychiatric, it is in his own interest to present both his strong and his weak points. A vitally important point is that the possibility of faking by no means entirely destroys the value of questionnaires, since assessments obtained from questionnaires are correlated with those from ratings and tests in which faking by the subjects plays no part whatever. The person who reports himself as anxious tends to be the same person whom others report as anxious in everyday life and he also tends to be the same person who gets into a dither during anxiety-provoking test situations in psychological laboratories. There is a great deal of difference between showing that questionnaires have serious drawbacks and proving that they have no validity at all.

Another important factor that influences questionnaire responses is 'acquiescence', the tendency of some subjects to say 'Yes' in preference to 'No' whatever the content of the question, e.g. more people approve than disapprove of an entirely fictitious Metallic Metals Act. As we all know, the ability to say 'No' when necessary is a desirable personal quality in professional life. This factor can be largely controlled by changing the questions to a grammatical form such that an equal number of 'Yes' and 'No' answers contribute to scores for the various traits. This is not as simple, however, as might appear, as many questions read awkwardly when requiring a negative answer. Also, the linguistic opposite of a question is not necessarily the opposite psychologically, e.g. a lot of people who would say 'No' to the question 'Do you like the Beatles?' would not reply 'Yes' to the question 'Do you dislike the Beatles', and some people would, quite logically, put 'No' to both questions.

3. *Objective Tests*

The problem of faking in questionnaires and the additional opportunities afforded by a new technique of assessment led Cattell to devise a large number of objective tests. In these the possibility of faking is much reduced by:

1. giving ability tests, but marking them for speed, persistence, etc.;
2. studying automatic responses such as speech and handwriting;
3. springing unexpected tasks on a subject, such as remembering the test instructions;
4. disguising the purpose of the test, e.g. marking the frequency of use of nouns, verbs, etc., in an essay;
5. giving tests in which socially desirable responses are not known to the subject, e.g. shading rectangles;
6. presenting the subject with an emotional situation which will force him to react naturally, e.g. keeping him longer than the official time;
7. using emotional content, e.g. photographs of car accidents;
8. administering physical and psychological tests known to correlate with personality traits.

IV. SOME LIMITATIONS OF PERSONALITY ASSESSMENT

As critics of our national life so frequently point out, there is a considerable resistance in this country to anything new and to anything embarrassing. Personality assessment by professional psychologists seems to many people to be an intrusion into their private lives, although they will accept the verdicts and pronouncements of untrained amateurs, such as doctors, magistrates, palmists and Auntie Mabel of Home Notes. This attitude has certainly slowed up progress in this branch of knowledge in Britain even among psychologists, but there are also more solid reasons for regarding this work with considerable caution. The testing of intelligence, almost as difficult a topic to convince laymen about, has nevertheless been applied by society on a vast scale in education, industry and the Services. Personality tests on the other hand are still at the developmental stage, and it has yet to be demonstrated that they are as valid and reliable as tests of cognitive capacity.

A major difficulty is that people's personality is much more labile than their intellectual capacity, although there is clearly an underlying constancy, otherwise we would not know the difference between one another. A moment's reflection about friends and relatives we have known well for many years will bring to mind the high level of overall consistency in their social behaviour and attitudes. Several influences, however, reduce the constancy of our behaviour, some of these influences appearing to originate within the individual himself and others to spring from the environment. Although moodiness (which varies, of course, from occasion to occasion) can itself be regarded as a personality characteristic, it affects all our behaviour and attitudes. In a good mood we tend to be stable, sympathetic extraverts, but in our bad moods we are irritable, grudging and withdrawn. Social behaviour also depends a great deal upon external events and good or bad fortune. Our personality may change permanently after bereavement or the onset of ill health, or it may change temporarily after passing events, as when we kick the cat because the home team missed a penalty. Moreover, we adjust our behaviour to circumstances, playing different roles in different situations. A young man, for example, behaves differently in the company of his girl friend, his colleagues, his mother, his boss and himself.

Another important criticism is that the correlations found between the various items and factors in personality questionnaires are not due to the fact that social behaviour is actually linked in any such manner but springs from a universal tendency to classify all material, psychological or otherwise, in certain standard ways. This tendency has been extensively studied by Osgood *et al.* (1957), who names it the semantic differential. His methods can be applied to all types of judgements concerned with anything from planets to film stars. Accordingly, the main factors he has established are:

1. Evaluation – the scales having the purest loading on this factor are good–bad, optimistic–pessimistic, positive–negative, complete–incomplete and timely–untimely.

2. Potency – hard–soft, heavy–light, masculine–feminine, severe–lenient, strong–weak.

3. Oriented Activity – active–passive, excitable–calm, hot–cold.

4. Tautness – this factor is labelled with considerable tentativeness – it comprises angular–rounded, straight–curved, sharp–blunt.

5. Novelty – new–old, unusual–usual, youthful–mature.

6. Receptivity – savoury–tasteless, colourful–colourless, sensitive–insensitive, interesting–boring, refreshed–weary, pungent–bland.

7. Aggressiveness – only the item aggressive–defensive had a sizeable loading on this factor.

There are certainly clear analogies between some of the semantic factors and personality factors, e.g. Osgood's Factor 1 is actually called 'stability', and can obviously be paired with Cattell's Anxiety, Eysenck's Neuroticism and Burt's Emotionality; Factor 3 'Oriented Activity' with 'active–passive' as its main loading is possibly linked with Extraversion; Factor 2 'Potency' with 'hard–soft', 'heavy–light', 'severe–lenient', 'strong–weak', 'tenacious–yielding' is similar to Cattell's second-order factor of Sensitivity (Tender *v.* Toughmindedness); and Factor 5, 'Novelty', with 'new–old' as its main loading and 'usual–unusual' markedly resembles Radicalism, so that the first four second-order personality factors have analogies among the first six factors in semantic space.

There are several reasons, however, why the semantic differential should not be regarded as invalidating work on personality assessment. Firstly, any universal tendency to classify concepts in certain ways seems more likely to be due to the fact that the external world is organized in that way than that it represents merely a tendency to organize verbal symbols. There is no obvious reason why some human beings should be *imagined* to be 'unstable' any more than some physical objects should be imagined to be 'wobbly'.

Secondly, even if the apparent structure of personality does spring from a tendency to organize human behaviour according to certain *a priori* verbal categories, such as potency and activity, and not from any regularities in everyday behaviour which could be verified by objective observation and recording, these classifications (not necessarily in the form of tests) would nevertheless have social reality and could continue to be used for a wide variety of educational and vocational purposes such as selection, allocation, streaming, interviewing, guidance, etc. However, the main objection to regarding personality assessment as due to semantic differentials is that a similar structure of behaviour appears in people's actual performance in laboratory tests, in which there is no question of the manipulation of words. Structure may be revealed, for example, by the relationships between performance in respect of speed, accuracy, trend, improvement and variability under various conditions with various types of material. Semantics play no part in the observed correlations and the factors which are derived from them. Yet these regularities observed in non-verbal behaviour are highly similar to those derived from verbal report questionnaires.

An interesting feature of work in the personality field is that research findings which at first appear to be contradictory are in fact in agreement when considered in relation to the cultural background of the subjects. For example, success as a teacher may correlate highly with introversion in Britain, but with extraversion in the United States. Bearing in mind, however, that the British way of life is more introverted than the American, it is clear that these results verify one another despite their statistical opposition, each demonstrating that society approves of its typical members as leaders of the young. This problem does not arise in the case of cognitive traits in which high ability is almost invariably found to be an asset, however diverse the social background of the subjects.

V. THE STRUCTURE OF PERSONALITY

According to the statistical analysis of results obtained from Cattell's voluminous work, questionnaires may be classified according to the following scheme of first and second order factors, the first order factors being designated by letters and the second order factors by numbers, as follows:

I ANXIETY

Q_3- Undependability *v.* Self-Discipline (low Self-Sentiment)
$C-$ Instability *v.* Stability (low Ego-Strength)
Q_4+ Tenseness *v.* Calmness (Id Pressure)
$O+$ Insecurity *v.* Self-Confidence (Guilt Proneness)
$L+$ Suspiciousness *v.* Broadmindedness (Paranoid Tendency)

II EXTRAVERSION

$H+$ Unreservedness *v.* Shyness (low Reactivity to Threat)

A+   Friendliness *v.* Aloofness (Cyclothymia *v.* Schizothymia)
E+   Dominance *v.* Submissiveness
F+   Surgency *v.* Desurgency
Q_2−   Group Dependences *v.* Self-Reliance

III TENDERMINDEDNESS
I+   Sensitivity *v.* Insensitivity
N−   Tendermindedness *v.* Toughmindedness

IV LIBERALISM
Q_1+   Radicalism *v.* Conservatism
M+   Unconventionality *v.* Conventionality

V MORAL ATTITUDES
G+   Moral Attitudes *v.* Expediency (Super-Ego Strength)

Guilford (1949a, 1949b) has also carried out several analyses of personality traits that call for a second-order analysis. Intercorrelations between his main thirteen primary factors were calculated by Lovell (1945). Her first factor was characterized by emotional stability, calmness, objectivity, freedom from depression, self-confidence, co-operativeness, lack of introspection, agreeableness and sociability, as opposed to instability, depression, nervousness, hypersensitivity, inferiority feelings, overcriticalness, quarrelsomeness, introspectiveness and social shyness. The close resemblance of this factor to stability *v.* neuroticism, is obvious, although there is not perfect agreement.

The second factor is equally clear. It contrasts inhibited disposition, inactivity, submission, social shyness, inferiority feelings, and depression with sociability, ascendance, self-confidence, freedom from depression and general activity. The similarity of this factor to extraversion–introversion is again marked.

Similar to Lovell's work is that of North (1949), who analysed the intercorrelations between the factors resulted in which the two rotated factors bear a marked resemblance to Neuroticism and Extraversion–Introversion. The first is characterized by C, emotional instability, depression, introspectiveness, and to some extent by social shyness. The latter is characterized by happy-go-lucky carefreeness on the extravert side and by social shyness on the introvert side.

Moreover, extensive work by Eysenck (1953) has established two major factors, Neuroticism and Extraversion, so that three major workers in this field carrying out completely independent analyses, usually on different materials, and covering between them an amount of research that has rarely been equalled in psychology (described by Eysenck, 1962, as 'millions of hours'), agree that the two major factors are anxiety (or neuroticism) and extraversion–introversion. These two factors may be taken as firmly established in the same way that general intelligence is established in cognitive psychology, and trait psychologists (clinical, vocational, educational, counselling, consulting, guidance) who ignore these findings and make up their own major categories are highly likely to be barking up the wrong tree, although, of course, we still need a great deal more detailed and reliable information about the structure of the contributory primary factors.

The general findings concerning Cattell's factors (together with the presentation of the typical questionnaire items and objective tests) are:

I. ANXIETY FACTORS

Q_3 + *Self-discipline* v. *Undependability* (*self-sentiment*)

High scorers in Q_3 are persons who can be relied on. They show socially approved behaviour, self-control, foresight, considerateness of others and conscientiousness. Q_3 is also positively related to ambition. The person who scores low in this factor is undependable and frequently fails to keep his promises. He lacks will control and character. He is not conscientious or considerate for others.

Questionnaire items

Concentrates easily; chooses his words carefully when speaking; likes to plan ahead; believes in insurance schemes; dislikes waste; does not put an argument forward unless he is sure of it; keeps his feelings under control; as chairman of a committee would wish to hear everyone's views before deciding on course of action; does things in deliberated, methodical way; perseveres in face of obstacles; is slow to change his interests; enjoys detailed work; in conversation likes to deal thoroughly with one topic at a time.

Tests

The conscientious person persists longer when undertaking a task, e.g. drawing a perfect circle freehand; is more accurate in all tasks, e.g. draws fewer lines touching the edges of mazes; shades geometrical figures more neatly; gives more exact temporal or spatial estimates, i.e. to the nearest second or 1/10 inch, or guesses the length of plane journeys to 5 minutes, takes fewer risks on gambling games.

C+ *Stability* v. *Instability* (*ego-strength*)

C *is* stability. As with physical objects, it is the capacity to remain unmoved and not to be knocked off balance by outside pressures. Some people, like some ships, have inbuilt stabilizers.

The person who scores high on Factor C tends to be emotionally mature and realistic about life. The person who scores low on this factor tends to be immature and changeable. Factor C is similar to the characteristic described by psychoanalysts as 'ego-strength'.

Questionnaire items

Satisfied with how he has lived his life; can meet emergencies; does not think modern life has many frustrating situations; does not avoid exciting situations; understands what people are talking about; thinks atomic discoveries will improve his future.

Tests

The essential feature of this factor is the ability to stand up to difficult or unexpected situations. It is assessed by tests such as backward writing (rigidity), the tendency to do better on difficult tasks than easy, on speeded than on untimed tests, on practised than on unpractised tasks, to have relatively high output when tired or under frustrating conditions, e.g. in a rhymes test in which Part I is easy, Part II impossible (words like 'month'), and Part III easy, the unstable person becomes rattled by failure and does relatively badly on Part III. Unstable persons are also suggestible, e.g. they make the flips go faster or slower as instructed in a reversible cube test. They cannot make up their minds in unfamiliar tasks requiring quick judgements, such as estimating a large number of dots inside two-inch squares or in identifying specimens of handwriting. In a risk-taking test the unstable person will be particularly upset by failure and have low scores following failure relative to his scores following success. Low C scorers tend to perform relatively poorly when the content of tests such as word association, memory, comprehension, is emotional, e.g. they shy away from horrific drawings and are unable to reproduce them accurately.

Q_4+ *Tenseness* v. *Calmness* (*Id pressure*)

The person who scores high on Factor Q_4 tends to be tense, excitable, restless, fretful, impatient and in a general turmoil.

Questionnaire items

Trivial things get on his nerves; becomes tense when thinking over events of the day; gets angry with people easily, is much irritated by small setbacks; his nerves get on edge and he finds it difficult to return to normal after an argument or near-accident; lets off steam when annoyed; is impatient at delays.

Tests

High Q_4 persons have high scores on 'annoyances', e.g. 'Are you annoyed by car honkers, burpers?' etc. They also tend to be impatient and hence do relatively badly on difficult tasks.

O *Insecurity* v. *Self-confidence* (*guilt proneness*)

In some ways the high O, anxious person is the opposite of the tense high Q_4 person, as he tends to be squashed flat and kept quiet by the exigencies of everyday life. It is an effort for him to keep going, and the fault lies (so he thinks) in his own weaknesses. He is intrapunitive, suffers from self blame, and feels unable to meet the demands of everyday life. He tends to be depressed, moody, a worrier, brooding, avoids people and is perturbed by his own mood changes.

The person who scores low on Factor O has an unanxious confidence in himself and in his capacity to deal with things.

Questionnaire items

Worries without reason, feels that he would never make a success of life, is depressed if people don't show appreciation; is discouraged by failure; feels guilty about unimportant things; is discouraged because life fails to work out as it should; feels lonely and inadequate in company; doesn't easily forget past mistakes; is disheartened by criticism; feels inferior to associates; takes medicines on his own.

Tests

A person who is unsure of himself makes longer estimates on the time he would require to do certain tasks, e.g. cleaning shoes, mowing lawns, writing letters. His estimates for himself are particularly low in relation to how long he thinks other people will take to do the same task. He has a low level of aspiration and makes lower estimates of his overall test performance. In projection tests of the 'what faces do you see in the fire?' type he sees a greater number of threatening objects. His unsureness leads him to give more 'don't know' or 'can't say' answers.

L+ Suspiciousness v. *Broadmindedness* (*paranoid tendency*)

This factor shows itself strikingly in abnormal populations in the form of paranoia. The person who scores high on Factor L is mistrusting and sceptical of idealistic motives in others. The person who scores low on this factor tends to be free from jealousy, concerned about other people's welfare, and a good team worker. In some ways criticalness may be a better name for Factor L, since among the educated it appears rather as the ability to carry out critical thinking, particularly of the destructive kind.

Questionnaire items

Believes most people dislike putting themselves out for others; hates being pushed around; worries if talked about behind his back; is 'contrary' if bossed; thinks most people are a little queer mentally; is considered hard-headed and critical; feels hostile towards rivals; can't tolerate braggarts or affected people; thinks people don't understand him; is suspicious of too friendly and honest people, believes people are honest from fear of being found out; thinks his parents' discipline was too strict, that most people are not open to reason; that the troubles of the times are due to ill-will.

Tests

The suspicious person is expected to give lower grades to examples of other people's work, such as a 10 year-old child's drawings; to criticize the time taken for a chemist to make up a prescription; to ascribe more luck to successful people in their occupations, especially top ranking professions; to be pessimistic about the reactions of the public to moral issues; to regard more types of social behaviour as abnormal; to volunteer for fewer activities; to resent helping other people, e.g. acting as a subject in a psychological experiment.

II. 'EXTRAVERSION' FACTORS

H+ *Unreservedness* v. *Shyness (reactivity to threat)*

The person who scores high on Factor H is sociable and spontaneous. He tends to be thick-skinned and adventurous and is able to face wear and tear in dealing with people and emotional situations without fatigue.

The person who scores low on this trait, is shy and withdrawn.

Questionnaire items

Speaks up on social occasions: is not shy in company or in the presence of superiors; doesn't mind being the centre of attention; is impulsive; blurts out things in company that later land him in difficulties; likes addressing a large group; would rather interview buyers than set up blueprints; doesn't mind people watching him work; would report to a superior by speaking to him rather than by sending a letter; is active in organizing clubs; thinks most people are glad to meet him at a party.

Tests

In all tests the high H person tends to be inaccurate but fast. He is relatively fast in difficult tests and in embarrassing tasks; he is more fluent about the future than the past; he is difficult to embarrass; takes tasks readily; has short-term rather than long-term goals.

A+ *Friendliness* v. *Aloofness* (*Cyclothymia* v. *Schizothymia*)

This factor stresses good naturedness. The person who scores high tends to be good-natured, easy going, ready to co-operate and attentive to people. He is generous in personal relationships. The person who scores low on Factor A tends to be stiff, cool and aloof. He likes things rather than people.

Questionnaire items

Would rather be a salesman than a physicist; a schoolteacher than a forester; a Y.M.C.A. secretary than an artist; a waiter than a carpenter; a banker than a chemist; a life insurance salesman than a farmer;

a personnel officer than a machinery expert; prefers debating to photography, and novels to non-fiction books; likes talking to people in trains, prefers popular resorts to country cottages.

Tests

This person has many friends and acquaintances, obtains higher scores in memory and association tests for items involving people rather than things; is less critical of the tester than the test (although not tending to be critical of either); complies with test instructions (in order to spare the examiner's feelings); volunteers to work longer.

E+ *Dominance* v. *Submissiveness*

The person who scores high on Factor E is dominant, self-assured, assertive and courageous in his approach to social situations. He dislikes conventions and abhors censorship.

Questionnaire items

Does not understate his powers; makes smart remarks at the expense of others; has been called stuck up; likes being knowledgeable enough to boss his companions; would bet money he was right after an argument; is satisfied with his capacities; does not think one should show much respect for people's pet ideas; does not feel nervous in the presence of his superiors; persists in a remark if other people overlook it; feels he excels others in some characteristics; is considered tough and practical, 'has it out' with anyone who hectors him; thinks he is generally right in an argument, tries out remarks to see if they shock people; will borrow something without permission; speaks his 'mind'; doesn't suffer fools gladly; speaks to important people at parties; expresses openly any disagreement with a teacher; bosses waiters and waitresses; likes having personal servants.

Tests

Is highly fluent about himself compared with others; uses a lot of personal pronouns; expects to engage in many more activities in the future, rates his present and potential skill highly and is confident of achieving a high level of performance in completely new activities, such as pelota or building ostrich sheds.

F+ Surgency v. *Desurgency*

Surgent people are lively, effervescent and bubbly. The person who scores high on this factor tends to be cheerful, talkative, expressive, quick and alert. He is given to cracking jokes and telling stories and mimicry, he likes a job with change and variety, prefers a lively party to a hobby, gets bored and craves excitement, and expresses emotions easily and naturally. This factor has an overall talkative, witty, lime-lighting Gallic quality. The person who scores low on Factor F tends to be taciturn, reticent, and introspective.

Questionnaire items

Likes dashing rather than sober dress; would rather be an actor than a builder; is considered lively and enthusiastic; is happy-go-lucky; takes life gaily; cracks jokes; is talkative; likes excitement; enjoys practical jokes; likes a job with plenty of variety and travel.

Tests

In tests the high F scorer is expansive; attempts more tasks; draws larger shapes; makes larger checkmarks; uses more words, particularly adjectives, in descriptive writing.

Q₂— Self-reliant v. *Group Dependence*

The person who scores high on Factor Q_2 is independent, accustomed to going his own way and making his own decisions. The high Q_2 person would rather work with one or two assistants than with committees, does not avoid doing things that might make him seem odd, and is not afraid of his own ideas just because they are unusual. He tends to avoid society because it wastes time, not because of any emotional rejection, and because experience has told him his thinking is well enough organized to solve problems for himself. High Q_2 is a matter of independence of mind and of individuality of action rather than confident social behaviour, since it goes with high introversion, not extraversion. For example, executives, scientists and criminals, all of whom have to take individual decisions, score high in this factor.

The low Q_2 person tends to be conventional and fashionable, enjoying social approval and admiration and preferring to work and make decisions with other people.

Questionnaire items

Likes to plan things without help; to learn from a book rather than by discussing; would rather work on his own than with a committee; likes a teacher who leaves him to himself; prefers photography to playing in a band; likes to solve problems on his own; likes to make his decisions alone; likes to travel abroad without a guide; detests organized tours or any sort of gaggle; gets more ideas from discussing a book with others than from reading it; avails himself more frequently of opportunities of help during a test session; volunteers to take part in team games rather than in individual exercises.

Tests

Objective tests of this factor are difficult to construct. The high Q_2 person should give a large proportion of unusual answers, i.e. those checked least often by others.

III. TENDERMINDEDNESS FACTORS

I+ Sensitivity v. *Insensitivity*

This factor contrasts the tender-minded person who eschews force as a means of gaining his ends with the tough who would always use force if he considered it necessary. The person who scores high on Factor I tends to be sensitive and tender-minded, a person with a labile, imaginative, delicate, aesthetic mind, introspective and fastidious. He is somewhat impractical in general affairs. He dislikes crude people, and rough occupations. The person who scores low on Factor I tends to be tough, practical and realistic.

Questionnaire items

Likes to have his privacy respected; does not like vaudeville humour; prefers cathedral choirs to Strauss waltzes, a select club to a noisy bar, fencing and dancing to football and boxing, visiting an art gallery to playing cards, holidays abroad to holidays in own country, poetry to prose, a good novel to a military or political narrative, religious controversy to marketing news; he does not think modern art is too eccentric and is sensitive to the artistic quality of his surroundings.

Tests

The high scorer in I should be more fluent in written and perceptual tasks, since his sensitivity springs in part from an intense emotional awareness of the situation (although not necessarily an intellectual understanding). Similarly he will tend to produce a greater number of original solutions to problems such as 'What would happen if everyone suddenly became incurably blind?' or 'Give some uses for a fountain pen cap (other than baling out a bird bath)'. He will also have more suggestions to make for improving tests. On the other hand, his sensitivity to the implications of a task should make him relatively slow on complex tasks such as questionnaires concerning political or moral issues or his own personal likes and dislikes; he is likely, for example, to have food fads.

N— *Unaffectedness* v. *Shrewdness*

The person who scores high in Factor N is polished, experienced and worldly. He is flexible in viewpoint, alert to manners and to social obligations and to the reactions of others. He is a clear thinker with a trained, realistic and often expedient approach to problems, motivated in part by social climbing.

The low N person is a vague, naïve, simple person who may get along well with people in a primitive heart-to-heart way, but has no skills in anticipating personality and socially expedient needs and reactions or the done thing. He is apt to be slow and awkward.

Questionnaire items

(The questionnaire items of the tests are indirect measures of this factor, since they are based on the social attitudes accompanying these personality traits.) Would vote for vegetarianism on the grounds of humane treatment for animals rather than for sterilization of defectives; opposes compulsory vaccination and strong national military forces; thinks it is unnecessary to use force to get things done, even for people's own good; objects to commercials on radio; believes in free discipline rather than corporal punishment in schools.

Tests

In tests on the appropriateness of certain punishments for certain crimes, the high scorer in N will not only tend to advocate light punishment, but also light punishment relative to his own evaluation of the seriousness of the crime.

Q_1+ *Radicalism* v. *Conservatism*

This factor is a non-political radicalism. The high scorer is inclined to experiment in everyday life and in social affairs. He likes changing things, whereas the conservative usually prefers to leave things alone. He is usually interested in social problems. He frequently takes issue with ideas, either old or new, and enjoys breaking the crust of custom and tradition, and leading and persuading people. He is inclined to question things everywhere and has the bit between his teeth whenever a better, more resourceful way of doing things can be perceived. Although this attitude sometimes springs from resentment of the success of others, it seems to be more often the case that the intellectual and general success he has enjoyed in the past favours this pitting of his own reasons against tradition. The person who scores low on Factor Q_1 tends to be conservative, cautious and unresourceful. He is patient in tribulation.

Questionnaire items

Believes one should not be ashamed of nudity; that birth control is necessary; that society should adopt new customs more readily; opposes strict Sunday observance; thinks explorers should have more news-space than athletes; considers divorce should be by mutual consent; would rather read H. G. Wells than see an historical movie; likes to solve problems by thinking them out rather than by accepting solutions.

Tests

In tests this person will be an innovator, with many suggestions for improvements; he will be in favour of most new things, such as electronic bacon-slicers and evening classes in urban anthropology. He will be more fluent in ideas for solving situations, or using things in a novel manner.

$M+$ *Unconventionality* v. *Conventionality*

This factor is akin to Bohemianism. The person who scores high on Factor M tends to be unconventional, unconcerned and bohemian.

The person who scores low on Factor M tends to be anxious to do the right thing, and is often rather narrowly correct.

Unconventionality is associated with verbal, artistic, literary, aesthetic, radical, tenderminded, theoretical, creative interests, and conventionality with more formal interests such as mechanical engineering, physics, statistics and economics. Neurotics, drug addicts, criminals, homosexuals and those with marital problems score well above average in this factor.

In contrast, the low M person lives very much in the external world, and is concerned to do what everyone else does. In extreme cases, this takes on an obsessional–compulsive character, with much attention to detailed ritual. It may be the temperamental basis for the compulsiveness that characterizes psychaesthenia.

Questionnaire items

Thinks many people worry about nothing; finds conventional people distressingly insensitive; thinks individual tastes should be paramount; finds his neighbours boring; likes to express personality in his dress; thinks one should express oneself rather than be conventional; believes in useless things; prefers serious thinking people to those with a businesslike turn of mind; doesn't mind untidy people.

Tests

In tests he will prefer the unfamiliar in all things from works of art to names for babies, and in general he will show less respect for other people's opinions.

V. MORAL ATTITUDES FACTOR

G+ Moral Attitudes v. *Expediency* (*super-ego strength*)

This factor closely resembles the 'super-ego' of Freudian theory. It is best depicted as a high regard for moral standards with the tendency to drive the ego and to restrain the id.

The person who scores high on Factor G tends to be strong in character, responsible, conscientious, well-organized and with a high regard for accepted moral standards. G has strong associations with deep religious and moral beliefs in contrast to the similar but more superficial self-sentiment factor (Q_3) which is typified by good altruists, socially approved conduct, but based on temperament rather than depth of conviction. The person who scores low on Factor G tends to be unprincipled, irresponsible, irresolute, unreliable and quitting.

Questionnaire items

Thinks people are not sufficiently well-mannered and law-abiding; guides his conduct by general principles; thinks people should have more respect for the law; would make certain that a quarrel between children was settled fairly; decides conduct after consideration of ethical principles; believes perseverance usually leads to success; is not easy-going; is not deterred by obstacles; is scrupulously correct in social obligation; values integrity above intelligence; checks the condition in which personal property is returned; sets a high standard in all his undertakings; will take a lot of trouble to show up injustice; thinks public should show more responsibility; would give most of his income to charity, if he was rich.

Tests

Chooses moral leaders as admirable; admits frailties; fails to cheat; takes a serious view of criminal offences.

VI. SECOND-ORDER FACTORS

The organization of the primary factors into second order factors is highly interesting. Cattell's first two factors, Anxiety and Extraversion, are highly correlated with the two major personality factors named Neuroticism and Extraversion by Eysenck. Moreover, Cattell's other two second-order factors of Sensitivity (Premsia) and Liberalism appear to be the analogues in the personality field of the two major social attitudes Tendermindedness *v.* Toughmindedness and Radicalism *v.* Conservatism found by Eysenck after exhaustive study. Thus work carried out in complete independence on the two sides of the Atlantic is in substantial agreement about the four major dimensions of personality. Cattell's fifth second order factor, Moral Attitudes, is obviously different from the other four, and it is not surprising that his five second-order factors, viz. Anxiety, Extraversion, Tendermindedness, Liberalism and Moral Attitudes have been shown to cover a very wide sector of human behaviour. Our mental hospitals are monuments to the existence of Anxiety; Jung's Extravert–Introvert dichotomy is one of the best attested of psychological concepts, and the remaining factors cover much the same ground as the important factors of political and religious attitudes.

With regard to the organization of primary factors within the second-order factors, Anxiety breaks down into five dimensions resembling: (i) Freud's tripartite categories of the *Super-ego* (Q_3+) (although G is even closer to the concept of the Super-Ego), the *Ego* $(C+)$ and the *Id* (Q_4+), and (ii) the well known distinction between intra-punitive $(O+)$ and extra-punitive $(L+)$ tendencies. Thus there is some agreement between clinical and psychometric work in this area, although the results have been arrived at by the completely different methods of therapeutic treatment of individual cases and the responses of groups of subjects to objective questionnaires.

The constitution of the second order factor of Extraversion is also worth noting. Eysenck postulates that the introvert conditions easily and that the extravert inhibits easily. Cattell makes a similar point in interpreting the primary Extraversion Factor H (Unreservedness), thinking it due to low reactivity to threat; the extravert going out to meet situations, particularly social situations, whilst the introvert tends to avoid them. Reactivity to threat is perhaps the common element in the second order factor of Extraversion, and may explain why these particular five primary factors go together, the introvert withdrawing from people in social situations $(H-)$ (Reservedness), from people in the usual everyday situations, social and otherwise $(A-)$ (Aloofness), from power relationships $(E-)$ (Submissiveness), from co-operative situations (Q_2+) (Independence) and from general experience $(F-)$ (Desurgency). This may explain the apparent contradiction between the introvert's submissiveness in personal relations and his independence of viewpoint and ideas, since both represent withdrawal from contact with other people. In the third second-order factor, Sensitivity, there is a distinction to be drawn between tolerant attitudes in private $(I+)$ and public $(N-)$ situations.

The fourth factor, Liberalism, goes, not surprisingly, with both radicalism and unconventionality, since the radical and the bohemian agree in favouring independent new approaches to old situations.

There is also some recent evidence that a third order structure exists as follows:

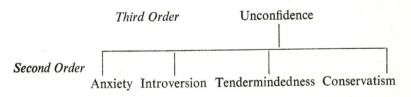

These five second-order factors of stability, extraversion, tough-mindedness and radicalism have a common element in that the high scorer in each attempts to control his environment rather than yield to it and tends to be capable, self-assured and reliant, his confidence showing either in the capacity (i) to remain stable in the face of environmental pressures, (ii) to show outgoing extraverted behaviour in social relationships, (iii) to express himself and to act in a tough forthright manner, (iv) to welcome the opportunity to make radical changes in his environment and to cope with the uncertainties that necessarily accompany change, and (v) to follow his own code of conduct rather than conventional morality. On the other hand, the person low in these qualities tends (i) to wobble under strain (instability), (ii) to withdraw into his carapace in social situations (introversion), (iii) to yield to the demands and views of others (tendermindedness, (iv) to fear change (conservatism), and (v) to act according to an extrinsic moral code (moral attitudes).

VI. SOME FURTHER COMMENTS

1. *The relationship between questionnaires and objective test factors*
Over 400 personality tests incorporating nearly 2,000 variables have been constructed in the University of Illinois alone. A very large number of plausible relationships can be postulated between these variables and the fifteen primary personality factor scores obtained from questionnaires. A great deal of consideration has been given to possible results, but it must be remembered that these preliminary hypotheses will need much revising in the light of the experimental findings.

Some hypotheses (expectation, suspicions, conjectures, guesses, hopes) concerning the relationship between objective test variables and questionnaire factors are fairly easy to make, e.g. between the questionnaire factor of *Unsureness* ($O+$) and 'acquiescence' the number of 'don't know' or 'can't say' answers, and variables such as 'greater number of excuses made for poor performance', 'more criticalness of self relative to criticalness of others'; 'less conviction of correctness of judgement' and acquiescence. Similarly between the questionnaire factor of *Instability* ($C-$) and distractibility; between Tenseness (Q_4+) and the number of common annoyances reported; (particularly extreme annoyances) between Suspiciousness ($L+$) and the proportion of luck said to be enjoyed by successful people (particularly the higher professions) and the tendency to criticize the tester more than the test; between *Dependence* (Q_2-) and readiness to volunteer for group rather than individual activities and willingness to accept help in answering test items; between *Radicalism* (Q_1+) and liking for new things and innovations; between *Unconventionality* ($M-$) and preferences for unusual names for dogs, boats, books, etc., and the tendency to give unusual answers. In all these cases it would be difficult to justify associations in the opposite direction.

Other hypotheses can be advanced with some degree of confidence, not because they appear plausible but because they have been found in a large number of previous researches, such as the positive correlation between Extraversion and fast speed and low accuracy or between Anxiety and the tendency to do well on easy rather than difficult tasks.

In other cases, hypotheses can equally well be made in either direction. For example, speed of association is usually thought to be slower following emotional words, particularly for emotional people. On the other hand, it is sometimes found that the effect of emotional cue words is to speed up the responses of anxious people. This is entirely a matter for experimental investigation. Similarly, we do not know on *a priori* grounds whether emotional (anxious) people tend to remember more or fewer emotional compared with non-emotional words and pictures (they appear to remember fewer), or whether moral persons answer questions concerning moral issues faster than other people because they have given them more consideration in the past, or slower because they tend to be worried about them.

Sometimes the results are unexpected: e.g. the use of extreme answers seems to go with stability and not with anxiety, as originally postulated. This is because the anxious are very reluctant to budge from 'safe' answers in the middle of the range, so that the correlation between stability and extremity stems from the fact that stable persons use extreme answers sensibly. And dishonesty tends to go with stability rather than anxiety, possibly because anxious people are afraid to do anything wrong, although it would of course have been equally plausible to put forward the opposite hypothesis, namely that anxious people will cheat because of an abnormally strong desire to succeed. Thus the principle of compensation can be used only too easily to justify negative findings, in much the same way as in Freudian psychology. Many interpretations are possible of variables such as 'risk-taking following success relative to risk-taking following failure'. Again, in slow drawing, in which the subject draws a line as slowly as possible, on the principle of the slow bicycle race, we cannot say whether the very, very, slow person is a cheat or is painstaking, without a great deal of analysis. And there is no very obvious connexion between the use of parts of speech in free writing, although in fact egocentric people appear to use a relatively large number of personal pronouns, and extraverts, with their outgoingness, tend to employ adjectives freely.

2. *Application to schools*

Since personality tests are partly fakable, they should not, in the opinion of the writer, be set in Britain in competitive situations, such as academic and vocational selection. They can probably be used, however, in any form of guidance in which the subject is actively seeking out advice. The major purposes of research into the temperamental reactions of children would appear to be (i) to clarify theoretical problems concerning the nature of personality, temperament, motivation and character which will eventually have important practical consequences in putting everyday educational procedures on a sound footing; (ii) to improve the efficiency of educational, vocational and psychological guidance, including the treatment of delinquent, disturbed, backward and possibly forward children (who are ahead of their peers in school work but who are not necessarily in advance in emotional adjustment); and (iii) to throw light on the procedures used in vocational and educational selection, where actual tests are unlikely to be used at all, except possibly to give supplementary information.

The main value of research into the nature and structure of personality characteristics lies perhaps in its contribution to our general understanding of human behaviour rather than in the specific application of tests or questionnaire for purposes of educational, vocational and clinical guidance. We should view the application of these methods to individuals with great caution (though not with too much auntiness). It should be borne in mind that even if these devices were never used directly for practical purposes they would remain of overriding importance in ensuring that all techniques for assessing the personality and vocational fitness of individuals were placed on a sounder footing. Thousands of judgements are made each day in schools and universities, in commerce and industry, in the Forces and the Civil Service, in the form of references, testimonials, interview grades and confidential reports. Their accuracy can make or mar a person's life, but at present they are almost invariably drawn up in an amateurish, slaphappy and uninformed way that would be tolerated in few other departments of life.

The ignorance of educationists in the field of personality makes a striking contrast to their ability to estimate educational and intellectual capacity, imperfect as that may be. As we have seen, research results in both Britain and the U.S.A. indicate quite clearly that the two major temperamental characteristics are, firstly a form of instability, designated neuroticism by Eysenck, anxiety by Cattell, and emotionality by Burt, and secondly, the well-known dichotomy of extraversion–introversion, first formulated by Jung. In primary school, neuroticism is most likely to show as nervousness, a tendency to show off, to tell lies and show 'spoiled child' behaviour, whilst extraversion is likely to appear as friendliness and a willingness to co-operate with the teacher. In the secondary school, whether grammar, technical or modern, these traits will also be related to academic achievement, stability appearing as perseverance, conscientiousness and effort, and introversion as a studious disposition and a liking for books and academic pursuits. By basing our judgements in the first instance primarily on these two major tendencies, i.e. by *separately* considering the roles of anxiety and extravert interests as the two most powerful yet radically different influences retarding scholastic achievement, we are more likely to come to fruitful and practicable opinions and to devise more realistic techniques of assessment which will be of value in the everyday work of the school, just as teachers who are cognizant of the overall structure of the abilities are more likely to assess their pupils' school work realistically.

3. Upshot

The understanding of children's personality and the teacher's ability to assess these traits is perhaps the most important topic in the whole field of education. Its urgency is taken for granted by all teachers and all parents and it is constantly referred to in discussion about individual children. In view of this the failure of educational psychologists to attempt to devise standardized tests of personality seems quite remarkable. Nearly every research that has been carried out in education in the past has assumed, in effect, that all children are equally anxious, equally introverted, and equally persistent, despite our personal knowledge that children differ widely in these respects, and that temperamental factors are of the utmost importance in achievement. In what condition would our education system be today if we assumed that all children were of equal intelligence, and if we had no means of assessing ability or achievement except by referring to what Mr Jones wrote on the school report or personal reference? There is a great practical as well as a theoretical need for extensive research on the structure of human personality.

4. *Concluding Remark*

It must be remembered that the psychometric approach to personality assessment is largely descriptive. It does not *per se* attempt to present explanatory principles that account for human behaviour, although it often leads indirectly to such interpretations being made. For instance, Eysenck relates personality theory to learning theory in associating anxiety with drive and extraversion with unconditionalibility, and Cattell has clearly been influenced by the purposivistic systems of McDougall and Freud, although he is more wary of what he calls 'blind theory' than 'blind empiricism'. 'To pursue theories which you cannot verify (or refute) is to chase uncatchable geese', and he would no doubt regard it as a compliment to be told that he has no pre-experimental theory. His choice of pertinent data and of the best questions to ask is nevertheless guided by the naturalistic observations of such writers as McDougall and by clinical hunches, as well as by the principles of 'representative experiments' (Warburton, 1959).

Despite its limitations, a descriptive taxonomy has the advantage of being close to real life and hence practicable. Hypotheses can readily be confirmed or refuted in terms of objective findings. Interpretations can be put forward that are understood by laymen, and action can be taken in everyday life, such as changes in the procedures adopted by boards of interviewers. Concepts of wider implication and fascinating theoretical interest such as the interpretation of social behaviour in terms of adaptation, homeostasis and maintenance of equilibrium are intellectually stimulating, but not much use in a classroom.

REFERENCES

BASS, B. M., and BERG, I. A. (1957). *Objective Approaches to Personality Assessment*. Princeton: Van Nostrand.

CATTELL, R. B. (1946). *The Description and Measurement of Personality*. New York: World Books.

CATTELL, R. B. (1950). *Personality: a Systematic Theoretical and Factual Study*. New York: McGraw-Hill.

CATTELL, R. B. (1957). *Personality and Motivation. Structure and Measurement*. New York: World Books.

EYSENCK, H. J. (1947). *The Dimensions of Personality*. London: Routledge and Kegan Paul.

EYSENCK, H. J. (1952). *The Scientific Study of Personality*. London: Routledge and Kegan Paul.

EYSENCK, H. J. (1953). *The Structure of Human Personality*. London: Methuen.

EYSENCK, H. J. (1962). The personality of Mensa members. *Mensa Correspondence*. **41**, 1–3.

GUILFORD, J. P. (1949a). *The Guilford Martin Personality Inventory*. Beverley Hills, Calif.: Sheridan Supply Co.

GUILFORD, J. P. (1949b). *The Guilford Zimmerman Temperament Survey*. Beverley Hills, Calif.: Sheridan Supply Co.

HALL, C. S., and LINDZEY, G. (1957). *Theories of Personality*. New York: Wiley.

LOEVINGER, J. (1957) Objective tests as instruments of psychological theory. *Psychol. Repts. Monogr. Suppl.* **30**, 1–104.

LOVELL, C. (1945). A study of the factor structure of thirteen personality variables. *Educ. Psych. Measurements*. **5**, 335–350.

NORTH, R. D. (1949). An analysis of the personality dimensions of introversion-extraversion. *J. Pers.* **17**, 352–367.

NOTCUTT, B. (1953). *The Psychology of Personality*. London: Methuen.

OSGOOD, E., SUCI, C. G., and TANNENBAUM, P. H. (1957). *The Measurement of Meaning*. Champaign: Univ. of Illinois Press.

VERNON, P. E. (1964). *Personality Assessment*. London: Methuen.

WARBURTON, F. W. (1959). Review of *Personality and Motivational Structure and Measurement* by R. B. Cattell. *J. Soc. Psychol.* **50**, 341–352.

WARBURTON, F. W. (1961). The measurement of personality. I. *Educ. Res.* **4**, 2–17.

WARBURTON, F. W. (1962a). The measurement of personality II. *Educ. Res.* **4**. 115–132

WARBURTON, F. W. (1962b). The measurement of personality III. *Educ. Res.* **4**, 193–206.

F

4

Personality and Adjustment

D. H. STOTT

I. APPRAISAL

1. *Direction in behaviour*

A MYSTIQUE has grown up around the word 'personality', as if it is a something-or-other inside a person which makes him what he is. If, scientifically, it has any meaning at all it is merely a convenient way of saying that each individual, within limits, behaves according to our expectations of him. We find that some people can be relied on to be cautious and others impetuous, some ambitious and others easygoing, some vain and others modest. These are generalizations about behaviour. When we set out to study personality or social adjustment, differences in behaviour are all we can observe.

Sometimes people behave in ways which are difficult to understand. A person may 'go to pieces', that is to say, revert to an undesirable mode of behaviour which is uncharacteristic of him. Or another person's behaviour may continually strike us as irrational, foolish, dangerous. To account for these exceptions we need a theory which can explain abnormal as well as normal behaviour.

We have first to reflect upon what behaviour is and what is its biological value. It is something more than just movement. We do not speak of stones or coal behaving nor, strictly speaking, do plants behave. To be true, a few plants, such as the sundew, close their tendrils over their insect victims. But by behaviour we mean something additional, a capacity to produce different responses to suit different situations.

Behaviour is an evolutionary speciality of animals, giving them tremendous advantages in the struggle for survival. A plant is rooted in one spot; it has access only to the food that its roots can reach, and

130

cannot escape from danger. An animal can move about in search of food. It can escape from flood or fire and other animals, seek warmth, build nest or shelter, store food, catch and eat other animals and use means of fertilization which are more efficient than reliance upon the wind or the visits of other animals. Man has gone furthest in the development of forms of behaviour which enable him to modify his environment, and it seems to have become part of his nature to experience an intrinsic pleasure in doing so. Although one may be accused of anthropomorphism in suggesting it, there is much evidence that the higher animals also enjoy exercising such effectiveness: birds seem to indulge in soaring for its own sake, and a cat or a seal will play with its prey before eating it.

2. *Perception and appraisal*

Along with behaviour two other characteristics of animalness evolved. It is not much use being able to move around in search of food or to avoid becoming the food of another animal without the means of knowing what is going on outside one's own body. It is essential to be able to recognize food, or one's enemy. There would not be much point in becoming aware that one was in danger of being eaten if one could do nothing about it. Sense organs, giving information about the outside world, must therefore have developed concurrently with the capacity to behave.

However, a series of reports carried to the brain is not enough. The animal has to take decisions about what it perceives. Its very existence may depend upon escaping from an unfavourable situation; its well-being will depend upon its ability to take advantage of a favourable one. All the time the animal has to be weighing up its situation in terms of favourableness or unfavourableness. Naturally, if the verdict is 'Unfavourable' – in the sense of 'I am about to be eaten', or 'I am sitting on a thorn', or 'My head is under water', action is taken if possible to rectify such an unpleasant state of affairs. If the appraisal amounts to 'favourable' – 'I am warm, safe, well-fed', etc. – no action is called for.

A preliminary sorting of sense impressions by criteria of their significance to the organism has been generally recognized. Adrian (1954) hypotheses that 'At some stage the complete report from the sense organs must be subjected to an editing which emphasizes the important items and sets the unimportant aside.' Hediger (1955) remarks how elephants 'would suffer the most severe disturbance from their fellows without even being wakened up, while they immediately started from sleep at the least disturbance from human beings . . . the incoming stimuli are filtered, so to speak, i.e. divided into biologically harmless ones from members of their own species, and potentially dangerous ones from human beings or other enemies'.

What has been less discussed are the criteria by which sense impressions are edited, filtered, or appraised (to use a more general and less metaphorical term). We know that young animals respond to extremely simple stimuli in a stereotyped way; if one touches the edge of a thrush's nest the young stretch their wide-open beaks upwards. But the higher animals, in their adulthood, have to interpret a vast diversity of sense impressions for their significance in respect of their safety, nutrition and shelter.

3. *General criteria of appraisal*

Any simple theory of response to stereotyped signs breaks down when we realize that, above a certain level of development, animals respond not only to stimuli which offer immediate satisfaction of visceral needs; they also recognize certain types of situation which give them general advantages for the satisfaction of such needs, or which constitute a threat to their well-being. Woodworth (1958) points to the biological value of curiosity: 'Anyone who has observed mammalian behaviour . . . will realize how great a proportion of activity is devoted exclusively to keeping in touch with the environment, finding out what's going on, keeping informed, getting acquainted with a strange environment or with changes and new objects in a familiar one.' Rats, even when hungry, will explore a new environment before they eat. Although in such cases we can only guess what goes on in the animal's mind, it is obvious that it appraises percepts by the rather abstract criterion of 'familiar' or 'not familiar'. Another example of this preference for situations which increase the chances of future satisfaction is the holding of territory, either individually or collectively, which is observed in nearly all species of mammals and birds.

The animal evidently has some means of appraising its situation as 'I am in control' or 'I am not in control', and for this there is no simple sensory sign. Many animals like to place themselves on a point of vantage which gives them a good overview, and a physical advantage if attacked. (Their young, like those of the human species, enjoy playing 'King of the Castle'.) It is almost universal among mammals and birds that individuals strive to achieve a dominant position over their fellows, which must bring nutritional and sexual advantages.

We cannot suppose that such general appraisals in terms of knowledgeability, territory-control and dominance are the result of learning, because the sorts of behaviour which have these results are observed in young animals before they could have any experience of the benefits they confer. Nor could animals work out logically the benefits, say, of dominance ('If I bully so-and-so, next time he catches a worm I shall be able to make him relinquish it to me without a fight'). We therefore assume that some sort of 'templates' for appraising situations in terms of general advantage must be provided instinctually.

The abstractness of such appraisal must be worrying to those psychologists who prefer to deal in materially definable variables. It becomes less difficult to accept when we realize that even simple sensory information such as the recognition of colour differences, or of everyday objects such as chairs and tables, is not dealt with mechanically. Lashley (1951) speaks of 'dynamic patterns, determined by relations or ratios', and the abstraction of 'similar relations'. Quite small children can deal with abstract relations such as smallness and largeness, and apply them to a variety of dissimilar objects.

4. *Effectiveness*

In man this seeking to establish advantageous or effective conditions for himself pervades all behaviour, even though an organic satisfaction is also directly involved. The present writer (Stott 1961) recorded the behaviour of his infant son which was unrelated to any organic or social need. It fell into the following five categories:

1. Recognition or discrimination (perceptual effectiveness).
2. Exploration (establishing a relationship of knowing).
3. Control (effective manipulation).
4. Completing a task (actualizing some mental scheme such as filling a bucket).
5. Producing some spectacular effect or change (such as making a novel noise, reducing an object to pieces).

The child's daily activity, during the times when he was well fed and rested, could be seen as establishing one or other of these general relationships, activities which did not produce the required result being soon abandoned. The intense motivation of the child was seen by his concentration, persistence, expressions of satisfaction when he succeeded, frustration when he failed, and even the neglect of organic needs or physical hurt. The endless succession of activities would at one time be directed to recognition, at another to manipulating some object, at another to producing a change for change's sake. What the child, and the normal human being of any age given the opportunity, does through life, is to seek to establish general relationships of effectiveness within his environment. White (1959) has made a very similar formulation in his concept of effectance – or competence – motivation.

This is not to propose an effectiveness *drive*, for this would be reverting to the animistic supposition that all movement or change is caused by a something-or-other. Science is based on evidence, and we have no evidence which leads us to conclude that a 'drive' as such exists; all we observe is that a large amount of behaviour seems to be directed towards attaining a position of greater effectiveness, or, of course, avoiding ineffectiveness.[1] The best way of ridding ourselves of the inclination to look for some driving force which provides the motive-power of behaviour is to think of a stimulus-appraisal-response sequence. In the course of evolution it has come about that animals react to certain classes of stimuli which have proved to be important for the species. According as how each situation is appraised, so the sort of behaviour results which by-and-large has been of value for survival. The only entity underlying this process of interaction is the neural organization through which perceptions are appraised and behaviour initiated.

Lest it be thought that this represents too passive and mechanical an explanation of behaviour, it should be emphasized that a completely negative, stimulus-deficient environment constitutes a highly unfavourable situation which will certainly provoke action. The process of appraisal in terms of effectiveness is a continuous and ongoing one. Thus it is not a question merely of reacting to stimuli but of demanding a dynamic relationship of activity *vis-à-vis* the environment.

If the opportunity for establishing effective relationships is absent, the person will normally seek some change in the situation which will provide it. This is sometimes formulated as 'seeking' the stimulus; but what is really sought are the conditions in which effectiveness can be exercised. Naturally, the same applies to the satisfaction of social and sexual needs.

Consideration of the origin of this effectiveness-seeking throws us into the midst of the controversy. At the present time it is often assumed, without any foundation of first-hand observation, that the behaviour to

[1] There is no harm in speaking generally of a need to be effective so long as we do not think of the 'need' as an entity.

which we refer is derived from 'primary' organic needs by conditioning. Such a view is put forward by J. Z. Young (1951) who has made a special study of nerve mechanisms in behaviour: 'The mother becomes gradually less co-operative and the child has to learn to get what it wants by ways other than crying.' The implication is that the unwilling, passive child is forced to widen the range of its responses by pressures from the external world. The opposite is nearer the truth: it is the child who normally takes the initiative in new feeding procedures despite the mother's wanting to continue feeding him in the old way. It can even be observed that in his insistence to feed himself the child, by his inaccuracy, or holding his spoon upside down, actually gets less into his mouth than if he let his mother feed him.

Systematic observation of a child forces one to conclude that its constant search for effective relations with its environment – in its play, feeding, dressing, its curiosity, experimentation, its liking for control and dominance, its delight in achievement – appears so early and with such spontaneity that it can hardly be accounted for by conditioning. An analysis of 48 manifestations of effectiveness-behaviour (Stott, 1961) in a young child showed that at least 30 of them could not be thus explained. Much of the experimentation was dangerous, destructive or annoying, and would have been discouraged by the parents. Many of the other new activities were of a kind that, although harmless, the parents never thought of evoking.

Naturally adults who have the job of training children normally practise a very thorough social conditioning; this channels their activities into acceptable means of fulfilment. The child is punished for drawing on the walls, but encouraged to do so on paper. But there is overwhelming evidence from the play of young children and of animals that the motivation is there to begin with. The neural organization which prompts the child to appraise the possibilities for effectiveness which his environment offers would seem to be genetically provided as part of our human nature, and so we can say that the need to establish effective relationships with our environment is instinctive.

5. *Need for a progressive effectiveness*

The young child's search for effectiveness follows a regular pattern. Experiment in a new activity may at first be largely a matter of trial and error: 'I hit that bright object dangling from the hood of my pram and I hear a rattling noise.' The child hits the rattle, probably again by chance, a second and third time; at some point it learns that it is producing an effect. Naturally such learning is a form of conditioning, but the noise would have no significance to the child unless its production gratified some pre-existing need. As soon as he realizes the possibility of producing the noise regularly – or of bringing about some other satisfying change like fitting something together or pulling something apart – he exploits the new-found form of effectiveness zealously for a few days. Then he loses interest; the activity no longer represents an achievement. Occasionally, in the following weeks, he will give the erstwhile craze a perfunctory trial, but without enthusiasm. The child needs a *progressive* effectiveness: he searches for new realms to conquer. In the intervals between tiring of one activity and finding another means of fulfilling this need he may be irritable and bored. This occurs very often during the fifth year, when all the possibilities for exercising effectiveness within the home have been exhausted, and he is not yet going to school.

This need for a progressive effectiveness persists through life. For lack of fulfilment it may become partially inhibited, or it may become canalized into some kind of group-achievement, such as following the fortunes of a football team, with a personal pride in attending their every match and knowing their history of successes. Alternatively it may degenerate into the easy achievements and excitements of gambling.

6. *The effectiveness-needs of the adolescent*

The adolescent is in a tricky position in the satisfaction of his effectiveness-needs. His sense of no longer being a child cuts him off from juvenile forms of self-expression, but he has little skill or status in adult forms of effectiveness. Consequently he is apt to pass through phases of frustration or boredom, and this is especially the case when the society in which he lives fails to provide him with the means of using his near-adult physical powers or with the opportunities for exercising leadership or participating in group-projects with those of his own age. Periodically a frustrated adolescent generation will spontaneously exploit some means of effectiveness which is disapproved by society at large. Such a movement swept Western Europe in the early 1950s. In Britain it took the form of the Teddy Boy craze. This, which chiefly consisted in adopting a special youth fashion of dress, in itself smart and neat, but intended – and interpreted by many of the mature generation – as a gesture of independence and possibly of defiance. As such it was innocuous, and older people who were incensed against it should have consoled themselves with the thought that the rising generation of working-class youth could have resorted to much more anti-social means of seeking effectiveness. In Germany, at about the same time, a wave of youth riots swept from city to city. They were set off by attempts to prevent groups of youths with motor-cycles from noisily congregating at certain outlying beer-gardens. The challenge was accepted, and crowds of youths began to assemble, on the word being passed around, in the main squares. Many minor acts of vandalism were perpetrated. Streets were blocked to traffic, sometimes cars overturned or pushed away, people were pulled off cycles, police cars were mobbed and their doors held fast so that the agents of the law were reduced to a state of indignity. Sensational newspaper reporting conveyed the pattern of misbehaviour to the youth of other cities, who felt they could do as well or better. But the mood of the rioting was high-spirited rather than ugly, and surprisingly little serious injury resulted. A study by a team of psychologists and sociologists (Bondy *et al.*, 1957) found that those arrested by no means answered to the popular conception of the 'hooligans'. They included a smaller proportion of youths belonging to the underprivileged occupational groups (unskilled workers) than in the cities as a whole, and a high proportion of apprentices, young artisans and office workers. Nor were they criminal or delinquency-prone elements: their record of previous court appearances was no higher than the average for their age-groups. The investigators attributed the disturbances to the lack of opportunities for progressive fulfilment open to modern city youth. Formerly, they pointed out, an apprenticeship involved being taught a wide range of skills by a master craftsman whom the young man respected. Now, engineering and other large-scale industries often require only a single specialized skill, which soon becomes monotonous. It will not escape the reader that the present wave of disturbances in British holiday resorts and the misbehaviour during sporting excursions points to the same state of effectiveness-deprivation. We shall see later that these responses are typical of situations where instinctive needs are frustrated.

7. *Appraisal of social attachment*

Observation of young children makes it apparent that another important and no less constant need exists beside the constant search for effectiveness. The child, from the age of a few weeks, likes to be sure that the guardian adult is at hand. Schaffer (1958, 1964) has shown that up to about seven months any adult will apparently do, but thereafter the child develops attachments to particular adults and becomes shy of strangers. Once again, although one adult may be preferred to another for the satisfaction of this social-attachment need, the need seems to be there to begin with, that is to say, is instinctive; and the particular forms that it takes at each age follow a regular pattern of maturation. It is a commonplace observation that a baby who is separated from an adult, even if only by being put down to sleep in a pram, often shows displeasure or frustration, and joy when the adult reappears. A child lost in a crowd at the seaside will howl unconsolably until restored to his family (unless, as occasionally is the case, his attachment-need is impaired through neural damage). With his growing desire to be independent and to explore further afield a child may become impatient of being kept too much under the adult's eye. Nevertheless he is not happy unless he knows the parent is within earshot or that he can find his way back home. We are all familiar with the sight of the toddler who trots off some distance, stopping at intervals to turn round and make sure that the parent is within sight, and then, when he feels he has ventured far enough away, runs straight back without stopping, uttering gleeful noises but showing a trace of anxiety.

8. *Summary*

We have seen that human beings, as social animals, seek to maintain two major types of *relationship* between themselves and their environment. The individual likes to establish effective relationships and to operate with a progressively greater effectiveness; he also wants to make certain that he is in contact with his own 'belonging-group' of members of his own species and has a secure relationship of acceptance with them. We do not know exactly how the brain copes with the problem of continually appraising the environment in order to make sure that these conditions are satisfied, but we do know that, in the normal human being, it does so very efficiently. By some means or other information received through the senses is constantly being checked against a number of situation-templates, rather in the same way as an inspector in an automobile factory goes round with his instruments to see that the vital parts of the car engines are up to standard. He will apply a number of tests during his inspection. We have similarly to suppose that the brain is, mainly unconsciously, appraising the outside world by a number of standard tests. As regards the effectiveness-test, the questions may be of the order of – 'Am I doing this job properly?' – 'Am I receiving the respect and consideration from other people which

I think is my due?' – 'Do I know my way about in this neighbourhood or building?' – 'Do I have to admit that this problem is too difficult for me?' If the answer to this process of appraisal is unfavourable, a danger-signal lights up, and there is an urge to take rectifying action.

II. CONFLICT

1. *Introduction*

Alongside the criterion of effectiveness the outside world will be subjected to appraisal by the second criterion (deriving from attachment), that of ensuring a secure relationship with the group. It causes us to ask ourselves such questions as: 'If I say what I think to so-and-so will he take it badly?' – 'If I take so-and-so's book or tool without permission will he feel hurt or slighted?' A number of other continuous acts of appraisal are being made at the same time. The individual will receive reports from his sense organs which he will interpret as meaning that he is hungry, or getting cold or is in a situation where he may suffer injury. It can be appreciated, therefore, that it may not be possible to satisfy all these criteria all the time, in which case a state of conflict ensues: 'Shall I join my friends in a party or shall I do some work for my exam?' – 'If my boyfriend is driving dangerously shall I reveal my fear or shall I just sit beside him and hope for the best?' – 'Shall I take a different side from my friend in a committee?'

How we resolve such conflicts depends in part upon our cultural conditioning. In some cultures primacy is given to agreeable face-to-face relationships even though this may entail deceit. In others a higher premium is put on honesty, even though it may give offence. In a non-aspirational group social climbing has a flavour of betrayal, and self-respect rests in large part upon one's standing with one's fellows (Young and Willmott, 1956). In an aspirational group it is often said that an individual 'owes it to himself' to further his own interests, even at the expense of others. Family ties count for so much in some cultures that an official is regarded as failing in his duty if he does not accept the bribes which would enable him to subsidize his relatives. A sense of guilt which might otherwise arise from harming other people is allayed by a process of rationalization: a trader selling a faulty article may dismiss the moral implication of doing so by saying 'That's the buyer's worry.' On the other hand, in times of intense political or religious struggle individuals will suffer torture and death rather than betray their principles or their associates. Their self-respect, based upon the standards of personal effectiveness subscribed to by their cultural group and reinforced by their group loyalties, is stronger than their sense of self-preservation. The value-system of each culture sways the individual's decisions in conflict-situations.

2. *The law of least cost*

In our everyday lives we seldom find ourselves in such acute dilemmas as those instanced above, so that we are able to strike a compromise between conflicting needs. This brings us to an important principle of adjustment. The normal individual resolves conflicts in a way that involves the minimum damage on balance to his relationships with the outside world. We do not jump out of the frying-pan into the fire. Incidental discomfort, rudeness, unfairness are put up with rather than suffer loss of dignity or other major disadvantage. A normal child learns which modes of self-expression may be indulged in without jeopardizing his standing with his parents; and normally he quickly learns their tolerance limit. As with most of us, his social attachments have primacy, so that if he yields to some impulse which displeases his parents he will probably humble himself by seeking forgiveness.

Adherents of Adler's theory of personality have held that abnormal and even anti-social behaviour may be a compensation for feelings of inferiority arising from a physical or other disability. Such an explanation is indeed sometimes put forward as an explanation of delinquent behaviour. It is understandable that feelings of frustration and inferiority might originate in this way, but – unless there are additional motives for anti-social behaviour – the individual concerned will be very careful to choose a form of compensation that will not get him into trouble. This is illustrated by two cases from among the non-delinquent controls of the Glasgow Probation Study. The first was a boy of $12\frac{1}{2}$ years in a special school who was a spastic and in consequence a cripple. His class teacher wrote of him that he 'is really pathetic in his desire to get on, in spite of both mental and physical handicap. . . . Equally pathetic is his desire to play football – and to do so as well as the strongest, most fit boy'. At manual work he 'is under-average, but tries desperately hard'. Yet despite the acute frustration and sense of inferiority of which this report is evidence, he had a score of only 2 on the Bristol Social Adjustment Guide, which put him in the 'stable' category. The two adverse markings were merely 'over-eager to greet', and 'very anxious to do jobs' – which are the reverse of anti-social behaviour. The second case was of a boy of 15 in a special school, who could not play football owing to poor muscular co-ordination. He refused to try to play, but compensated for the disability by acting as secretary to the school football club. Thus he associated himself with the game in a socially useful role. His social-adjustment score was similarly only 2, the adverse indications consisting solely of his avoidance of athletic activities. Despite intense feelings of inferiority arising from their physical incapacities neither of these boys jeopardized their personal relationships by resorting to anti-social modes of compensation. They chose outlets which did not involve sacrificing their social attachments.

3. *Compensation*

During every day of our lives, if we wish to maintain a reasonable adjustment, we have to resort to various compensatory devices in order not to take incidental situations of minor ineffectiveness so seriously that we react against them to our disadvantage. Any car driver has continually to be compensating mentally for the petty annoyances caused by other drivers who behave selfishly; he does so by priding himself that he is a better and a safer driver, while looking down upon the inconsiderate driver as a fool or a psychopath. It would be a quite intolerable state of affairs if every driver tried to get his own back. We are in effect provided, as human beings, with a general technique for preventing ourselves from responding to petty frustration in ways that we would afterwards regret.

The problem in general terms is how, when the appraisal-mechanism registers a situation which is unfavourable in terms of effectiveness, this does not automatically evoke a response. In popular language we say we exercise an act of *Will*. But how do we translate Will into psychological processes? Is it that man possesses some godlike quality which lifts him above the laws of stimulus and response to which animals are subject? Many people like to think that this is the case, pointing to the freedom of choice which we are able to exercise. It is not a question of denying such relative freedom, but of understanding psychologically what it consists of.

Human beings are reactive to stimuli and the pattern of their reactions is a function of their experience. But we have the ability within limits to choose which situations to respond to. We can do this by mentally *enlarging the stimulus-situation*. A frustrating incident then becomes only a small stimulus among more powerful stimuli, and by being thus dwarfed loses its capacity to evoke a reaction. There are two main ways in which this can happen. The first consists in a re-evaluation of the significance of the incident. Let us suppose that a sensible driver, keeping a safe distance from the car in front, is subjected to the momentary annoyance of having the driver of the car behind slip in ahead of him. Rather than give free play to bad temper or feelings of frustration he will, as we say, maintain a sense of proportion or humour. He may reflect that the inconvenience to which he has been subjected is of a very minor sort compared with the regular means of fulfilment that he enjoys in his life as a whole. Of course he is unlikely to think in this highly abstract manner, but he may say to himself, 'Well, it doesn't matter to me if I get to my office a few seconds later.' He reduces the incident to its due proportion in his wider life-situation, and is thus enabled to ignore the momentary disadvantage as too petty to bother about. He may even re-interpret the incident as evidence of his superiority over the other driver, whom he regards as ill-mannered or subject to an irrational compulsion to push ahead of others. The second device we use for reducing the power of an adverse stimulus is to prolong the situation into the future. The motorist envisages not only the incident itself, but the consequences of reacting to it in this way or that. In short he applies the same procedure of appraisal, in terms of favourableness or otherwise, to these consequences as he does to the contemporary situation. A time-dimension has been introduced which, once again, dwarfs the importance of the incident. The annoyance is seen as insignificant compared with the loss of status which would be incurred by giving vent to one's annoyance. Hearnshaw (1956) has termed this a capacity for *temporal integration*, and draws attention to its value in the control of behaviour.

The Iliad contains a classic literary example of this process of enlarging the stimulus-situation through time. After a successful affray with the Trojans, Agamemnon, the overlord of the Greeks, and Achilles, their doughtiest fighter, each claim a captive damsel. It transpires, however, that Agamemnon's young lady is the daughter of a high priest, and she has to be returned to her father lest the wrath of the god be visited upon the Greek host. Agamemnon then exercises his overlord's right and commandeers the damsel allocated to Achilles. In his fury Achilles is on the point of challenging Agamemnon to single combat, knowing that he would have no difficulty in slaying him. Only one thought deters him: he would then be guilty of regicide, the most heinous of crimes among the Greeks, and be condemned to roam the earth as an exile. So he compensates by prolonging the situation into the future. He will refuse to fight for the Greeks until, defeated as he reckons they will be without him, they come and beg on their knees for his help.

III. DYSFUNCTION OF THE APPRAISAL MECHANISMS

We have viewed behaviour, not as actuated by a number of 'drives', but simply as the outcome of a continuous situation-appraisal. It is a multi-stage process in which a complicated hierarchy of neural structures play their part. For the behaviour to be appropriate the brain has consequently to be reasonably well developed and intact, well supplied with oxygen, well nourished and uncontaminated by toxins. Its function may be impaired because one or more of these conditions is not met. The resulting neural dysfunction is seen in a failure of behavioural adjustment. If we review the stages as outlined briefly above, by which a perceived stimulus results in behaviour, we can see how dysfunction at any stage produces its characteristic form of behaviour disturbance.

1. *Effectance-deficit*

Let us suppose first that something has gone wrong with the process of appraisal in terms of maintaining personal effectiveness. An important part of the motivation of behaviour is cut away or reduced to a lower level. A child affected thus will have little curiosity because he will be content not to know about things. He will not feel the challenge to solve problems, or to keep up with other children in play or learning. He will not have the 'go' to experiment with fresh activities or to venture further afield. Nor will he be ashamed of remaining dependent upon his parents and timid of strangers. This is a description of the *unforthcoming* or *effectance-deficient* child. Often he passes just as dull, and indeed his mental development is usually poor. The ability to solve complex problems depends upon knowing about the objects and materials one is dealing with. It also depends upon how much experience one has had in solving problems of a similar type. The effectance-deficient child has had few such mental experiences, and so has not developed the concepts required for good mental function. In fact he is seldom as 'dull' as his test, which, by its nature, involves solving unfamiliar problems, for it is just these that daunt children of this sort.

2. *Impairment of Attachment-behaviour*

When the mechanism for the appraisal of social attachment is impaired the results may be still more serious. The children most seriously affected in this way may be diagnosed as autistic, but this term is becoming rather loosely used and it is better to stick to what can be observed. As with effectance-deficit, impairment of attachment-behaviour can be found in all degrees. Quite a number of apparently otherwise normal young children do not appreciate cuddling. Others, as toddlers, do not worry about losing contact with their familiar adult, and become 'wanderers'. It is not known what proportion of these unaffectionate young children recover spontaneously, since this can only be found out from following the development of a large sample of children over a number of years. But mothers of maladjusted children frequently report that they were strange, unaffectionate and difficult to get to know almost from birth.

The persistence of the social-attachment deficit may result in a failure of moral development. It has been seen that a normal child learns to avoid means of satisfying his effectiveness-needs which evoke the disapproval of his parents, and as he grows older, that of his age-peers. He accepts the values and moral standards of his group and adjusts his personal desires to them. Anxiety about social disapproval becomes generalized into what we call a sense of right and wrong, or conscience. If, however, a child is indifferent to approval, social conditioning has nothing to build upon. He knows that stealing is regarded as wrong, but he does not view it in terms of human relationships. If he is a strong child he may gratify his need for dominance by bullying weaker children. All that deters him is the punishment on being caught. But since, with reasonable care, the chances of this are small, he becomes conditioned, not against wrongdoing, but against making mistakes which may lead to his detection. Teachers describe him as 'hard to catch'. Naturally a child who is impaired in this way excites the reverse of sympathy, and may be regarded as 'just wicked'. It is seldom realized that he may be suffering from neurological impairment and is a socially handicapped person.

3. *Failure of temporal integration* (*inconsequence*)

So far we have dealt with defects of the appraisal mechanisms. We now turn to that type of neural impairment which results in failure of temporal integration. Since in this condition the past and future are, as it were, blinkered off, the child thus affected is at the mercy of every momentary stimulus. His distractibility renders him incapable of purposeful behaviour. Owing to his lack of concentration he does not learn about the properties of materials, nor does he gain experience in solving complex problems. Like the unforthcoming child, he remains at a low level of concept-development and is deemed unintelligent. Failure to take the consequences of behaviour into account will, of course, often land a child in trouble. His seeking for effectiveness may be normal, but he gratifies it by whatever opportunity presents itself. If his ball goes over a spiked railing he may injure himself or tear his clothing by trying to climb over it. He is easily dared by other boys into foolish acts. In school he may play the clown and be a bane to his teacher. When failure of temporal integration results in such forms of behaviour-disturbance it may be termed *inconsequence*.

The inconsequential child is hard to condition. Either he never reflects for long enough upon previous corrections and punishments for it to 'sink in', or his experiences are never called to mind. Just as he is unconditionable in the ways of wisdom, so he does not become conditioned towards resentment or hostility. He does not take badly the frequent punishments and rebuffs that he incurs. He is in short an irrepressible, puckish child who is often in trouble but seldom disliked.

The form that inconsequence takes also depends upon the strength of the child's other needs. The normal child becomes conditioned against pestering or demanding undue attention of adults. When she is tired or busy his mother would often have told him to leave her alone, and would probably have got irritable or angry with him if he did not. But the inconsequential child may never acquire a sense of how much affection and attention it is wise to demand. His unconditionability makes him appear an attention-seeker, and is sometimes wrongly attributed to lack of home affection.

A child may be impaired both in his attachment-needs and in the capacity for temporal integration. He may then indulge in grossly inconsequential and anti-social acts. A boy convicted of laying a sleeper across a railway line in order to derail a train could have been multiple-impaired in this way. If a child suffers from an effectance-deficiency any failure of temporal integration which may also be present may hardly attract attention, because he will lack the initiative to commit foolhardy acts and just appear as a very dull child. Indeed close observation of mentally subnormal children suggests that their thinking processes are not necessarily damaged, but that they have never been brought into use.

4. *Failure to inhibit attack-response*

In the ability to widen the stimulus-situation we have seen one of the ways in which the inhibition of inappropriate responses is effected. A general failure of inhibition is characteristic of certain types of neural impairment. A young child who cannot get his way or is denied some treat may respond by striking the adult. If he cannot make his toy work he may lose patience and break it. But normally he will quickly become conditioned against such exhibitions of temper by the disapproval or punishment which they bring in their train. If, however, the mechanisms for inhibiting such behaviour are impaired there will be frequent outbursts of rage over trivialities. In later childhood and adolescence, if the defect persists, the failure to inhibit this attack-response to frustration may result in serious damage or violence. It has often been attributed to brain damage, although the modern tendency (Birch, 1964) is not to make this assumption unless, as in epilepsy, there is direct evidence of damage to brain tissue, but to speak of neural impairment or dysfunction. There are also reasons for supposing that in most cases neural dysfunction as observed in behaviour is due not so much to tissue damage as to adverse factors affecting the working of the nervous system. (Stott, 1966.)

5. *Extroversion-introversion*

We are now in a position to consider a popular way of classifying behaviour deriving from Jung (1924), of which little has been said so far. This is the dimension of introversion-extroversion. One of the difficulties in accepting these terms as representing fundamental modes of behaviour is that, in their modern use, they are not induced, as any scientific concept should be, from the direct observation of the differences in the behaviour of a large number of people. Rather, they have been accepted *a priori,* and have then had self-rating inventories built around them which naturally appear to confirm the concepts. It is indeed difficult to find explicit definitions or descriptions of what is meant by extroversion and introversion as seen in the behaviour of real life. If one attempts an analysis of the items in the Maudsley Personality Inventory which are scored for extroversion they are seen to indicate a tendency to lively, confident action, with a sprinkling of inconsequential tendencies. The items scored as introversion are those indicative of lack of spontaneity, inaction and misgivings. Jung himself found that he had to make various sub-classes of each category, and when it comes to first-hand empirical study of variants of behaviour, and above all of behaviour disturbance, the extroversion–introversion dimension is found to be too crude an oversimplification.

People can of course be classified phenomenonologically as under- or over-reactors, but within each group would be many who under- or over-react for quite different reasons. The unforthcoming child will be an under-reactor because his effectance-needs are deficient. He makes few demands on life in terms of assertiveness and doing new things. But the depressed or exhausted child will also be an under-reactor. Similarly, because he responds to every passing stimulus, the inconsequential child will be an over-reactor. But so will someone who is very subject to anxiety, or who has been so deprived of gratifications that his appraisal-mechanisms are constantly registering 'unfavourable', and goading him to do something. It does not help us to understand the processes of adjustment to lump all these types of people together as 'extroverts'. For example one sometimes meets a woman who admits that she is an 'anxious type'; she can never relax and must always be fussing around doing something. But her house is kept meticulously and she looks after her family only too well, usually spoiling and over-protecting her children. She is the reverse of inconsequential. On the other hand one finds feckless mothers who live from hand to mouth without anxiety; although affectionate they neglect their children. Their 'extroversion' is better thought of as inconsequence.

People scoring highly for extroversion on a self-rating personality-inventory often show poor conditionability. This is also very characteristic of inconsequential people, and it is possible that this admittedly not strong relationship between poor conditionability and extroversion is due to the inclusion of a number of inconsequential individuals in the sample. If a more sophisticated classification of behavioural modes were made it should be possible to achieve higher correlations and to see poor conditionability as an integral part of the definition of a type of behaviour disturbance.

IV. THE EXECUTIVE-MECHANISMS

1. *Introduction*

We must now return to an examination of normal behaviour in order to study what happens when an appraisal of 'unfavourable' is registered. Characteristic patterns of adaptive reaction can be observed. These are so universal, both among sub-human animals and man, that they tend to be taken for granted. What prompts an animal to flee, for example, when it senses danger? If each generation of young animals had to learn afresh that flight was necessary, the mortality among them would be enormous. It is evident that the impulse to flee is instinctive. The survival value of such an unlearnt behaviour-pattern must have been so great that one might say its evolution was a foregone conclusion. It can be argued that each species is equipped genetically with a whole array of similar executive-mechanisms. The advantage they confer is to provide ready-made, or unlearnt general modes of response to certain standard types of situation. This does not prevent them from being adaptive and even intelligent. It just means that a large part of any decision is laid down in advance. Moreover, although each animal species has its own equipment of executive-mechanisms, the differences between those possessed by the higher animals are more of detail and of degree than of kind. This again points to their extremely ancient and instinctive origin.

2. *Attack or quit*

There would be no point in an animal's being able to call upon any one of an array of executive-mechanisms unless it has the ability to recognize the type of situation for which each is the appropriate response. Consequently, besides summing up a situation as favourable or unfavourable, it has to carry out supplementary acts of appraisal. Neurologically this probably works by a system of binary choice after the fashion of an electronic computer. Let us suppose that an animal is molested or threatened by another animal. Its response depends upon whether its opponent is appraised as 'stronger than me', or 'weaker than me'. If the first, the flight mechanism comes into play, if the second the attack-mechanism. From his experience in the domestication of the woolly monkey Leonard Williams (1965) wrote, 'In monkey logic anything that hurts spells danger, and there are only two ways of dealing with it: either go as far away as possible, or kill it, if you can.'

The decision *how* to flee or *how* to attack will depend upon further appraisals of the situation. For example the attacking behaviour may only be half-serious or of the nature of a threat-posture if the opponent is a member of the same species. In such instances, also, the animal may be unable to decide whether it is stronger or weaker, and so get into a state of conflict.

Even though the frustration comes from some inanimate object, basically the same judgement of stronger or weaker is made. The creature decides either that it can master the obstacle, or that the problem is too difficult. The response is attack – that is to say having a go at it – or avoidance. We do indeed speak of attacking or tackling a problem, and sometimes 'aggressiveness' is used in the sense of a willingness to tackle problems resolutely. As has been seen, this attacking response appears in its most elemental form in the violence of very young or of neurally impaired children when they meet with frustration.

3. Redoubling of effort

However, few problems are solved by elemental violence. The usual mode of approach is rather to apply some well-tried solution, or one which has worked in somewhat similar circumstances. If this does not bring success the next in the hierarchy of executive-mechanisms comes into play. This is *redoubling of effort*. The person, or animal, feels himself placed in a state of ineffectiveness and becomes determined to master the problem – to such an extent that the original purpose may be subordinate to the need to restore the balance. When we have lost something quite trifling we may obstinately go on looking for it, expending far more effort than the object is worth because we do not like being beaten. The reinforcement of effort may take a physical or intellectual form. If one's car won't start one gives it repeated bursts on the self-starter. If after a time this proves of no avail one starts to think what might be wrong – no petrol, oiled-up plug, etc.

In personal relationships this 'trying harder' is seen in the efforts made by an affectionally deprived child to gain the attention of an adult. He may attach himself to a milkman or other roundsman and serve as his unpaid helper, or pal up with road-workers or anyone who is easily available.

4. Normal avoidance

The 'man-in-the-street' seldom finds himself face to face with failure because he shuns any task which he is not confident of being able to carry out successfully. When the routine procedures of the craftsman do not suffice, he reports to the foreman rather than try the job and make a mess of it. Fiddly or tricky problems are disliked, and where possible avoided. They are appraised as 'stronger than me'. (Exceptions are games and gambling, but in them success and failure are the point of the exercise, and the latter involves no loss of face.)

As an executive-mechanism *avoidance* has value in steering us away from failure-situations and so minimizing frustration. This constant process of selection takes place below the level of consciousness, as indeed do all mental operations in the first place. It is therefore not remarkable that we all indulge in unconscious avoidance. We fail to understand a point of view which we sense to be against our interests and, equally unconsciously, find dubious reasons for the things that we want to do. The well-known process of rationalization is the result of the normal process of unconsciously selecting and rejecting ideas.

At a more elemental, instinctive level, avoidance has been observed in the animal world, notably by Tinbergen, although he sought to explain it as an overflow of neural impulses into an inappropriate response-system. A herring gull, in a state of conflict as to whether to defend its nest site or to yield to its fear of an intruder, may tug impulsively and bad-temperedly at a near-by tuft of grass. King John, forced to sign Magna Carta, is reported to have thrown himself on the floor and bitten the rush mats. Most often avoidance-behaviour consists merely in appearing temporarily to forget all about the dilemma. The gull may suddenly stop making threatening gestures at its adversary and begin to preen itself. Similar *displacement-activities* can be observed in man. When confronted with an awkward problem we may pass a hand through the hair or tap the desk. Such acts do not facilitate thought, but only serve to distract our attention (by movement or sensation) from the unsolved problem. The essence of what we may call mental, as opposed to physical avoidance, is that the unfavourable situation is not attended to, or the distressing thought is kept out of consciousness. This is possible because of the unconscious selection or 'editing' of all our thinking that was referred to above. (It is unnecessary, and indeed inaccurate, to describe the process as 'repression', because the disagreeable thought is not allowed to get into consciousness in the first place.)

5. *Pathological avoidance*

The need to banish extremely distressing memories centring around his family-situation may dominate a child's life and result in abnormal behaviour. The simplest way of banishing a nagging anxiety from consciousness is to keep the attention filled with intense sensation, physical movement and substitutive tensions and excitements. A boy under such a compulsion will often begin to dash about madly and seek all sorts of easy excitements. He will find any closed space such as a schoolroom or workshop intolerable because he is denied the constant variety of sensation he needs. (The exception is when he can retreat

into such realistic fantasies as to become oblivious of his surroundings.)
The kind of job he is happy in is that of a vanboy, where he can be
jumping off and on, hold on precariously at the back and be bumped
and jolted about.

The need for substitutive excitements is one of the most frequent
motivations of delinquency (Stott, 1950). Several such cases are reported
in *Studies of Troublesome Children*. One was of a boy of 13 years whose
younger brother was killed outside the family home by a van, following
which the mother had a nervous breakdown. In his efforts to blot
out the memory of the distressing event from which his family troubles
dated he became a severe truant and committed senseless acts of
delinquency. Running past a shop, he would dive in and grab something.
With a gang of other boys he would make quite considerable journeys
by rail during which they would commit minor offences and nuisances.
Another boy began a career of burglary before the age of 8 (when he
could be charged in court). His mother had died when he was 6, and he
was neglected and ill-treated by his father. His abnormal behaviour
included throwing bottles at passing cars and ill-treating animals.

6. *Hostility*

The following anecdote is related by a woman student in an examination answer: 'I remember I was given a doll's house when I was about
six years old. One day, for some reason which I can't remember
(presumably because I misbehaved) my mother threatened to take this
out of my possession, to give it away to someone who would appreciate
it: in a rage I systematically destroyed it. What I couldn't have, but
wanted, I deliberately destroyed.' Renouncing something that one
wants badly can never be a cool and unemotional decision. It hurts less
if one swings to the opposite extreme by working oneself into a state of
hatred for the love object.

The same destructive response is evoked when the need for social
attachment is frustrated. A child requires a stable human setting in
which to grow up, that is to say, he should be able to take his membership of a family, or his attachment to an adult who acts as his parent,
for granted. If it is impressed upon him – by neglect, attempts to get rid
of him, threats of the parent to put him away or to desert the home –
that he has no such reliable adult-attachment, he finds himself in a
basically unfavourable situation. The more positive and normal
executive-mechanism of trying harder will probably be first brought
into play. He will do everything he can to make himself acceptable and

the home less burdensome to his mother. His anxiety will prompt him to help her by doing her housework for her, minding the baby, buying her expensive presents and – if he is earning – wanting her to accept more of his wages than is customary. If these measures are of no avail and the anxiety about losing his parent becomes intolerable, he may adopt what on the surface seems the irrational and senseless course of setting out to smash the love-relationship with his mother (or with the father or whichever adult he has looked to most). He may act in a way which secures his own rejection, such as by stealing from her, often things which are of no use to him but which cause her inconvenience. He behaves generally in a moody and defiant manner. This is the reaction of *hostility*. It differs from ordinary naughtiness – by which the child tests how far he can go – in that the purpose of the hostile acts is to secure rejection. The merely naughty child takes the risk of a bad relationship with his parent. The hostile child sets out to make one. As a teacher once said of a hostile girl in her class, 'She seems to wait until you are watching her before she does something wrong.' It is not, as sometimes thought, that hostile children get themselves into trouble because they feel inwardly guilty and want to be punished. Their purpose is to put an end to an unreliable love-relationship. As with the jilted lover, the unrequited love-feelings can only be killed by summoning up all the hate possible.

7. *The removal impulse*

Continued physical existence in a family is intolerable to the child who feels that he is likely to be thrown out or deserted. Consequently, besides resorting to hostility, he may seek ways of removing himself from a situation which is a constant reminder of his deprivation. Along with hostile acts, therefore, we find a removal urge. The child runs away from home, fails to come back for hours after school, and truants. He may make attempts to get away permanently from home by joining the merchant navy or the Forces, and have fantasies of attaching himself to a travelling fair or circus. When these devices fail, as they usually do, he may, consciously or unconsciously, secure his removal from home by getting convicted of offences. This is in fact a very common motivation for delinquency. Its most tell-tale sign is that the crimes are of an obvious and apparently foolish nature – for the motivation behind them is to be caught. The writer recently heard of a boy who repeatedly stole bicycles but rode them round to the police-station and confessed his theft. Sometimes a boy, in order to make sure that the magistrate will remove him from home, commits further offences while waiting for his case to be heard. Naturally the Bench conclude that they have before them a hardened sinner, and oblige by committing him to an approved school.

8. *Anxiety*

We have finally to consider what happens when no executive-mechanism proves of avail. The person finds himself in an unfavourable situation to which he has no suitable response. If animals had just been able to put up with states of affairs like this, the whole system of appraising situations and resorting to behaviour in order, as Nissen (1954) put it, to maintain near-optimum relations with the environment would be pointless. There would be no sense in knowing that one was in danger, or in a position of disadvantage, unless one was prompted to do something about it. We know that such prompting takes place in the form of unpleasant feelings. If the threatening object is appraised as 'weaker than me' and the attack-mechanism is aroused, the accompanying feeling is that of anger or rage. If the reverse, and the flight-mechanism comes into play, fear is felt. Should no course of action appear of any avail, the feeling is that of anxiety. It arises when the normal responses to an unfavourable situation are blocked. In a state of conflict, for instance, straightforward solutions by attack or flight may each bring disadvantages as great or greater than the danger feared. The best evidence for this view of anxiety is the observation that as soon as a course of action is embarked upon, however unrealistic or forlorn, the feelings of anxiety vanish. Maier (1949) found that although the constant ringing of an electric bell was normally so intolerable to his experimental rats that they had fits, if the bell was attached to the rat's back so that it could take some action in the form of running, no fits occurred even though the rat did not escape from the noise. The above view of anxiety also explains why the feeling of anxiety is accompanied by mental perturbation, restlessness, and an inability to concentrate upon any other interest. The so-called needling of anxiety consists in repeated reminders from the appraisal-mechanism that the unfavourable situation is still present. Under the promptings to take some action quite silly ideas come into the mind and are hastily rejected. If late for a vital appointment one may toy with the idea of getting off the train prematurely, only to realize that that would make one later still. When the anxiety is acute or intolerable it may result in foolish actions. Even though its cause is mentally avoided and unconscious, the behaviour-prompting mechanism will continue to needle, so that the anxious person is preoccupied and cannot settle down to any purposeful activity. Thus anxiety interferes with learning.

This definition of anxiety also explains the lack of it in the inconsequential person: having no foresight, he does not experience any conflict between what he wants to do at the moment and the results of such action. Hence he seldom or never finds himself in the state of helplessness or response-inhibition which is an essential feature of anxiety.

None the less, anxiety is associated with excessive activity, and it is this which has led to its being regarded as a 'drive' or a 'motive'. The paradox is resolved when we appreciate that the biological function of the unpleasant feelings which we call anxiety is to make it difficult to remain in a critically unfavourable situation. The action is generated, not by the anxiety, but by the stimulus-appraisal-response mechanism as a whole.

The development of a monitor-system which registers states of fulfilment or the reverse is a sure and economical way of ensuring that a 'thriving' relationship is maintained between the organism and its environment. In the higher animals this takes the form of conscious feeling. In the case of a threat to actual bodily tissue the monitoring system of consciousness causes us to feel pain (except in desperate situations where behaviour has to go on despite the tissue-damage). When the unfavourable relationship is of a more general, non-organic type and resists immediate solution, it has been seen that anxiety is registered. The attribution of a motivating power to anxiety arises from a confusion of the monitoring feeling-state with the basic behaviour-arousing processes. Subjectively and introspectively, the actions associated with anxiety appear to spring directly therefrom; objectively they are attempts to rectify the unfavourable situation.

In experimental psychology the term anxiety is often used in the sense of apprehension of physical pain, and avoidance-behaviour is seen to result by conditioning against the situation with which it is associated. Strictly this is fear rather than anxiety, but parallel reactions are found in situations which induce anxiety proper. Prominent among these are the mechanisms of avoidance discussed above, which, as has been seen, can reach extremes of unreality and fantasy. The mental avoidance of the distressing situation necessitates a blocking of all reminders of it, and this is done by filling the attention with substitutive sensations, emotions and behaviour. If the stress becomes unbearable, the behavioural system explodes, as it were, in an irrational resort to some violent activity or other which will change the whole situation. At times this has the effect of bringing about the disaster that was the subject of the anxiety, on the principle that the worst that can happen is more bearable than the suspense. A boy threatened with being turned out of the home if he is brought to court may commit another offence in order to test the reality of the parents' threat. The self-banishing reaction of hostility is also one of these responses of desperation.

V. PROBLEMS OF MEASUREMENT

1. *The basic predictability of human behaviour*

This outline has so far consisted of a general description of the various modes of human behaviour. These modes have been discerned by observing that in similar situations people tend to act in rather similar ways. This may seem a rather surprising statement, knowing as we do how different people can be. But the differences in the behaviour of individuals are more noticed because we take the similarities for granted, and because it is of greater practical value to know the personal quirks of those we have to deal with than it is to reflect upon all the ways in which their behaviour is ordinary. It is only when we find an individual who deviates from this basic sameness – who, for example, makes no attempt to attain competence in anything, or who betrays no need or liking for any kind of companionship – that we realize what a degree of similarity and predictability there is in normal human behaviour. And this regularity in our response-patterns seems to point to the existence of a fairly uniform piece of neural machinery which is genetically determined.

It is the first task of the scientist, when approaching phenomena such as a number of human beings behaving, to put his observations into some sort of a system. The more fundamental his classification the better it will fit any additional observations he may make. Naturally, also, once he has detected causes and effects which occur regularly, he will be in a position to make predictions. Moreover he will be able to say what is usual or unusual, normal or abnormal.

2. *Origins of unadaptive behaviour*

Even in dealing with abnormal behaviour he may be able to perceive a certain regularity or lawfulness. For example, in observing certain symptoms of hostility he may learn to expect others, and get to know the kind of situation that provokes them. When we study maladjust-ment by methods of systematic observation it becomes apparent that it is not a matter of mere behavioural disorganization, or as people say, of breakdown or 'going to pieces'. Exposed to adverse circumstances beyond the limits of his tolerance, an individual reverts to recognizable types of stress-behaviour. It may seem to go too far to suggest that their relatively uniform character similarly points to a common genetic origin, because it is hard at first sight to see what survival-value there could be in hostile behaviour which secures rejection and banishment, or in depression which removes its victim from active participation in life or may even lead him to suicide. Nevertheless it can be argued from similar behaviour in animal-species (Stott, 1962) that such self-destruc-tive impulses do have survival-value – not of course for the individual but for the local population. The theory is that they are mechanisms for keeping population-numbers within a safety-level. Under natural conditions it is the stresses of high population which bring the character-istic self-destructive stress-behaviour into play. What we see, therefore, as maladjustment in human beings may be a survival of genetically built-in provisions for curtailing the numbers of primitive man. This would account for the characteristic forms which maladjustment takes. It also explains the law of multiple congenital impairment. If a child has one type of inborn defect, whether of mind, physique, health or temperament, he stands a more than average chance of having a second; if he has two he has a still greater chance of having a third, and so on in a rising curve. The population-limiting mechanisms result in the birth, under conditions of social stress, of larger numbers of children who are mentally, physically and behaviourally impaired, so that their chances of survival in a primitive community would have been small.

3. *Measuring adjustment by self-rating inventories*

In science there is little point in formulating a theory unless it can sooner or later be verified. For us this means in the first place develop-ing the instruments by which behaviour can be measured. The aspect of behaviour with which we are concerned here might be described as its appropriateness. To verify our theories about how behaviour some-times goes wrong we must be able to measure inappropriateness, or maladjustment.

Our facts are those about people behaving and misbehaving in the situations of real life. It is not good enough to measure how people *say* they behave or how they think they would in hypothetical circumstances.

They may give quite a false account of their actual behaviour for several reasons. In the first place, we all know that we very often *feel* like doing something which we do not in fact do when it comes to the point. It is not a person's feelings that make him maladjusted, but his acts. If, therefore, we ask someone, in a self-rating personality-inventory, 'Do you sometimes feel like doing so-and-so?' and he is perfectly candid, he may get a rating as a very maladjusted person. Consequently the score for 'neuroticism' in such an instrument may represent nothing more than a person's candour-rating. This is no doubt why, in a well-known personality-inventory, criminals appear as less neurotic than ordinary people, and university students, especially the women among them, come out as twice as neurotic as criminals (Bartholomew, 1959). To account for this incongruous result the topsy-turvy explanation has been put forward that educational success, and even the ability to keep out of prison, are the result of neurosis and anxiety. Such a theory only makes sense provided the 'neuroticism' diagnosed by the personality-inventory has nothing in common with neurosis as we generally understand the term, that is to say, failure and personal ineffectiveness. The most likely explanation is that academic ability normally carries with it a sense of personal security and confidence – which means that one can afford to be candid, and so gain a high neuroticism score. On the other hand the criminal with his suspicious, anti-social tendencies will be ultra-defensive and make a low score. Tests with other self-rating personality-inventories give equally unbelievable results: delinquent boys come out as having a greater sense of personal responsibility, being emotionally better adjusted, having more satisfying work and recreations and having better family and community-relations than non-delinquents (Stott, 1963).

Even normal people, it was found by Edwards (1957), tend to put a gloss on their own behaviour when asked to complete a self-rating personality-inventory. We give ourselves the benefit of the doubt and rate our behaviour as more socially desirable than it really is. The upshot is that such indirect means of measuring behaviour, besides breaking the first rule of science that one must observe directly what one wishes to know about, contain weaknesses which produce a systematic distortion.

Although the way in which a person replies to a question is an objective fact, this is not to say that the content of his answer is factual. Before we can hazard an interpretation of what a particular answer indicates in terms of personality we should have to correlate it with the individual's behaviour in real life. For example, the finding that the

more successful, thriving and law-abiding sorts of people get high
'neuroticism' scores must be interpreted as meaning that 'neuroticism'
is the reverse of neurotic. In fairness to some who use self-rating
personality-inventories it should be pointed out that in certain circumstances they seem to give reasonably reliable results. The first of
these is in comparing different types of mental patient; the critical
distinction between the neurotic and the psychotic is that the former
retains an awareness of his abnormality and how it appears to the world,
while the latter does not. The psychotic is therefore more likely to give
a candid report upon his feelings and impulses. The second is in studying
hospitalized patients, who generally accept the convention of being
frank to the doctor and can do so without losing face because it is
expected in the doctor–patient relationship.

4. *The direct observation of behaviour*

There is, in short, no other way of getting our data about behaviour
than by the direct observation of behaviour. The reason why greater
progress has not been made in doing this is that the data are very complex. How is a bit of behaviour isolated or defined, so that different
observers will agree in the same way as two physicists will report a
similar reading on an instrument? It is obvious that, at the present
level of our technique at any rate, we shall have to content ourselves
with a lesser degree of objectivity than is demanded in the older sciences.
One solution might be to describe behaviour in purely physiological
terms. But let the reader try to break down, say, a willingness to help
into a number of movements and facial changes. A little thought makes
it apparent that such a procedure would be not only intolerably cumber-
some but also impossible: a willingness to help might be expressed in
quite dissimilar physical movements in different situations. But we have
no difficulty in deciding whether a particular individual is showing
willingness to help. A group of people engaged in common activity
could probably assess each other's willingness to help fairly accurately,
and there would consequently be good agreement among them. Their
reports would be general statements about a series of facts regularly
observed. This is quite different from asking them to rate each other
for a trait of character such as 'willingness'. We have no right to assume
that such traits exist as components of personality. Whereas a person
may be observed to be willing, or confident, or sociable, in one situation,
this is not to say that he will be so in another. This is why teachers find
it so frustrating when asked to rate their pupils by traits. What rating

for sociability is a teacher to give to a boy who associates very sociably with a group of anti-social youths, but is very unsociable to other boys of his age? A further objection to the assessment of personality in terms of traits is that these are usually provided ready-made by popular characterology and tend to echo the classic virtues and vices. No scientist would get very far by merely accepting traditional categories and attempting to force all his observations into them. On the other hand, we are provided with a reasonably reliable instinctive ability to interpret people's attitudes towards us by observing their facial expressions or gestures. Whether a smile is sincere or not, or a scowl deep-felt, there is seldom any doubt about what these expressions are meant to convey. They are attitude-signals, or sign-releasers as students of animal behaviour call them, and they are universal among the social animals as means of communicating friendliness or unfriendliness. For practical purposes, then, the information which we gain about people by such signs are facts, and in so far as there is reasonable agreement among independent observers about them they have objectivity.

5. *Situation-attitudes*

When we come to measuring an individual's capacity for behavioural adjustment we meet a further complication. We have seen that behaviour consists essentially in responding to situations. A person may be able to adjust himself to one type of situation, but be thrown off balance by another. If, for example, someone has a streak of jealousy in his nature this will only show itself in particular circumstances. The most we can do is to measure *situation-attitudes*. In studying the social adjustment of children we can note their attitudes to particular standard situations, and so compare one child to another. By keeping systematic records we can discover what the normal, expected kind of response is, and so learn to distinguish those that are abnormal.

The above were the principles upon which the Bristol Social Adjustment Guides were developed. Strictly, they afford standard means of recording the bits of behaviour, observed but uninterpreted by an adult, which individual children exhibit in certain defined situations. They are measures of situation-attitudes rather than of the mysterious thing 'personality'.

6. *Response consistency and variability*

It may be asked of what enduring value it is to measure the

responses of a child just in one type of situation at a particular phase of its development. The answer is that there is a considerable degree of overlap between the ways in which a child reacts in all situations. A child who has been rendered hostile from having lost faith in his parents may also show hostility to the teacher in school. The reasons why a child exhibits a particular situation-attitude go back far into his past – his experiences of other people, and the sort of temperament he has been born with. Consequently a degree of consistency is to be expected. A child who has been subjected to adverse conditioning or who has suffered impairment of temperament is much more likely to react in a maladjusted manner in a stressful situation than a normal child. Being more vulnerable he is liable to show a greater variability of response. Physically handicapped children, a large proportion of whom would be neurologically impaired in a way that affects their behaviour, are particularly prone to such liability. Any measuring instrument which did not show such objective changes would be lacking in sensitivity. Despite these factors making for variability Lunzer (1960) found that when sixteen disturbed children were re-assessed on the Bristol Guides after a year the pattern of their maladjustment generally remained the same even though the number and severity of their symptoms might be reduced. In only one case was there a virtual reversal of patterns.

One inevitable source of variation in a record of a child's behaviour is that the adults in charge are themselves part of the situation and may provoke different reactions. We may, in short, be measuring the situation rather than the child. There is no way of overcoming this difficulty, and once again, if it were not reflected in the instrument something would be wrong. This source of error can, however, be exaggerated. In studies in which the Bristol Guides have been marked independently by two teachers correlations of about 0·7 have been found in the total scores. What is more important is that in only some 2½ per cent of cases did a completely divergent pattern of maladjustment emerge as between pairs of teachers marking the Guide independently. The divergences will be mainly in the responses of the situation-vulnerable children. A child of stable temperament can be relied upon to show reasonable consistency: if he finds a teacher difficult to get on with he will take greater care to behave circumspectly. Further evidence of inter-situation reliability was obtained by comparing the scores of twelve senior approved school boys on the (so far unpublished) Youth Club edition of the Bristol Guides with their scores on the Residential edition marked by different members of the staff; this gave a rank correlation of 0·90.

7. *Observer-subjectivity*

The imputation has been made, nearly always by those who have not been teachers themselves, that the prejudice of a teacher against a delinquent or a truant will colour his or her marking of the items on the Guide. In practice, the factual nature of the items, related as they are to situations, induces a concentration of attention upon what the child actually does; it is broad interpretative statement which opens the door to prejudice and halo-effect. Recently, in an all-British survey of truants, a lucky chance made it possible to test this objection of teacher-prejudice. Some of the truants were not known to be such by their class-teachers; none the less their average number of 'disturbed' items was nearly as great as those of the known truants. When allowance is made for the probability that truancy which had not yet been brought to the class teachers' notice would have been of a less serious type, the factor of teacher-prejudice is reduced to virtually nothing.

There is undoubtedly a truly subjective element in teachers' markings arising from their powers and skill of observation. It is very difficult to know how great this is. It should be possible to reduce it to a minimum by regularly including training in observation in College of Education courses. This would also have a practical value: once a teacher can recognize hostile or unresponsive behaviour or extreme 'laziness' as indicating maladjustment he or she is fortified against reacting emotionally against it and can develop a sense of responsibility towards the child as one who needs help rather than punishment. Wherever the Bristol Guides have been re-used after an interval in the same school it is found that the children come out as somewhat less disturbed. This is a therapeutic 'intervention-effect'. In completing the Guides the teachers' attitudes to their troublesome children have been rendered more tolerant; and the latter, sensing greater interest and less rejection, respond with more co-operative behaviour.

8. *Prediction of delinquency*

It is important to bear in mind that all a test of social adjustment can measure is a cross-section of a developing pattern of behaviour. Nevertheless, because in any individual the way he reacts to a given situation is the result of influences reaching back as far as his birth and even earlier, it is possible within limits to predict his future behaviour. To do so has considerable value when it is a matter of detecting those tendencies which indicate a proneness to anti-social acts. It has

G

been found (Stott, 1960a) that between 40 and 45 per cent of delinquent children are maladjusted by the criterion of a score of 20 on the Bristol Guides. Another 30 per cent may be described as unsettled or unstable, and only about 25 per cent show reasonable stability as observed in school (some of whom however may be maladjusted outside school or at home).

It was further observed that the delinquents were more prone to certain types of maladjustment than to others, notably hostility to adults, unconcern for adult approval, hostility to other children, and anxiety for the approval of their age-peers. These were made the basis for a Delinquency Prediction Instrument (Stott, 1960b, 1960c) by weighting the indications of behaviour-disturbance most characteristic of delinquents according to their relative frequency among the delinquents and non-delinquents. The resulting score should serve to pick out those children who possess the kinds of attitudes likely to result in delinquency. This technique cannot of course predict anything but a proneness. Whether a child actually becomes delinquent or not depends upon all sorts of future events – those of his family life, how he gets on at school, even the sort of girl-friend he acquires – none of which can be predicted. What the instrument none the less does diagnose with fair certainty in the more extreme cases is that the boy has developed anti-social attitudes and needs skilled help in overcoming them.

REFERENCES

ADRIAN, E. D. (1954). The physiological basis of preception. In: J. F. Delafresnaye (ed.), *Brain Mechanisms and Intelligence*. Oxford: Blackwell.

ALLPORT, G. W. (1937). *Personality: a Psychological Interpretation*. London: Constable.

BARTHOLEMEW, A. A. (1959). Extraversion-introversion and neuroticism in first offenders and recidivists. *Brit. J. Delinq.* **10,** 120.

BIRCH, H. G. (1964). *Brain Damage in Children: its Biological and Social Aspects*. Baltimore: Williams and Wilkie.

BONDY, C., *et. al.* (1957). *Jugendliche stören die Ordnung*. Munich: Juventa-Verlag.

EDWARDS, A. E. (1957). *The Social Desirability Variable in Personality Assessment and Research*. New York: Dryden Press.

HARLOW, H. F. (1953). Mice, monkeys, men and motives. *Psychol. Rev.* **60,** 23–32.

HAYES, C. (1952). *The Ape in Our House*. London: Gollancz.

HEARNSHAW, L. S. (1956). Temporal integration and behaviour. *Bull. Psychol. Soc.* **30**, 1–20.

HEDIGER, H. (1955). *The Psychology and Behaviour of Captive Animals in Zoos and Circuses*. London: Butterworth.

JUNG, C. G. (1924). *Psychological Types*. London: Kegan Paul.

KOHLER, W. (1927). *The Mentality of Apes*. London: Kegan Paul.

LASHLEY, K. S. (1951). The problem of serial order in behaviour. In L. A. Jeffries (ed.), *Cerebral Mechanisms in Behavior*. New York: Wiley. (Re-printed in S. Saporta (ed.), *Psycholinguistics*, New York: Holt Rinehart & Winston, 1961).

LUNZER, E. A. (1960). Aggressive and withdrawing children in the normal school. *Brit. J. Educ. Psychol.* **30**, 1–10.

MAIER, N. R. F. (1949). *Frustration: the Study of Behavior Without a Goal*. New York: McGraw Hill.

MAIER, N. R. F. (1956). Frustration theory: restatement and extension. *Psychol. Rev.* **63**, 370–388.

MCDOUGALL, W. (1923). *Outline of Psychology*. London: Methuen.

MURRAY, H. A. (1954). Toward a classification of interactions. In Parson, T. and Shils, E. A. (ed.) *Toward a General Theory of Action*. Cambridge: Mass.

NISSEN, H. W. (1958). Axes of behavioral comparison. In Roe, A. and Simpson, G. G. (ed.) *Behavior and Evolution*. New Haven: Yale Univ. Press.

NISSEN, H. W. (1954) The nature of the drive as innate determinant of behavioral organization. In Jones, M. R. (ed.) *Nebraska Symposium on Motivation*. Lincoln: Univ. of Nebraska Press.

SCHAFFER, H. R. (1958). Objective observations of personality development in early infancy. *Brit. J. Med. Psychol.* **31**, 174–183.

SCHAFFER, H. R., and EMERSON, P. E. (1964). The development of social attachments in infancy. *Mon. Soc. Res. Child Devel.* **29**, No. 94.

SKINNER, B. F. (1953). *Science and Human Behavior*. New York: Macmillan.

STOTT, D. H. (1950). *Delinquency and Human Nature*. Dunfermline: Carnegie U.K. Trust.

STOTT, D. H., and SYKES, E. G. (1956). *The Bristol Social Adjustment Guides*. London: Univ. London Press.

STOTT, D. H. (1958). *The Social Adjustment of Children* (third edn. 1966). London: Univ. London Press.

STOTT, D. H. (1960a). Delinquency, maladjustment and unfavourable ecology. *Brit. J. Psychol.* **51,** 157–170.

STOTT, D. H. (1960b). The prediction of delinquency from non-delinquent behaviour. *Brit. J. Delinq.* **10,** 195–210.

STOTT, D. H. (1960c). A new delinquency prediction instrument using behavioural indication. *Internat. J. Soc. Psychiat.* **5,** 195–205.

STOTT, D. H. (1961). An empirical approach to motivation based on the behaviour of a young child. *J. Chil. Psychol. Psychiat.* **2,** 97–117.

STOTT, D. H. (1962). Cultural and natural checks to population growth. In Montagu, M. F. A. (ed.) *Culture and the Evolution of Man.* London: Oxford Univ. Press.

STOTT, D. H. (1963). Delinquency proneness and court disposal of young offenders. *Brit. J. Criminology.* **4,** 37–42.

STOTT, D. H. (1965). Method and motivation. *Forward Trends.* **9,** 149–157.

STOTT, D. H. (1966). *Studies of Troublesome Children.* London: Tavistock Publication.

WHITE, R. W. (1959). Motivation reconsidered: the concept of competence. *Psychol. Rev.* **66,** 297–333.

WILLIAMS, L. (1965). *Samba and the Monkey World.* London: The Bodley Head.

WATSON, J. B. (1925). *Behaviourism.* London: Kegan Paul.

WOODWORTH, R. S. (1958). *Dynamics of Behaviour.* London: Methuen. New York: Holt.

YOUNG, J. Z. (1951). *Doubt and Certainty in Science.* Oxford: Clarendon Press.

YOUNG, M., and WILLMOTT, P. (1956). *Family and Kinship in East London.* London: Routledge.

5

Handicaps in Learning

A. CASHDAN

I. SOME GENERAL CONSIDERATIONS

1. *Towards a definition of learning handicap*

SUCCESS and failure in learning are relative things. In a professional family a child who does not secure a university place may be regarded as dull; in another milieu the adolescent who can stumble haltingly through the sports page of the newspaper may be considered the bright one. Furthermore, terms such as dull, backward, subnormal, retarded – all frequently used in this field – have none of them a precise scientific meaning. In any particular study or discussion where precision is needed the terms have to be defined anew. For their meanings are affected not just by dictionary definition, but also by the population being studied, the point in time and the skill under consideration.

A child whose arithmetic is below average today might, ten years ago and with the same attainments have compared favourably with his peers if, for example, standards have since risen. However, by today's standards, the child is backward. This is a descriptive statement, telling us that his attainments are below those of (say) half the population of children of his age. It should not be confused with a prescription – that is, with the decision as to how advanced in arithmetic children of that age *should* be. Looked at in wider perspective, standards in arithmetic might turn out to be anything from unnecessarily high to very low. So that by a more objective evaluation the 'backward' child we have been considering might be doing very poorly or quite well.

What constitutes a learning handicap is thus seen to be a question of social demands, both in the sense just discussed and in a further one also. Different skills acquire different valuations. Thus, in our society, literacy is highly prized but musical attainments, though approved of, are not considered essential. An educated man can cheerfully confess to an inability to sing in tune or play a musical instrument; if he could

165

not read, his claim to be educated would be derided. So teachers make tremendous efforts to get children reading, but are relatively casual about musical performance. By the objective standard of what could be achieved given equal amounts of educational attention, the population as a whole is probably underfunctioning musically and overfunctioning in terms of literacy.

If a child has an intellectual handicap there are three aspects which need clarification: the severity of the handicap, how general it is, and what progress or improvement is likely or possible. Progress and improvement will be dealt with at the end of this chapter; for the present it is enough to point out that almost all children, however handicapped, make intellectual progress, though often not enough to change their standing relative to other children.

The severity of the handicap is normally defined by the use of standardized tests and the application of reasonable, albeit arbitrary, conventions. Thus at the junior-school age a child is considered backward if his attainments are below the average for children a year younger – say, a gap between chronological age and attainments of approaching two years. However, a gap of two years is obviously of lesser significance for older children (at age 6 a two-year gap produces a quotient of 67, whereas at age 15 this would be 87). So a better convention is probably that of standard score. Using this, one might call attainments one standard deviation below the mean (usually a quotient of 85) mild handicap, and those two deviations below average (70 or less) more serious.

The generality of the handicap may be estimated by comparing the child's performance at different skills, say reading and mathematics. More frequently, a poor showing on an intelligence test is held to indicate general limitation even if the child's scholastic showing is average at some skills. Estimates of general intelligence do, of course, show high correlation with school attainment, but there are some pitfalls in using the IQ as a sole, or even main, index of handicap. Children who over-function in relation to their IQ may often be interesting problems but it would be slightly odd to describe them as cases of learning handicap.

However, the obverse – the child of average or superior intelligence who is under-functioning – frequently leads to muddled thinking. It does not follow that because a child's mental age is higher than, say, his reading age, he ought to be reading better. To claim this is to deny that abilities at particular skills depend on anything but a single general factor rather than on both general and specific ones. Or, to put the point in another way, one must beware of overrating the predictive powers of the intelligence test. Usually, the intelligence test is little more than a disguised set of tests of attainment so designed as to be rather less dependent on specific training than are ordinary attainment tests. Recently, this concept of retardation (M A higher than Attainment Age) has been further questioned in a factorial study by Curr and Hallworth (1965). They found that although social variables such as adjustment, home background, delinquency, showed definite loadings on a backwardness factor (low I Q), this was not true for retardation: retardation is thus a statistical concept which has yet to prove its meaningfulness.

So far no mention has been made of emotional and motivational factors in learning. Much learning failure or difficulty is undoubtedly due to faulty attitudes and poor (or even negative) training. However, there seems little advantage in treating emotional and intellectual difficulties in learning in separate compartments. The implication is usually that intellectual difficulties are permanent and irremediable, whereas emotional blocks can be cleared up by suitable social, educational or medical treatment. Behind this lies the further assumption that intellectual powers are pure and 'given' but that everything else is acquired. But in practice emotional difficulties rarely melt away at speed and intellectual weaknesses can nearly always be at least partly reduced.

To conclude this section, one might suggest that a child has a learning handicap worthy of further investigation if at some socially valued skill he performs at a level below that of three-quarters or more of children of his age. This corresponds roughly to a quotient of 85. But there is great variability in normal development, a steady progress curve being probably the exception rather than the rule; so that one need not suspect any long-term difficulty if the child performs at a low level for a short period. But when the difficulty, general or specific, persists and the child falls back to a level two deviations below the mean (70 or less) one thinks in terms of serious handicap.

2. *The content and scope of this chapter*

The detailed discussion of every type of handicap with its psychological and educational implications is beyond the scope of this chapter. It is proposed, therefore, to deal briefly with recent work and theory in the aetiological field, particularly as these are seen by psychologists. This will be followed by some consideration of specific difficulties, with particular emphasis on learning to read. Physical handicaps will then be considered briefly: the special problems of the blind and deaf are largely outside the chosen scope of this chapter, but some reference will be made to the problems of spastic and other brain-damaged children.

Children with general and severe difficulties – the subnormal and severely subnormal – will be discussed in some detail, for their study has proved of general interest and significance to psychologists and educators as well as being valuable in its own right. Finally, the problems of children with difficulties will be discussed in terms of educational provision and of the practical application of research findings.

II. CAUSAL FACTORS IN LEARNING HANDICAP

1. *Heredity and environment*

It has been customary to divide the causes of handicap, particularly subnormality, into two groups, a variety of typologies being suggested. These include 'endogenous' and 'exogenous', 'pathological' and 'subcultural' and so on. Nowadays, most psychologists would probably prefer a threefold classification: inherited, due to physical pathology, and socially determined. But attempts, either in general theorizing or in particular cases, to apportion these causes can lead to arguments which are unfruitful and often irrelevant. To develop Hebb's (1949) point of view, we might say that practically no one has perfect hereditary endowment and no one at all receives absolutely ideal environmental support and stimulation. As many studies have shown (see Clarke and Clarke, 1965), subnormal children are particularly likely to suffer adverse environmental conditions whether as primary or secondary factors in their condition. Certainly, recent thought (e.g. McV. Hunt, 1961) favours an environmentalist approach, so that one is nowadays inclined to look at a child's social history at least as carefully as at hereditary factors. Among the severely subnormal, physical pathology can at times be demonstrated, though surprisingly often nothing obvious is found. Among the more mildly subnormal the position is quite different. In an interesting study, Stein and Susser (1963) found that among those ESN children who showed physical abnormalities all social classes were represented, but of those who were 'clinically normal' none came from outside the 'demotic subculture'. Thus they see mental retardation in the clinically normal as a social phenomenon.

2. *Pathological causes – minimal brain damage*

This chapter is not the proper place for a full discussion of the whole problem of brain damage, but it is important to note that alongside the generally increasing emphasis on cultural factors new information has also come to light on the pathological side. Essentially this consists of studies of children who are very nearly normal clinically but who nevertheless have suffered minor brain-damage either before or during the birth process. This, it is suggested, reveals itself only in very careful examination (if at all: the diagnosis may be largely presumptive). But children who have suffered in this way may exhibit long-lasting, if not permanent, learning disabilities and/or behavioural disturbances. Thus, Stott (1959), in a study embracing nearly two hundred subnormal and retarded children, found a significant correlation, which could not be explained in any other way, between maternal illness and stress during pregnancy and a passive, withdrawn, unsuccessful personality in the child, which he labels 'unforthcomingness'.

Again, Prechtl and Stemmer (1962) found a syndrome of minor neurological signs which they call the 'choreiform syndrome' exhibited by children with intellectual and emotional problems. By both retrospective and prospective techniques they were able to link this with similar disturbances dating back to the new-born period. However, the significance of this finding would be reduced if similar signs could be found in otherwise normal children. Rutter *et al.* (1966) quote a later unpublished work by Stemmer in which a population study did not confirm the earlier findings, nor did Rutter and his co-workers find confirmation for them in their own Aberdeen study. On the other hand, Wolff and Hurwitz (1966) quote three or four studies (albeit of rather lower scientific rigour than that of Rutter *et al.*), all of which tend to confirm the Prechtl findings. More work is obviously needed in this field – at present one can only say that some children who at first sight appear to have difficulties of psychological or subcultural origin, may in fact have suffered pathogenic insult at a very early age. However it is not clear whether these syndromes are sufficient, let alone necessary, causes of later difficulties.

3. *Early relationships*

The importance of early relationships for healthy intellectual and emotional development no longer needs stressing. It is now well established, both through studies of animals (e.g. Pfaffenberger and Scott, 1959) and work with human infants (see Ainsworth, 1962) that where primary socialization is very delayed or inadequate, development can be difficult or stunted, though the effects are not necessarily completely irreversible, as was at first thought (see Moltz, 1960). Clearly, adequate earlier relationships form a substratum of confidence which makes it possible for the child to develop intellectually as well as emotionally. Without this, he is quite likely to have emotional and possibly also intellectual difficulties. In cases of severe subnormality where laborious distinctions between mental illness and mental deficiency are apt to break down, it can be difficult to put much meaning into discussions of differential diagnosis. If the child makes no or very distorted relationships and at the same time shows little capacity for learning, either factor might be the primary one, though the conventional diagnosis is still likely to be subnormality. The recent growth of interest in autistic symptoms has somewhat blurred this picture, but Russell Davis (1961) has argued for some time that even without the presence of 'psychotic' symptoms, subnormality may often be the end product of a 'burnt-out' psychosis – the child having come through an early period of unbearable stress.

Critical periods for learning particular skills will be mentioned later in this chapter. These certainly exist in animals (see Moltz, 1960), but their status in child development is rather less clear. Here, they are best described as optimal learning periods; they obviously last longer in children than in animals and it is hard to separate the social difficulties in learning a skill at the 'wrong' age from the neuro-developmental ones. Most often, too, the unfavourable learning conditions exist both before and after the particular critical period.

4. *Stimulation and affection*

As we have just noted, the child's early relationships with other adults, particularly the mother, set the tone for his whole emotional, and hence also intellectual, development. Hence the concentration on investigating the continuity and quality of the early mother–child relationship. This is often best approached indirectly by studying the mother's attitude to her child. But another major dimension of the mother–child relationship is what the mother actually does (or fails to do) with the child and the experiences, cognitive as well as emotional, with which she presents him. In a study of normal children in the first year of life Blank (1961) found stronger relationships between stimulation variables and development than between affectional measures and development. Whatever the reason for the subnormality, it seems likely that mothers of subnormal children may not provide enough or appropriate experiences for their children. This may be because of feelings of guilt or rejection, through a desire to protect the damaged infant from further strain, or through an inadequate appreciation of the child's special needs. It may also be through the sheer overwork and practical difficulties caused by having a handicapped child in the family (see J. and E. Newson, 1966). In an ongoing study Cashdan and Jeffree (1966) are looking at these factors in a group of severely subnormal children.

5. *Language and development*

As ours is essentially a linguistic culture – as any advanced culture is bound to be – poor language development and control is likely to be both a cause and a sign of intellectual failure, whether mild or severe. Language training begins immediately after birth. By the time a child is ready for school the pattern of his development may be largely set. So the language training the child receives from those about him at home – again mainly the mother – is crucial. The mother is not responsible only for the child's diction, accent and vocabulary. She also teaches him (as she does in emotional relationships) what to expect of linguistic communication.

Bernstein (1961) suggests that in working-class subcultures language is frequently restricted to crude and essentially general uses. It is not used, as in the dominant culture, as a means of expressing and in fact creating fine shades of meaning, conceptual thinking and awareness of one's own status and feelings. Thus many children may come from a background which has doubly impoverished them. They may lack vocabulary, complex language structures and skill in using language; in addition, they may not expect to acquire sophisticated language skills, for they have not been trained to perceive them. As education at school becomes progressively more demanding linguistically, children from these subcultures may fall further and further behind. As many recent surveys have shown (e.g. Douglas, 1964), the educational system progressively discriminates against the working-class child; this may not be just for reasons of social prejudice, but also because as he grows older he is increasingly less capable of meeting the educational demands made of him.

III. SPECIFIC DISABILITIES

Parents (and teachers) frequently describe children's difficulties in terms of difficulty or failure in one area only. The child is generally bright, and average at arithmetic, but is doing very poorly at reading. Such cases certainly exist, but they are much less common than first reports would indicate. More typically, the child turns out to be of below average intelligence and poor attainments generally. Frequently also, he is suffering from emotional problems and it can be very difficult to determine whether these have caused, or are consequent upon, the learning difficulty. In this section we shall look first at reading difficulties in general, then at the problem of highly specific reading disability; this will be followed by a brief examination of difficulties in arithmetic and other learning areas.

1. *Backwardness in reading*

Among the many causes of reading difficulty the most frequently quoted is low intelligence. However, as suggested earlier in the chapter, the ascription of reading failure to low intelligence is less informative than it might seem. Children of low intelligence do mostly make poor progress at reading, but the link between the two may be as much associative as causal and one wants to examine the root causes of both. In older children, of course, it may be the poorness in reading which depresses the intelligence test score.

While it may never be possible entirely to separate acquired from congenital factors, one can nevertheless distinguish two rough aetiological groups. First, there are congenital and physical causes. Poor readers are likely to be less mature mentally than good readers. They will have poorer memories, retarded language development and weaker conceptual powers; though these may not be purely inherited or even congenital, they may be determined early in life. Poor readers are more likely also to have visual and auditory defects.

As Vernon (1957) suggests, very few children lack the visual perceptive powers needed for learning to read; these may in fact be present in many children by 2 years of age (see Lynn, 1963). Nor do many more lack the requisite auditory powers although the complex skills needed in the phonic analysis of words may be beyond many 7-year-olds – as Bruce (1964) has shown – at any rate without specific coaching. Naturally, the understanding of reading difficulties is linked with the proper analysis of reading skill – a task barely begun (see, however, Vol. II, Chapter 7). Birch and Belmont (1964, 1965) have recently analysed children's ability to translate auditory into visual stimuli and have found that retarded readers do not do this as well as normal readers.

Untypical laterality patterns (left or mixed dominance) have often been blamed for reading difficulties, sometimes on rather slender evidence (see Zangwill, 1960). Belmont and Birch (1965) recently found no association between left dominance or cross-laterality and reading difficulty, but they did find that poor readers showed greater confusion in right-left orientation (awareness of right and left on one's own body and on others). Similarly, in a recent survey of over 1,200 retarded readers (Cashdan, Pumfrey and Lunzer, 1967) no over-representation was found of children with mixed or left dominance; nor did these groups show either greater retardation or poorer response to remedial treatment. As Belmont and Birch (1965) point out, the difference between these and the earlier studies lies probably in the fact that the earlier studies used small, highly selected, clinical groups, whereas both their study and the Manchester survey are in effect population studies.

A second group of factors are social and educational. Many children do poorly at reading because they have been unlucky in their educational experiences. They may have missed school, had too many changes of teacher, or been badly taught. Their difficulties are often increased by their being given worse educational facilities rather than specially favourable treatment (see Morris, 1966). It has also been suggested that children who miss learning to read at the appropriate age may have greater difficulty in doing so later. But such difficulty may be less related to inherent difficulties (or critical learning periods) than to rigid and inflexible classroom procedures where children who miss an important process are not afterwards given a chance to learn it thoroughly.

But perhaps the most important in this group of factors is the social background of the child. Many children come to school with attitudes which are at best indifferent to school attainment and at worst positively hostile. The child has not had the background experiences which are prerequisites of learning to read, he has no proper expectation of what will happen at school, and he sees no particular advantages to himself in making educational progress. If the teacher lays appropriate foundations for learning and supplies both the intellectual and motivational background that has not been given at home, the child may make good progress. If these are not supplied he is very likely to become retarded. Thus the home background and the school provision may be seen to be mutually interdependent.

The normal provision for helping retarded children is to set up small remedial classes or groups with anything from one to half a dozen or so children, each group being taught once or twice a week by a specialist remedial teacher who may have a special qualification for such work. Typically, the children make fairly good progress at first, perhaps improving their reading age by two years in a year of coaching. Early reports showed this with some satisfaction (see Birch, 1948–9 and Ace, 1956). However, since 1961 when Collins published the results of a careful study in this field, later followed by similar findings by Lovell (1962, 1963), it became clear that much of this earlier optimism was not justified. Ignoring those studies whose methodology failed to stand up to Collins' scrutiny, the general consensus may be expressed as follows: the treated children make good initial progress but this improvement is not sustained. Moreover, control groups of untreated children recover spontaneously (though a little more slowly), so that they eventually attain similar levels to the treated children. It seems that the remedial teaching has little long-term effect on the children.

Three things seem to be necessary for successful remedial work: the children should be brought to an appropriate frame of mind emotionally; linguistic and perceptual skills should be strengthened where necessary; and appropriate systematic teaching should be given. Unfortunately, many remedial teachers seem to focus (often unwittingly) on one or two of these aspects to the detriment of the third. Some concentrate on building up appropriate attitudes and motivation without ever teaching systematically; others provide excellent formal teaching without really reaching the children. When more appropriate material has been designed, programmed instruction may be of particular value in remedial teaching; with taped material, auditory as well as visual skills can be built up. But here, too, teacher control will be very important, so as to allow for the child's background and current reactions.

Even when teaching satisfies all the above criteria, it is still not surprising that progress is not better sustained. The remedial teaching is often poorly integrated with the child's regular classroom experiences, and it is very rare for any attempt to be made to modify parental and home attitudes. Furthermore, the remedial teaching, owing to pressures on the service, is often discontinued before the child's reading skill is really firmly established. If all these factors could be adequately dealt with, remedial teaching would probably be much more successful than at present; but the cost of the service might then be so uneconomical that one would do much better by strengthening general classroom facilities and paying more attention to reading difficulties in the preparation of the ordinary class teacher.

2. *Specific reading disability*

There has been a recent resurgence of interest in a proposed condition known variously as dyslexia or word blindness, coupled often with one or more of the descriptions 'congenital', 'specific' or 'developmental'. Estimates of the incidence of this condition vary from 1 per cent to 60 per cent of retarded readers. The children are described essentially as being of average or above average intelligence, as having no emotional disturbances (or only secondary ones), and as finding it very hard, or almost impossible, to learn to read. Recent surveys may be found in Money (1962) and Vernon (1962).

There are, perhaps, two schools of thought in this field. One, represented by McDonald Critchley (1964), insists that the true case of dyslexia exhibits no signs of brain pathology and shows no deficiency in any skills other than reading and other forms of the interpretation of symbols (e.g. musical notation). This position seems to the writer *a priori* very extreme. One wonders what kind of a defect can be so subtle as to affect only reading without showing itself even in experimental 'reading-like' skills (such as Birch's auditory-visual tests). In the actual case however, the position is much more complex. For one can never really be sure that emotional and educational causes have been fully excluded.

The other position is represented by Lovell (1964, in two papers) and probably also by Prechtl, Birch and some of the other contributors to Money's (1962) review. They agree that some children have 'specific' reading difficulties, which are not due to social, psychological or educational causes, but unlike Critchley they expect to find neurological damage and/or other signs of behavioural dysfunction in addition to the reading difficulty. Lovell, for example, examined groups of children of near- and above-average intelligence and found that poor readers often showed other disabilities such as directional confusion and poor visual perception. Blank and Bridger (1966) similarly have argued for a deficiency in verbal labelling in retarded readers.

One suspects that on closer examination sufficient reason for the retardation may often be discovered in the children's cultural, educational and emotional backgrounds, as suggested by Morris (1966). In some cases it may be the perceptual and linguistic deficiencies which are secondary to the reading failure. Nevertheless, there probably are a small number of children, some of whom may well fall into the minimal brain-damaged category (see Prechtl and Stemmer, 1962), in whom the reading disability may be called organic or specific and where it is primary.

However it is probably a mistake to regard these children as a separate category for remedial purposes. It is commonly claimed that 'dyslexic' children have a special need for systematic phonic and letter training. But there is every likelihood that this is the best approach for a high proportion of retarded readers, who have become confused and need to build up systematic skill. Similarly, with all types of retarded readers it may be helpful to discover their strong and weak channels for learning (e.g. visual, kinaesthetic, etc.) and plan the remedial programme accordingly. Bartlet and Shapiro (1956) have demonstrated such an analysis in the case of a child with severe emotional difficulties. In any case, remedial work with any retarded child should ideally be based on an individually designed programme – there is no such thing as an 'ordinary' retarded reader, just as there are no 'ordinary' subnormal children.

This objection to the over-ready use of labels such as dyslexia and word-blind is based mainly on practical considerations. For research purposes, it is well worth looking at series of cases and attempting to arrange them in groups and going on to examine the possibility of their having different aetiologies or prognoses. Kinsbourne and Warrington (1963) have tried this by segregating two groups, one with a high verbal/performance ratio of abilities, and the other with higher performance skills. Further and more rigorous studies of this type may prove fruitful.

3. *Other disabilities*

Difficulties in writing and spelling tend to be considered with reading problems, though it is not uncommon for a child who is a competent reader to spell badly or to show extreme clumsiness in his attempts to write and draw. In some cases these problems may be associated with emotional upset or hostility to school work, but commonly there may be minor perceptual difficulties, often allied with undiagnosed sensory loss (such as high frequency deafness). The child may also have developed bad habits, as perhaps in the case of children taught exclusively by look-and-say methods who have never appreciated the relationship of heard sounds to printed symbols.

Poor progress at arithmetic is particularly thought to be due to emotional factors. Sometimes, however, there is confusion between the acquisition and the practice of skills. Emotional difficulties may interfere more in a subject like arithmetic where the child is constantly being asked to learn new structures and processes, whereas once he can read he is, in most arts subjects, being asked to exercise an already learned skill. Failure in other school subjects has received relatively little attention, partly because the child who has successfully learned to read is not likely to show obvious and alarming retardation in other subjects, and if he does, social explanations are likely to be looked for (e.g. reaction to the teacher, father's hostility to the subject, etc.); partly also for the reason given at the beginning of the chapter that much the strongest social pressures are for the acquisition of basic skill at reading and mathematics.

In all these specific disabilities boys are more strongly represented than girls, often in a ratio of two or three to one. At first sight this might appear to support a social hypothesis – the boy's characteristic response to stress is aggression, negativism and refusal, whereas girls are more docile and when under pressure react in other ways than by school failure. Such differences must be due in good part to differences in social training; at the same time it is equally well established that boys are far more susceptible than girls, especially early in life (right from the perinatal period), to illnesses and traumata. So that, on an organic hypothesis also, far more boys than girls would have suffered minor brain damage and might therefore have impaired learning abilities.

IV. PHYSICAL HANDICAPS

Many physically damaged children have no primary intellectual handicap. Nevertheless, physical handicap is very often accompanied by poor attainment, emotional problems and intellectual impairment. This may at times be due to extraneous reasons, such as schooling missed through hospitalization; but very often the physical handicap has more direct effects. If it makes the child less mobile then he is cut off from a wide range of stimuli and normal pursuits. Opportunities to explore bring not only direct information, but also new language in their train. Moreover, when the central nervous system is affected, there may be mental as well as physical handicap.

1. *Blind and deaf children*
   Although visual and hearing defects are frequently associated with other handicaps, it is of course possible to be simply blind or deaf without any other physical (or mental) handicap. Special procedures for educating such children and for alleviating their handicaps constitute whole areas of study and as such are outside the scope of this chapter, which is concerned with more general and primary intellectual handicaps.
   But blind and deaf children also have major secondary handicaps,

through the fact that they cannot learn in the same ways as normal children and will inevitably fall behind in attainment even in ideal home and school environments. Surprisingly, deaf children can be much more handicapped than the blind; for however much we value sight, ours is in fact largely a linguistic culture, requiring hearing and speech. With early detection and intensive social and educational help, deaf children make far better linguistic progress than they otherwise might (see Ewing, 1957). They are not nowadays encouraged to neglect any possible means of communication. Thus, finger-spelling used to be discouraged on the grounds that it might be used as a complete substitute for direct speech, thus limiting the child unnecessarily. But some workers, particularly in the Soviet Union, have reported great success with young deaf children, using finger spelling (see in Kent, 1964), and its use could again well become popular.

Partial sight and hearing present different, but not always milder problems. If the child with only moderate hearing loss is not diagnosed until late, he may have suffered a long period of frustration and many undeserved censures. There is, too, the special frustration of partial ability where complete inability might at times be accepted with more resignation.

2. *Children with brain damage*

As Birch (1964) explains in an interesting discussion, there are many different types of brain damage, and our knowledge both of aetiology and of diagnosis is woefully incomplete. As he points out, the psychologist often relies on the neurologist's opinion, only to find that the neurologist is basing his opinions on the psychological evidence! Educators in this field have fared little better. Thus, Strauss and Lehtinen (1947) give a list of aspects in which brain injured children function poorly, but also blithely state that the children may suffer in any, all or none of them.

Children who have specifically motor handicaps are normally referred to as cerebrally palsied, though this term includes a number of different conditions. Such children are very frequently of below average intelligence, as Dunsdon (1952), among other investigators, has shown. There is, of course, the special difficulty of testing such children and of distinguishing the different disabilities which may underlie apparently similar test performances. This has been well analysed by Abercrombie (1964). Three types of disorder may be distinguished: visual, where the child does not see objects properly, but might conceivably suffer from no central disturbance; motor handicap, where the child is unable to control his action (he knows what he wants to do but his hand won't move in the right direction); finally, in perceptual disorders, the visual and motor systems may be relatively intact, but the child is unable to make a correct analysis of (say) the model he is to copy. His drawing then shows perceptual, not motor difficulties. For some children, however, the actual copying procedure seems to introduce extra difficulty and the same child might be able to select the right one when offered alternative matches for a drawing (ibid., p. 11), though seemingly unaware that his own copy is defective.

Obviously, in such cases correct diagnosis is a prerequisite of educational planning. Kephart (1960) describes a number of general procedures and Frostig (1964) has worked out a programme for children with visual/perceptual disturbances. Nevertheless, it is still unclear to what extent one should attempt to remedy or to circumvent defective processes.

V. GENERAL DISABILITY

Unlike many of those discussed in the two preceding sections, some children suffer from all-round intellectual impairment such that they fall markedly below the average in most aspects of social and intellectual development. This includes those who are placed in schools for the educationally subnormal – about 1 per cent of school children – as well as the severely subnormal who are to be found in junior training centres and subnormality hospitals – a much smaller number. If one takes an IQ of 70 or below as roughly defining this group, one would expect, on purely statistical grounds, to find $2\frac{1}{4}$ per cent of the population coming within it. In fact, repeated surveys have shown an actual incidence of rather over $2\frac{1}{2}$ per cent: the 'bump' in the normal curve is probably due to the incidence of pathological cases who fall outside the limits of normal variation. This means that in this country about half of such children remain within the normal school system and indeed the Department of Education and Science recognizes that up to 10 per cent of the population is sufficiently mentally handicapped to need some special provision.

1. *Psychological profiles*

In considering educational placement it is not always possible or even desirable to use purely intellectual criteria. Thus, multiple-handicapped children, who may have physical or emotional handicaps in addition to their intellectual ones, are more likely to be placed in special schools than are more straightforward cases of intellectual subnormality, even if this practice is not always welcomed by the school. However, for the purpose of scientific study the single criterion of IQ is useful, provided one bears in mind the cautions expressed at the beginning of this chapter.

Binet was well aware that his intelligence scales provided information about the relative standing of children rather than telling us much about their functional characteristics. If subnormal children are not intellectually identical with younger normal children, it ought to be possible to discern characteristic patterns of strengths and weaknesses. At the same time one must bear in mind that subnormal children differ widely among themselves, so that there may be no one pattern of deficit but a number of different patterns.

The easiest way of approaching this task is to take Binet test results and discover which subtests differentiate clearly between normal and subnormal children at equivalent mental ages. In a careful large-scale study Thompson and Magaret (1947) found a number of such items and Zazzo (1960) has carried out a similar exercise. But the second stage of this type of study has not proved as effective; that is, the grouping of the distinguishing subtests so as to show up characteristic patterns. Of the four or five hypotheses which they tested Thompson and Magaret were successful with only one – the items failed by the subnormals showed higher loadings on McNemar's 'general first factor'. But this is only to say that the subnormal are poorest at the items which make the heaviest intellectual demands.

Zazzo (1960) also reports on a more general type of profiling that he has attempted. Using a large battery of tests he found that children whose Binet-type scores are about 70 are likely to have rather better scores (though still below average) on tests of psycho-motor efficiency (e.g. cancellation tasks). This is not surprising, as the Binet score probably represents the original selection criterion and one would expect other types of test to produce results nearer to the general population mean. Interestingly, however, the children produce spatial organization scores which are on average ten points below the Binet score, showing particular difficulty in such tasks as the Bender figures. This should repay further study.

More circumscribed profiles include the Illinois Test of Psycholinguistic Abilities in which McCarthy and Kirk (1961) have followed Osgood's model in classifying linguistic ability along three dimensions:

processes, namely encoding and decoding; channels, such as auditory and motor; levels, that is automatic and representational (see Figure 1). By comparing subtest scores one might discover that a child could decode well when dealing with auditory but not with visual material. Alternatively, he might show intact automatic skills but be poor at representation. The battery provides individual clinical profiles which may prove

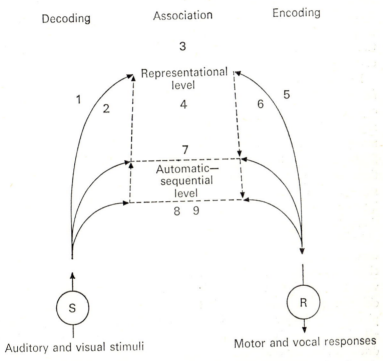

Fig. 1. A model of psycho-linguistic abilities

of use in the planning of special educational programmes for individual children, but it has not yet been used successfully in finding common patterns in specific diagnostic (or other) groups of subnormal children. Similarly, Frostig's (1961) test of visual perception provides differential information about a child's visual skills.

The weakness of studies in this field is that they have usually been conducted on mixed samples rather than on distinct aetiological and diagnostic groups, so that although Thomson and Magaret, for instance, used over 400 subnormal subjects it is not surprising that they failed to show any clear patterns.

2. *Theories of subnormality*

As suggested in the preceding section general theories are not likely to be entirely successful in dealing with the problems of subnormality. Furthermore, the recent spate of empirical researches, some of which will be mentioned in the next section, do not yet lend themselves to any simple fusion into an overall theory. Nevertheless, there are one or two theories which are sufficiently interesting to be worth at least brief consideration.

Kounin (1943) was the main member of the Gestalt school to argue for the theory of psychological rigidity in the subnormal. In his conceptual framework one imagines the young child to have few functional regions and only thin boundaries between them. Thus the child is at the mercy of the strongest impulse of the moment, but can switch easily from one activity to another. As he grows older differentiation increases; there are now more regions and the boundaries between them are stronger (see Figure 2). More activities are now possible and they interfere less with each other. In the subnormal, differentiation remains that of the child but the boundaries are more rigid than in the normal older person. Mental function is thus simple but circumscribed. Kounin used satiation experiments to support this theory. Thus, groups of children were asked to draw cats. When they tired of drawing cats they were told to draw turtles, and so on. By comparison with normal children the subnormal subjects drew the turtles and subsequent pictures for longer periods in relation to the time spent on the first set of drawings of cats. The subnormal children were less 'satiated', by drawing cats, for drawing in general than were the normals and would therefore happily continue with other types of drawing whereas normal children would draw other figures less.

Kounin's theory has not remained unchallenged. For instance, Werner (1946) pointed out that in an earlier investigation by Lewin, apparently opposite results had been explained by arguing that normal children could shift from one activity to another more easily! The controversy continued in papers by Brand *et al.* (1953) and Solomon (1954) in which attempts were made to determine whether the rigid behaviour was in fact a function of institutionalization rather than of the subnormality *per se*. Solomon concludes that rigidity is not a function of institutionalization. Recently, however, the whole concept

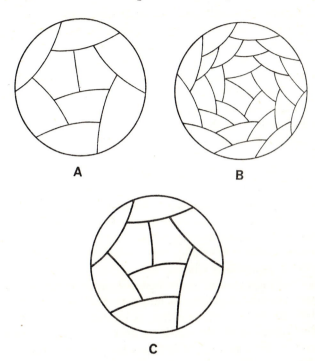

Fig. 2. Psychological differentiation: A, normal child; B, normal adult; C, feeble minded person (after Kounin, 1943, p.181)

has been re-examined by Zigler (1962) who argues convincingly that the phenomena attributed by Kounin and his followers to rigidity can be better explained in terms of the child's life history and his reaction to the adult experimenter. Thus, for example, the subnormal subject who finds the session with the experimenter a rewarding experience will do a long set of drawings for him on the second occasion; the more independent normal child does not need such reassurance.

Zazzo (1960) does not propound a theory of subnormality, but he does make two points of general interest. First, he points out that the subnormal child is frequently a 'slow-learner' in that he may spend two years passing through stages of development that take a normal child one year. The process becomes a vicious circle, for if the child remains for too long at a stage normally passed through quickly, habits may become stamped in over-firmly when further progress depends on developing or discarding them. Thus the child's difficulties are cumulative and in some areas he may even come to a complete stop.

Zazzo's other contribution is the idea of *hétérochronie*. As he sees it, the subnormal child is in some respects like the younger normal child and in others like his age-mates. His total performance is thus heterochronous, being appropriate to no normal chronological age level. Thus, in a cancellation task the subnormal may combine the inaccuracy of a young child with the speed of an older child and progress may present special difficulties.

3. *Studies of learning in the subnormal*

The last twenty years have seen an increasing volume of empirical studies of language development, learning, transfer and problem-solving in the subnormal, much of it carried out in this country as well as in the United States and the Soviet Union. Good reviews may be found in the works of O'Connor and Hermelin (1963) and Clarke and Clarke (1965, particularly Chapter 13).

Luria (1961) has stressed the subnormal child's difficulties in developing the regulative functions of language. Such children have much more difficulty than normal children in learning to use verbal signals to inhibit behaviour. In the classic experiment a child has to squeeze a rubber bulb when a red light is shown but remain still if the light is green. Normal children find it easier to inhibit the action if they say 'No!' aloud, but the subnormal have great difficulty in managing this.

O'Connor and Hermelin (1963) have extended this work and Bryant (1964) has carried out a series of interesting experiments. In summary, these workers find that subnormals can be helped by verbal instruction but that general instructions may not be much help and seem in any case to be quickly forgotten. Specific verbal instruction carefully adjusted to the needs of the situation does, however, help considerably; although, as Hurtig (1960) has demonstrated, the effect of the help may be to raise the level of performance in the particular setting, rather than to increase the child's general potential. O'Connor and Hermelin (1963) have also shown that subnormals' learning is often not mediated by implicit verbal structures. This makes their learning less stable and, paradoxically, in one experiment led to their being able to 'reverse' a response more readily than could normal children who had learned the initial response-set more thoroughly. As Bryant (1964) puts it, subnormal children 'are relatively incapable of abstracting general rules from learning specific instances'. They learn what is given but do not go beyond it. If, however, the original situation is such that the subnormal child's attention is inevitably drawn to general features of a display, Bryant showed that the learning can be more general.

In a review of learning studies Denny (1964) argues for a general defect of inhibition in the subnormal which results in particular difficulty in discrimination learning. House and Zeaman (1960, in Clarke and Clarke, 1965) are more inclined to attribute these difficulties to an attention defect. The position is summarized in a recent short discussion by O'Connor (1966) in which he stresses that a variety of different types of study nearly all point to an 'input-deficiency'. This idea is linked with work which suggests that in the subnormal short-term memory traces decay quickly and that the consolidation of new learning by its transfer to the long-term memory store is thus particularly difficult.

Studies of vocabulary and language in the subnormal tend to confirm O'Connor and Hermelin's (1963) view that subnormal children have normal (if retarded) language structure and semantic skills, but that they are less likely to make spontaneous use of the language skills they actually possess – thus slowing up progress still further (see Mein, 1961). This may reflect not just inherent defects but also the constricting effect of the unstimulating environments in which many such children are brought up, both in and out of institutions.

Birch and Lefford (1963) have suggested that intersensory skills – the ability to translate signals from one sensory (or motor) channel to another, say, in recognizing an auditory stimulus in visual form ('house' and a picture of a house) – represent a particularly advanced and uniquely human achievement. Failure or weakness in this area may be associated with brain damage, specific disabilities in learning, or with subnormality. O'Connor and Hermelin (1963) have investigated these skills (which they term cross-modal coding) in the subnormal and find that where subjects are forced to code cross-modally they perform better than in like-modal situations; the forced coding may act as an extra pressure on the subject to attend and inhibit automatic, stereotyped response-tendencies.[1]

On a more optimistic note, attention is drawn to the series of experiments on transfer reported by Clarke and Clarke (1965), and Clarke and Cooper (1966). They have been concerned to show that the ability to transfer learning both within a class, as in Harlow's (1949) work on learning sets, and between different classes also, is a major factor in

[1] See also the discussion in Volume I, p. 246 and footnote.

human development. Their research findings indicate that subnormals possess good transfer abilities and that with suitable training they may use these to make unexpected progress. One point these workers make is that transfer is more likely if practice situations are complex and that simple practice may be worse than none at all. When these findings can be successfully applied to the education of the subnormal they may have far-reaching results; in this connexion programmed instruction techniques may prove particularly valuable.

In general, one may say that the subnormal child's main weaknesses are in attention, set and cue-selection – in other words the subnormal child is poor at 'getting the hang of' what is wanted of him, and his input deficiency makes this initial stage in new learning particularly difficult to surmount. In addition, his lack of spontaneity, particularly marked in poor language use and representational thinking means that he does very little to explore or make links himself. New knowledge has to be brought to him and the situation specially structured. But if this is done successfully the child can learn relatively well and retains his knowledge.

On the other hand subnormal children have been found to possess virtually all the skills and abilities enjoyed by non-handicapped children. Nor is there much evidence that their intellectual development proceeds along radically different or distorted lines in comparison with that of the normal. In fact, studies based on Piaget's analysis of child development (see, for example, Woodward, 1963) show even very subnormal children progressing through the same stages and in the same order as he has set out in studying normal children, though they sometimes seem to cease developing at quite early stages (see Jackson, 1965). Thus the Piagetian studies provide better evidence of an 'arrest' in development than do traditional intelligence tests.

In conclusion, it should be emphasized that nearly the whole of the experimental work described in this section has been carried out on severely subnormal subjects (with IQs usually below 55), often in institutions. It is tempting to expect that the strengths and weaknesses so far discovered may be paralleled in the less severely subnormal children in ESN schools and classes, but on a smaller scale. On the other hand, it may be that the profile which is beginning to emerge in these studies is essentially that of the pathologically damaged child (for whom the Russians use the term oligophrenic) and that 'subcultural' cases may have a different pattern of function. Much more investigation is needed.

4. *Psychotic and autistic children*

At the beginning of this chapter it was pointed out that emotional disturbance might well be highly relevant to intellectual dysfunction. In fact, as we have just seen, many of the difficulties of the severely subnormal could well be interpreted as at least partly due to poor motivation and an unwillingness to learn from others, amounting often to an avoidance of the whole social situation. Children who are severely mentally disturbed may exhibit some of these characteristics in a very extreme form. They show no affective contact with human beings, often appear deaf, are completely withdrawn and may exhibit other bizarre symptoms. Such children are sometimes referred to as schizophrenic or more frequently nowadays as cases of infantile or childhood autism (see Rimland, 1965, for a recent view). There is, however, considerable uncertainty as to the definition and aetiology of this condition. Creak (1964) was chairman of a working party which attempted to clarify the position by proposing a nine point diagnostic list and suggesting that a child should exhibit most of these symptoms to be classified as a case of autism.

In terms of test performance autistic children are nearly always in the severely subnormal category, but they show signs, in the opinion of many clinicians, of 'islets' of normal or superior ability, suggesting that were the 'disease' cured, they would prove of at least normal intelligence. Attempted treatments have ranged in the educational field from the extremes of psychoanalytically-derived therapeutic approaches to behaviouristically rooted conditioning methods. Improvement is usually slow and incomplete, though a few children make fairly good recoveries; these are usually the ones who have some speech, perhaps established in early life before the onset of the condition. Although small intensive studies provide useful insights, systematic surveys such as the one carried out at Smith Hospital (see Whittam *et al.* 1966) are badly needed. Without them we can only agree with Tizard (Chapter 7 in Clarke and Clarke, 1965) that the widely differing prognoses in these children may reflect the fact that we are dealing under one title with a number of different diseases, some perhaps organic in origin, others due to pathogenic social experiences.

VI. EDUCATIONAL TREATMENT

1. *The application of research findings*

The immediate application of any new research finding in classroom practice is fraught with dangers. For one thing, the new idea may soon be contradicted, or at least modified, by later research. Again a general finding may not be easy to apply to individual children, or may have much less generality than the teacher expects. Half-understood ideas also may do more damage than good. There is too the backwash danger – if the psychologist feels called upon to produce practical classroom ideas he may sacrifice basic long-term research in favour of hasty and meretricious analyses.

Nevertheless, there is by now a body of knowledge, particularly in dealing with the severely subnormal and with brain-damaged children, which is still only being applied in a small minority of schools and centres. In the case of the severely subnormal this is in part due to the lack of well trained personnel, but even in the ESN schools there is far too little experimental work. Books like Kephart's (1960) are full of interesting suggestions, as for instance on the strengthening and development of basic motor skills. Even if some of these fail to justify themselves entirely they are still worth trying. Particularly useful might be a demonstration school or schools associated with a university department or research unit.

One general lesson may be drawn from research work, particularly from that done by the Clarkes and by O'Connor and Tizard (1956). All their work shows that handicapped children can achieve more than has frequently been expected of them. The attempt to teach a discrimination or a skill is often abandoned after a few unsuccessful trials; but if a far greater number of attempts are made there can be surprising success. This is not to suggest, however, that poor learners should be given long periods of repeating impossible tasks, nor that their attitudes should be ignored. The much repeated idea that subnormal people positively like monotonous, repetitive work would probably soon be discarded if they were brought up from the beginning in a more permissive, creative and unregimented atmosphere (see Hulme and Lunzer, 1966; Cashdan and Stevens, 1966). Such myths (like those about the behaviour of mongols exploded by Blacketer-Simmonds, 1953) can so easily be self-perpetuating; for children tend to live up to what is expected of them.

2. *Segregation and integration*

Much thought has been given both in this country and elsewhere to the question of educational provision for children with learning handicaps. Schonell *et al.* (1962) have collected a number of descriptions and opinions on current practice in many countries. On the question of whether handicapped children should be integrated with their normal school-fellows or segregated in special schools, no clear-cut decision is possible. Some children need the protection of the special milieu and régime while many others would benefit from closer contact with normal children. The problems of rejection and of stigma are also rarely completely solved. The solution, as Tansley and Gulliford (1960) say, must lie in a whole range of different types of provision; but, whatever the setting, some children will need individually designed programmes coupled with individual and small group work. If the child is given the right kind of work in an atmosphere of acceptance, his need for individual attention will progressively lessen. But there is no doubt that the specialist teacher of handicapped children needs to be particularly strong at diagnostic work and to be provided with help from psychologists and medical personnel. The most common error is not to take the unsuccessful child sufficiently far back, and thus to restart with remedial work at a point where the child will still fail. Before progress can be made, fundamental skills and attitudes have to be securely established. In this context the Brooklands experiment in this country (see Tizard, 1964) and Kirk's (1961) work in the United States on early education both demonstrate amply the gains that can be made if this lesson is properly applied.

REFERENCES

ABERCROMBIE, M. L. J. (1954). *Perceptual and Visuo-motor Disorders in Cerebral Palsy*. London: Spastics Society with Heinemann.

ACE, P. W. (1956). A remedial teaching scheme: introducing a new reading method. *Brit. J. Educ. Psychol.* **26**, 191–193.

AINSWORTH, M. (ed.). (1962). Deprivation of maternal care. *Public Health Papers, No.* 14. Geneva: W.H.O.

BARTLET, D., and SHAPIRO, M. B. (1956). Investigation and treatment of a reading disability in a dull child with severe psychiatric disturbances. *Brit. J. Educ. Psychol.* **26**, 180–190.

BELMONT, L., and BIRCH, H. G. (1965). Lateral dominance, lateral awareness, and reading disability. *Child Develpm.* **36**, 57–71.

BERNSTEIN, B. (1961). Social structure, language and learning. *Educ. Research.* **3**, 163–176.

BIRCH, H. G. (ed.). (1964). *Brain Damage in Children*. Baltimore: Williams and Wilkie.

BIRCH, H. G., and BELMONT, L. (1964). Auditory-visual integration in normal and retarded readers. *Amer. J. Orthopsychiat*. **34**, 852–861.

BIRCH, H. G., and BELMONT, L. (1965). Auditory-visual integration, intelligence and reading ability in school children. *Percept. Mot. Skills*. **20**, 295–305.

BIRCH, H. G., and LEFFORD, A. (1963). Intersensory development in children. *Monogr. Soc. Res. Child Develop*. **28**.

BIRCH, L. B. (1948–9). The remedial treatment of reading disability. *Educ. Rev*. **1**, 107–118.

BLACKETER-SIMMONDS, L. D. A. (1953). An investigation into the supposed differences existing between mongols and other mentally defective subjects with regard to certain psychological traits. *J. ment. Sci*. **99**, 702–719.

BLANK, M. (1961). *Some Effects of Maternal Behaviour on Infant Development*. Ph. D. thesis. Cambridge: University of Cambridge.

BLANK, M., and BRIDGER, W. H. (1966). Deficiencies in verbal labeling in retarded readers. *Amer. J. Orthopsychiat*. **36**, 840–847.

BRAND, H., BENOIT, E. P., and ORNSTEIN, G. N. (1953). Rigidity and feeblemindedness: an examination of the Kounin–Lewin theory. *J. clin. Psychol*. **9**, 375–378.

BRUCE, D. J. (1964). The analysis of word sounds by young children. *Brit. J. Educ. Psychol*. **34**, 158–170.

BRYANT, P. (1964). Verbalization and flexibility in retarded children. *Proceedings of the International Copenhagen Congress on the Scientific Study of Mental Retardation*. 359–365.

CASHDAN, A., and JEFFREE, D. M. (1966). The influence of the home background on the development of severely subnormal children. *Brit. J. Med. Psychol*. **39**, 313–318.

CASHDAN, A., PUMFREY, P.D., and LUNZER, E. A. (1967). A survey of children receiving remedial teaching in reading. *Bull. Brit. Psychol. Soc*. **67**, 17 A.

CASHDAN, A., and STEVENS, M. (1966). Social education in the junior training centre. *J. ment. Subnormality. Mongr. Supp*., 1–10.

CLARKE, A. D. B., and COOPER, G. M. (1966). Age and perceptual motor transfer in imbeciles: task complexity as a variable. *Brit. J. Psychol*. **57**, 113–119.

CLARKE, A. M., and CLARKE, A. D. B. (1965). *Mental Deficiency*. London: Methuen.

COLLINS, J. E., (1961). *The Effects of Remedial Education.* Edinburgh: Oliver and Boyd (for Univ. Birmingham Inst. of Education).

CREAK, M. (1964). Schizophrenic syndrome in childhood. Further progress report of a working party. (April 1964). *Develop. Med. Child Neurol.* **6,** 530–535.

CURR, W., and HALLWORTH, H. J. (1965). An empirical study of the concept of retardation. *Educ. Rev.* **18,** 5–15.

DAVIS, D. R. (1961). A disorder theory of mental retardation. *J. ment. Subnormality.* **7,** 3–11.

DENNY, N. R. (1964). Research in learning and performance. In Stevens, H. A., and Heber, R. (ed.), *Mental Retardation.* Chicago: Univ. Chicago Press.

DOUGLAS, J. W. B. (1964). *The Home and the School.* London: Mac-Gibbon and Kee.

DUNSDON, M. I. (1952). *The Educability of Cerebral Palsied Children.* London: Newnes.

EWING, A. W. G. (ed.). (1957). *Educational Guidance and the Deaf Child.* Manchester: Manchester Univ. Press.

FROSTIG, M. (1961). *Marianne Frostig Developmental Test of Visual Perception. Teachers' Guide.* Chicago: Follett.

HARLOW, H. F. (1949). The formation of learning sets. *Psychol. Rev.* **56,** 51–65.

HEBB, D. O. (1949). *The Organization of Behavior.* New York: Wiley.

HULME, I., and LUNZER, E. A. (1966). Play, language and reasoning in subnormal children. *J. Child Psychol. Psychiat.* **7,** 107–123.

HUNT, J. MCV. (1961). *Intelligence and Experience.* New York: Ronald Press.

HURTIG, M. (1960). Etude expérimentale des possibilités d'apprentissage intellectuel d'enfants debiles et d'enfants normaux. *Enfance.* **45,** 371–383.

JACKSON, S. (1965). The growth of logical thinking in normal and subnormal children. *Brit. J. Educ. Psychol.* **35,** 255–258.

KENT, M. S. (1964). Language needs for the child with deafness – some factors influencing development. In *Report of the Proceedings of the International Congress on Education of the Deaf.* Washington: U.S. Govt. Printing Office.

KEPHARD, N. C. (1960). *The Slow learner in the Classroom.* Columbus, Ohio: Merrill.

KINSBOURNE, M., and WARRINGTON, E. K. (1953). Developmental

factors in reading and writing backwardness. *Brit. J. Psychol.* **54,** 145–156.

KIRK, *The early Education of the Mentally Retarded.* Illinois: Univ. Illinois Press.

KOUNIN, J. S. (1943). Intellectual development and rigidity. In Barker, R. G., Kounin, J. S., and Wright, H. F. (ed.). *Child Behavior and Development.* New York: McGraw-Hill.

LOVELL, K., BYRNE, C., and RICHARDS, N. B. (1963). A further study of the educational progress of children who had received remedial education. *Brit. J. Educ. Psychol.* **33,** 3–9.

LOVELL, K., JOHNSON, E., and OLIVER, D. E. (1964). A further study of some cognitive and other disabilities in backward readers of average non-verbal reasoning scores. *Brit. J. Educ. Psychol.* **34,** 275–279.

LOVELL, K., JOHNSON, E., and PLATTS, O. (1962). A summary of a study of the reading ages of children who had been given remedial teaching. *Brit. J. Educ. Psychol.* **32,** 66–71.

LOVELL, K., SHAPTON, D., and WARREN, N. S. (1964). A study of some cognitive and other disabilities in backward readers of average intelligence as assessed by a non-verbal test. *Brit. J. Educ. Psychol.* **34,** 58–64.

LURIA, A. R. (1961). *The Role of Speech in the Regulation of Normal and Abnormal Behaviour.* London: Pergamon.

LYNN, R. (1963). Reading readiness and the perceptual abilities of young children. *Educ. Research.* **6,** 10–15.

MCCARTHY, J. J., and KIRK, S. A. (1961). *Illinois Test of Psycholinguistic Abilities.* Experimental Edition. Illinois: Univ. Illinois Press.

MEIN, R. (1961). A study of the oral vocabularies of severely subnormal children. *J. ment. Defic. Res.* **5,** 42–59.

MOLTZ, H. (1960). Imprinting: empirical basis and theoretical significance. *Psychol. Bull.* **57,** 291–314.

MONEY, J. (ed.). (1962). *Reading Disability.* Baltimore: Johns Hopkins.

MORRIS, J. M. (1966). *Standards and Progress in Reading.* London: Newnes with N.F.E.R.

NEWSON, J., and NEWSON, E. (1966). Child rearing in socio-cultural perspective. In Loring, J., and Mason, A. (ed.). *The Spastic School Child and the Outside World.* London: Spastics Society with Heinemann.

O'CONNOR, N. (1966). Backwardness and severe subnormality. In

Foss, B. M. (ed.). *New Horizons in Psychology.* Harmondsworth: Penguin Books.

O'CONNOR, N., and HERMELIN, B. (1963). *Speech and Thought in Severe Subnormality.* London: Pergamon.

O'CONNOR, N., and TIZARD, J. (1956). *The Social Problem of Mental Deficiency.* London: Pergamon.

PFAFFENBERGER, C. J., and SCOTT, J. P. (1959). The relationship between delayed socialization and trainability in guide dogs. *J. genet. Psychol.* **95,** 145–155.

PRECHTL, H. F. R., and STEMMER, ch. J. (1962). The choreiform syndrome in children. *Develop. Med. and Child Neurol.* **4,** 119–127.

RIMLAND, B. (1965). *Infantile Autism.* London: Methuen.

RUTTER, M., GRAHAM, P., and BIRCH, H. G. (1966). Interrelations between the choreiform syndrome, reading disability and psychiatric disorder in children of 8–11 years. *Develop. Med. and Child Neurol.* **8,** 149–159.

SCHONELL, F. J., MCLEOD, J., and COCHRANE, R. G. (1962). *The Slow Learner: Segregation or Integration.* Queensland: Queensland Univ. Press.

SOLOMON, P. (1954). A note on rigidity and length of institutionalisation. *J. clin. Psychol.* **11,** 294–297.

STEIN, Z., and SUSSER, M. W. (1963). The social distribution of mental retardation. *Amer. J. ment. Def.* **67,** 811–821.

STOTT, D. H. (1959). Evidence for the pre-natal impairment of temperament in mentally retarded children. *Vita Humana.* **2,** 125–148.

STRAUSS, A. A., and LEHTINEN, L. E. (1947). *Psychopathology and Education of the Brain-injured Child.* New York: Grune and Stratton.

TANSLEY, A. E., and GULLIFORD, R. (1960). *The Education of Slow Learning Children.* London: Routledge.

THOMPSON, C. W., and MAGARET, A. (1947). Differential test responses of normals and mental defectives. *J. abnorm. soc. Psychol.* **42,** 285–293.

TIZARD, J. (1964). *Community Services for the Mentally Handicapped.* London: O.U.P.

VERNON, M. D. (1957). *Backwardness in Reading.* London: C.U.P.

VERNON, M. D. (1962). Specific dyslexia. *Brit. J. Educ. Psychol.* **32,** 143–150.

WERNER, H. (1946). The concept of rigidity: a critical evaluation. *Psychol. Rev.* **53,** 43–52.

WHITTAM, H., SIMON, G. B., and MITTLER, P. J. (1966). The early

H

development of psychotic children and their sibs. *Develop. Med. and Child Neurol.* **8,** 552–560.

WOLFF, P. H., and HURWITZ, I. (1966). The choreiform syndrome. *Develop. Med. and Child Neurol.* **8,** 160–165.

WOODWARD, M. (1963). The application of Piaget's theory to research in mental deficiency. In: Ellis, N. R. (ed.). *Handbook of Mental Deficiency.* New York: McGraw-Hill.

ZANGWILL, O. L. (1960). *Cerebral Dominance and its relation to Psychological Function.* London: Oliver and Boyd.

ZAZZO, R. (1960). Une recherche d'équipe sur la débilité mentale. *Enfance.* **4–5,** 335–364.

ZIGLER, E. (1962). Rigidity in the feebleminded. In Trapp, E. P., and Himelstein, P. (ed.) *Readings on the Exceptional Child.* London: Methuen.

PART TWO

Environment and the Learner

Introduction

J. F. MORRIS

THE FOCUS of attention now moves from the study of individual differences in abilities and personality traits to the social contexts of education. In this section of the book there are three chapters: a brief introduction to the sociology of education, by Professor Blyth, of the University of Liverpool School of Education; a case study of inter-personal relations in a secondary modern school in Northern England, presented by David Hargreaves, of the University of Manchester Department of Education; and an account of some of the leading themes in the social psychology of learning, by John Morris, of the University of Manchester Business School, late of the Department of Psychology at the same University.

If sociological and psychological theories were more coherent and more fully developed, or if the editors had better powers of integration, the following chapters would form part of a continuous exposition. The shifts in topic would be self-evident, and the moves from one level of analysis to another would be accomplished elegantly and without loss of focus. Unfortunately, the theories are piecemeal and varied (though improving all the time; this will go down in the histories of the behavioural sciences as the Era of the Revival of Interest in Theory). The problems of moving from one scale to another are hard to achieve, because the units in such a scale are by no means agreed on. And the editor responsible for this part of the book (Morris) found his ideas of the purpose of the section changing as the work progressed. The aim of this brief introduction is to give some account of the contents of the chapters, the relationships between them, and ways in which the reader may care to use them.

The first chapter written was that by Alan Blyth. He had been asked by the editors to write a sociological essay on the contexts of development and learning. At the outset of the book, when only one fairly plump volume was envisaged, before it took on a life of its own and developed into three substantial volumes, the aim was to lead gently from the predominantly psychological chapters, through a social-psychological chapter, to a finale which would introduce the

197

psychological reader (particularly the reader from those departments of education and psychology still fairly remote from sociology) to the 'institutional point of view'.

In his own words, 'The term *institution* . . . does not necessarily mean something founded or instituted in any explicit sense. Rather, it refers to all the relatively enduring, socially sanctioned features of collective behaviour within a society. . . . One thing they all have in common: they can be thought of without reference to particular individuals or groups.' This clearly sets off the treatment in his chapter from that in the more psychological chapters, which do not wish to lose sight of the individual, unless it is by fractionating his individual behaviour into small segments. Nevertheless, the author provides a very accessible introduction to his subject, not by attempting a potted survey of the rapidly growing field of educational sociology, but by showing the range and complexity of the social environment, widening out as the child grows, and never ceasing to influence him, whether he is aware of it or not.

The phrase 'field of educational sociology' comes readily to hand, and can easily be used unreflectively. But consideration of the implications of the word *field* suggests that we would do better with a word that avoids the implication of hotly defended territory, with boundary skirmishes and invasions. Though this has an excitingly dramatic aspect, it does violence to the fact that all the behavioural sciences, sociology and psychology included, share the same subject-matter; namely, the processes and products of organic activity, usually human activity.

But there is still plenty of room for conflict, especially constructive conflict. When the word *field* is replaced by *perspective*, we find sharp and profitable differences of opinion on the most appropriate perspective from which to view particular problems, such as breakdowns or retardation in development. Even those who adopt the same perspective find themselves disagreeing on just what it is that they have seen, and especially on its implications. As perspectives widen, there are fascinating problems of linking together the results of observation. Ideally, the pieces would fit together like a well-constructed jigsaw puzzle. But the picture on the box is unfortunately missing, and there is great diversity of opinion on the picture that is likely to emerge from the widened perspective.

Alan Blyth's viewpoint is clear, because deliberately simplified and generalized. That in David Hargreaves' case-study is also clear, but for a different reason. Here the perspective is that of a field worker wishing to understand the conditions influencing the individual attitudes and group norms of one age-group of boys in a secondary school in the North of England. Behind this specific concern there is a more fundamental interest in the problems of young people in school, and the difficulties that many of them encounter because the school has not been designed to meet their particular needs. The school, in this treatment of learning and development, is seen as a system with a logic of its own, as all systems have. An important part of the structure of this type of school is 'streaming', which divides the pupils into separate classes, using the criterion of competitive performance in the subjects of the school curriculum. A study is made of the attitudes and group norms of the different streams in the fourth-year of the course of studies. It is found that there are striking differences in these. In the highest stream, the attitudes and norms of the pupils are congruent with those of the staff, in respecting the need to learn what the teachers have to offer and the need to have a formal co-ordination of activities. In the lowest stream, there is opposition between teachers and pupils, and teachers have to phrase their own attitudes and activities to counter or contain this opposition.

Hargreaves stays firmly within the school, and does not attempt a systematic link between school, home and social-class, though he is well aware of these linkages. What he does do, however, to the great advantage of his readers, is to set his study in a wider context of research literature, focussing particularly on the relationships between teachers and pupils from the perspective of authority and power. He uses some of the useful distinctions currently made in the behavioural sciences between different forms of social power, and shows very clearly how these relate to closely observed situations.

This case study is an excellent example of the use of sociological and psychological perspectives in the illumination of some of the real-life problems of a particular school; problems which are by no means limited to this school, or even to schools in general. As he starts off by reminding us, many of these problems of conflicting norms and attitudes in organizations were first encountered in studies of industrial organizations.

It is interesting to compare the technical terms shared by Blyth and Hargreaves: terms such as *role* and *group norms* and *peer group*. In the more obviously sociological chapter, these are seen broadly, as categories that can embrace thousands or even millions of people at a time. In the study of a particular school, some indication of differences in the roles of the 'A' stream teacher and the 'D' stream teacher in the same school begin to be made evident. This is in no way to suggest that roles in this study are more adequately defined than in Blyth's analysis. It merely reminds us that a common vocabulary in the behavioural sciences does not always, or even often, imply a common scale of treatment.

This difference in scale – with the same word being used to describe a small group of specified individuals in one case and millions of people, extending over many different societies and living in different historical periods, in another case – has led some writers to propose the use of a more differentiated technical vocabulary, with different terms for each scale of analysis. In our view, this would be unhelpful at the present stage of development of the behavioural sciences. In most instances, the context of discussion invariably makes the bounds of a concept quite clear. But it is useful to remember that contexts vary greatly, and that a study of 'the role of the teacher in modern industrial society' may call on one of the teachers at Lumley School as an illustration, but is likely to do so briefly. The diverse roles taken on by the teachers at this one school, however, would take more than a book to describe and analyse, as Hargreaves's more extensive study (Hargreaves, 1967) brings out very clearly.

This gives a brief review of two of the three chapters in this second part of the present volume. The third, which comes first in sequence because it stays rather closer to traditional psychological themes than either of the other two chapters, is an attempt by one of the editors, John Morris, to indicate the range and complexity of the social influences on learning.

Morris's chapter relates not only to the others in this part of the book, but to two other chapters in the first two volumes. In the first volume, Chapter 6 attempts to relate the common-sense psychology of motivation to observational and experimental studies of motivation, both human and infra-human. The case is made for seeing the concept of attitude as the most useful motivational concept in the study of human activity. Some attention is given in this chapter to the learning of attitudes, and to the significance of the self-concept in determining the organization and relative importance of attitudes. Since attitudes are strongly evaluative, some discussion of the development of morality was included.

In Volume II, Chapter 11, several of these points were developed from a slightly different angle. The main concern of the chapter is with social learning in childhood and adolescence (taking up from an earlier chapter on the origins of social learning, by Dr Schaffer). Once again the importance of the self-concept as an internal reference point was stressed, and attention was also given to the learning of social roles. These themes were followed through later childhood and adolescence, and discussed in the context of a possible 'crisis of identity' during the adolescent period. Since each of the three volumes in this work is intended to stand alone, even though it is hoped that they will often be read as a whole, a certain amount of overlap between the chapters in Volumes I and II was unavoidable.

Turning now to the chapter in the present volume, 'The Social Psychology of Learning', the emphasis is on the social influences on learning, and particularly on the directed learning that goes on in educational establishments. As this chapter was written last, it has been possible to make the cross references to other chapters fairly plentiful. The main conceptual scheme used in the chapter is that of a series of interacting structures guiding activity: structures which are on different scales. Starting, as the psychologist always does, with the individual in all his individuality, one sees that his behaviour is linked, in all cases where he is not acting under duress, with a set of attitudes, all of which have been shaped by his social experience.

Looking at these attitudes on the individual level of analysis, it becomes apparent that the 'learning-history' of each person is in various important respects unique. He does not take over the established attitudes of the 'significant others' around him in a passive, purely reproductive way. He selects, organizes, and (within limits) integrates them.

This individuality of attitudes, including all the attitudes relating to learning (both the subjects of learning and the level of aspiration) provides the educational system with a formidable problem. It can either ignore this individuality, and cope as best it may with the resulting problems of apathy and deviance, or set itself out to direct behaviour externally, with an elaborate system of 'incentives', or finally and in our opinion desirably, attempt to devise a system of education within which this individuality can flower.

Having firmly established the fact of individuality, it became necessary to show that human behaviour at any given time is not only a function of individual attitudes. Individuals spend their lives in groups and organizations, and these have sets of rules (sanctioned by a variety of rewards and punishments) guiding the conduct of their members.

These group norms constitute a subject of study in their own right, and it must not be thought that norms and attitudes always co-exist amicably.

Finally, the very useful but complex concept of *role* was once more employed to throw light on the activities of people in the educational system. The roles of teachers and pupils were considered, illustratively rather than rigorously, from the social-psychological point of view. That is, the role as enacted by a variety of diverse individuals was studied, not the role on a higher level of abstraction. The main difference between the treatment of the roles of pupils and teachers by Hargreaves and that by Morris lies in the focus of interest. Hargreaves is primarily interested in the ways in which teachers handle power and authority, in relation to the norms and attitudes of the pupils. Morris is primarily interested in the diverse materials that can constitute the subject matter of education, and attempts to classify these systematically, from the point of view of their possible relationship to the individuality of the learner.

It might be helpful to end this introduction by suggesting some of the ways in which readers might care to use the next three chapters. If a reader wants to move from the psychological to the sociological perspective in easy stages, with a good deal of cross-reference, he will read the chapters in their present sequence. If he prefers to see sociological and psychological thinking at work on particular problems, with wider references closely keyed in to these problems, he will start with Hargreaves, move on to Blyth for a broad sociological perspective, and back to Morris. If he would like a simple, lucid introduction to some of the main concepts used in the three chapters, he will start with Blyth, then continue with Morris, and end with Hargreaves. It will be noted that all of these suggestions take for granted a reader who will be prepared to read each of the three chapters. But one could hardly expect an editor to think otherwise!

REFERENCE

HARGREAVES, DAVID H. (1967). *Social Relations in a Secondary School*. London: Routledge and Kegan Paul.

6

The Social Psychology of Learning

J. F. MORRIS

I. INTRODUCTION

THE PREVIOUS chapters in this volume have been concerned with the nature and assessment of abilities and personality traits, and the problem of handicaps in learning. These are all matters in which individual differences are of great educational importance. The educational system must find ways of dealing reasonably effectively with the great variety of individual differences, and the teacher is confronted with a selection of these differences (however attenuated they have become as the result of selection) within his classroom. Educational psychologists have traditionally devoted most of their attention to these matters, and an impressive contribution has been made to our knowledge, though not all of this knowledge is yet embodied in educational practice.

In this section of the volume, the perspective changes to the social factors influencing learning, an area which has, until recently been quite seriously neglected (as the chapter by Hargreaves shows). This chapter and the two following chapters can be taken as a relatively unified whole – starting with a consideration of the social influences that are brought to bear on the individual pupils, shaping attitudes and values that are of crucial importance in the whole process of learning, and then illustrating the impact of these influences by the examination of one school, and a number of fourth-year forms within it. Finally, the chapter by Blyth indicates the complexity, both in scale, richness of interconnexion and rate of change, of the social institutions related to education.

As Homans (1961) remarks in his study of the elementary forms of social behaviour, it is a great pity that we cannot give a picture of the full complexity of social relationships, but have to proceed a step at a time. This pedestrian approach will, it is hoped, enlarge our understanding of social processes that can otherwise only be dealt with intuitively. Before we start analysing aspects of the social factors influencing

203

learning, it might be of value to remind ourselves of the complexity of an ordinary child in an everyday learning situation by sketching a case. The girl whose life we will be glancing at is a composite person, drawn from personal observation and recent studies.

II. A CHILD AT SCHOOL

Natalie Cole is an 11-year-old first-form pupil in a grammar school. She comes from a comfortably-off family (her father is a departmental manager in a medium-sized engineering firm) and both she and her parents took it for granted that she would move from the local primary school to the near-by grammar school, although only about one in five pupils succeed in doing so. Why were they so confident? Partly because Natalie's parents had learned from talking with other parents that the top ten or so in the 'A' stream of the primary school would almost certainly become grammar school pupils. Natalie's teachers had confirmed this.

Natalie had been placed in the 'A' stream at the beginning of her primary school career and she had been consistently in the top four places of the form list. In her class, she had been friendly with four or five other girls and one or two boys. They came to her parties and she went to theirs. These friendships seemed entirely spontaneous, and in one sense of the word most certainly were so. That is, they lacked premeditation, but were influenced by the congeniality that goes with re-cognizing that a person is from one's own social background. All Natalie's friends came from solid middle-class families: all their parents had attended grammar schools. They all attended the parents' association meetings and regularly visited the school on 'open days'.

In the grammar school, Natalie was disturbed at finding herself in the 'B' stream of a four-stream entry. Although she had not expected to be at the top of the 'A' stream, because she allowed for the fact that she was entering a much bigger school, she had certainly expected to be in the top stream. Her parents told her that this was nothing to worry about, pointing out that the grammar school could not really be compared with her primary school, because it was much more selective. Natalie was fairly well convinced by this, but was much more reassured by finding two of her friends in the same form (though another was in the 'C' stream and one in the 'A' stream). At the end of the first term, Natalie had settled down rather well. At least, that was the view of her parents, and most of her teachers.

If we look at her now, coming to the end of her first year, a number of comments can be made. She has learned to take a reasonably effective part in a much more complicated educational programme than she had experienced in the primary school. She has recognized, and adapted to, the individual differences between members of staff who teach her. And, not least, she has made a successful shift from the small social world of the primary school, in which she was a person with some authority, to the larger world of the grammar school, in which she is almost at the bottom of the hierarchy. In other words, Natalie has begun to cope effectively with a new network of groups, similar in many ways to those in which she worked and played in the primary school, but consisting of a new set of people, in more diverse and complicated relationships than before. But, as before, they are not all of equal importance to her. Some are more real than others. She sees them in detail, sharply aware of their individuality. Other people, on the fringe of her social life, are somewhat blurred: one is inclined to lump them into groups, such as 'the prefects', or into personality types, such as 'swots'.

Her teachers are more impersonal than those at the previous school. For one thing, there are more of them, and they are much more specialized, and attach great importance to their individual subjects. They behave more formally, though they do occasionally step out of role when they feel at ease with the class. In general, the whole school seems brisk, and matter-of-fact. There is a strong sense of purpose. Although Natalie had been accustomed to working quite hard at her previous school, and there was a certain excitement in her last year in looking ahead to the secondary school, she had not expected to have such a full programme. It takes up the whole of the waking day, or so it seems, until the week-end, when there is some opportunity of relaxing.

Nevertheless, for a newcomer, this astringency has certain advantages. It may fit well with parental views of a worth-while education. It is evidence of seriousness, of achievement. So, looking back over her first year, Natalie herself would probably claim to be highly satisfied. On the formal life of the school, the part that grows up spontaneously within the staff-planned curriculum, she finds, as in the primary school, a loose-knit system of expectations and traditions among the pupils. The traditions are not incompatible with fads and fashions; in fact, variability of interests is itself a tradition. This informal system gives an additional measure of support, and many of the teachers intuitively allow for it, so there is relatively little conflict between the two. Not that the school is lacking in contrast and even conflict. Like all systems of organized human behaviour, it contains many areas of disorganization. For example, the sixth-formers seem in many ways like a group of college students, with very little contact with the other pupils. Some of the boys, especially, seem like members of staff, though more belligerent and officious. To Natalie, the prefects are often quite outrageous, and seem to have no regard for anyone.

Many of the younger members of staff seem to have a very friendly, informal manner, quite unlike that of the older teachers. While some teachers are sticklers for homework, others are casual. The headmaster seems very much more easy-going than the deputy headmistress, and it sometimes appears that there is very little agreement on the disciplinary style to be adopted by the teachers, though all of them know a great deal about their subjects.

The pupils' informal system, even in the younger forms, who are inclined towards a greater social conformity, is by no means wholly unified. There are marked differences in attitudes to work between the different streams, for example (a theme developed in some detail in the chapter by Hargreaves). Some groups of pupils think it is their duty to help enforce school rules, particularly the rules dealing with respect for persons and property. But most pupils feel it to be the teachers' task to check violators of rules, without help from pupils. Another example of a conflict of values, also between groups of pupils, is provided by disagreements between different cliques in the form on how hard to work for examinations. These cliques do not always align themselves along the familiar swots *v.* slackers dimension, but show complex differences of motivation and behaviour.

These conflicts are *structural* from the point of view of the sociologist, and can be studied as ways of containing diverse social interests that would otherwise be expressed more destructively (Gluckman, 1955; Coser, 1956). To the social psychologist, they can be readily studied on the attitudinal level, as conflicts of individual beliefs and commitments, within groups or specific individuals. The situation can be further developed if we look at Natalie's attitudes to the different subjects of study in the school curriculum.

We may note, for example, that her interests are much more closely akin to those of her mother than of her father. Her father finds it difficult to understand why an 'obviously intelligent' girl like Natalie finds mathematics so difficult, and has made a number of abortive attempts to teach her himself. Her mother, on the other hand, found the subject difficult herself at school, and feels that she has missed very little in later life from her very low level of achievement. Natalie's mother is a lively, talkative woman who has always enjoyed talking with her children about a wide range of topics of interest to her. She reads very widely, and is a keen member of a book club and the local public library. Natalie reads a good deal, too, including many adult books.

She finds some of the books read at school extremely juvenile, but is nevertheless a regular reader of a number of comics, some of which she was reading in the junior school. Natalie's parents are mildly disapproving of the piles of comics lying around the house, but feel that she needs some relaxation from school work. They do, on the other hand, subscribe to a monthly publication of popular knowledge that will ultimately form part of an encyclopaedia in several volumes. They also encourage her to study languages, because they hope that she will be going abroad on exchange visits quite soon, and they feel that she should be able to take advantage of opportunities that they have missed.

Some of their attitudes to school subjects are made quite explicit; others are embodied in behaviour without verbal comment. Natalie's father has made it clear, without saying anything in particular, that he has no time for the subject called Religious Education, and regards religious beliefs as discredited and pre-scientific myths and legends. Her mother is sceptical of the value of Domestic Science, and feels that the scientific part is irrelevant and the domestic part is her own province. She has been particularly caustic about some of the exercises that Natalie has been set and feels that the school should not waste precious working time on such straightforward homely matters.

To these parental attitudes (not all of which are expressed in Natalie's own attitudes) are added the attitudes of Natalie's classmates, and especially her close friends. These are based on a mass of experiences, few of which are capable of being recognized and evaluated by Natalie herself, but are nevertheless influential.

If we followed her on her career through the school, as one of the majority of pupils who spend their whole secondary course at one school, we should be able to note changes in these attitudes. Partly, they will become increasingly complex, and slightly more coherent and explicit. Gradually, the school will become a familiar place to her, its size apparently diminished and its hard outlines softened. Socially, it will become more complex, because she will become more aware of the number and individuality of the people outside her immediate clique. In all these and many other ways, the school will be a miniature world

for her, a differentiated social world of teachers and pupils, of first-formers and sixth-formers – and all the gradations in between, varying subtly in rights and obligations – of boys and girls, bright and dull, friends and enemies, 'us' and 'them', Drake House and Frobisher, and the immutable arrangements of the timetable, like a great wheel, or perhaps a slow spiral turning, bringing its predictable sequences of morning assembly, history, French, English, Domestic science, games and the rest.

The ways in which this world can be described, and felt, are legion, and as Natalie grows older and more experienced, she will probably become more adept in coping with its intricacies, even to the point of becoming clearly aware that the world of the school is only a small part of a much greater world; in some senses quite a small, rather self-important part. She will have moments in which she is sorry for the teachers, who will stay on at the school to teach other Natalies, while she herself goes on and outside and up into the greater life beyond the school. She may have more than a little contempt for the eager, earnest, rather priggish first-form pupils with their new clothes and gleaming equipment.

All this, then, is the social psychology of learning as a first-former meets it – a network of groups, all of them composed of highly in-dividual people, young and old, but all of them none the less part of a society which influences them all. As we move back from the individual person we see more clearly the firm outlines of this society. We see in social institutions discernible regularities of attitude and behaviour which keep their shape over generations, if not centuries. Members of the society have attitudes which are not inborn, but acquired in a social context, the results of patterns of interaction which are in a deep sense impersonal. Natalie as a recognizable individual disappears from view and we have, on a different scale, a perspective of 'the educational system', with the secondary grammar school as a relatively prestigeful and long-established institution (though with an uncertain future). But as we move closer, she and her classmates re-appear, posing questions to us as observers, if not to themselves, about the processes by which they acquire some measure of individuality, and become people of importance to their intimates and associates, in the course of taking on established roles in school and family life.

By starting with an individual person who is in no sense a 'problem' in the everyday meaning of the word, but who implies very interesting problems of social selection and adaptation (discussed in a wider context by Douglas, 1964, and Fleming, 1959), we have indicated the level of description and analysis on which social psychologists typically move, a level which enables a clear view to be taken of individual diversity and social influences. Each level of observation requires appropriate concepts to match its scale and purposes. The most appropriate concepts for our purposes are *attitude, group norm*, and *social role*. While each of these is flexible enough to be used in different contexts and even on different scales of analysis (a comment applying particularly to the protean word *role*), they all permit attention to be paid to individuality and the selective aspects of learning, not only social learning but learning of almost every kind. In the following sections, an attempt will be made to raise a number of questions of interest to those concerned with learning, and to throw light on them by using these concepts.

III. ATTITUDES AND THE LEARNING PROCESS

In the brief account of Natalie settling in to life at her new school, a number of attitudes have already been indicated. There is the rather strongly positive attitude of Natalie to school and most of the things that it implies. There are the varying attitudes of her parents to particular school subjects: Mr Cole has a negative attitude to Religious Education, and Mrs Cole feels much the same way about Domestic Science, but on different grounds. Natalie has negative attitudes to prefects and to Mathematics. Mrs Cole is with Natalie on Mathematics. but Mr Cole's attitude is positive.

The grammar school teachers have a less personal attitude to their pupils than the teachers at Natalie's primary school. They also have a more positive attitude to individual achievement. Natalie, too, has a positive attitude to achievement, shared by her parents. But her parents have seen fit to attempt to moderate Natalie's attitude where it seemed to them to be inappropriate to changed circumstances, as in her disappointment at not being in the 'A' stream of the grammar school.

From this very rapid survey of some of the attitudes mentioned in the last section, it appears that attitudes are dispositions of people towards other people, towards things or indeed towards anything that can be conceptualized, real or imaginary. These dispositions are most obviously categorized as positive or negative. A positive disposition is associated with a tendency to move towards its object, to spend valued resources, such as time, money, or materials on its maintenance and development (or, in some cases, on its incorporation into the subject, as with a positive attitude to food and drink). A negative disposition, on the other hand, is associated with a tendency either to avoid its object or to move towards it with the aim of attacking, destroying or conciliating it.

As noted in Volume I, Chapter 6, the concept of attitude has much in common with certain uses of the term *drive* in animal studies. There are many differences, of course. Human attitudes, through learning, can ramify indefinitely and form complex systems. Also, because much human behaviour is concerned with anticipating the behaviour of others, and with modifying the behaviour of others, attitudes are often defined in terms of 'incipient' cues or responses. In other words, we come to think of attitudes almost as pre-motivational, and of drives as sustaining behaviour. In the discussion here, attitudes will not be limited to states of readiness, but will be seen as associated with ongoing behaviour as well. This said, the link between drive and attitude is close, given the differences in the scale of complexity (there is no implication here that infra-human behaviour is simple: the differences are relative, but nevertheless striking).

Both of the terms are clearly dispositional, both involve the organism as an agent, and both have a wide variety of objects (though this is not to suppose that the object can necessarily be reported on by the subject) and both can be measured on an approach-avoidance dimension.

Just as drive is of crucial interest in throwing light on animal behaviour, so the concept of attitude might be expected to throw light on human behaviour. In Volume II, Chapter 11, an attempt was made to examine the development of social learning in childhood and adolescence in terms of the learning of social roles and the growth of the 'self-concept'. Both of these are very relevant to attitudes. Social roles are not just an assemblage of overt responses, built up through piecemeal imitation, or by Skinnerian 'shaping', but are elaborate constructions of attitudes and values, permitting a wide range of adaptive responses, with an underlying consistency. The learning of these attitudes and values is linked with the processes of identification, which turn out, on close examination, to be highly complicated.

Complexity is also the most obvious characteristic of the 'self-concept', which can be seen as a complex system of attitudes and values to one's own attributes and activities, particularly as these relate to the attributes and activities of 'significant others' (to borrow Mead's helpful phrase; Mead, 1956).

It is not part of our purpose here to develop the theme of social learning any further. The social psychology of learning and education is concerned to go beyond social learning to social influences on all learning. The technical knowledge and skills that enable a bridge to be designed and constructed are only social in an attenuated sense. But, clearly, the attitudes to the development of such techniques are socially mediated; and the changing social attitudes to technical education bring this out very clearly (see, for example, Venables' detailed and penetrating study of technical education in Britain; Venables, 1955). Again, social learning is powerfully influenced by group interaction. Group interaction generates regulative tendencies, influencing the behaviour of individual group members. These tendencies are usually termed 'group norms' in sociological and psychological studies. Our aim here is to show how attitudes (and, in a later section, group norms) shape the process of learning; not only social learning but learning of every kind.

From the point of view of the teacher, it is useful to consider attitudes to learning under two related headings: the *content* of learning and the *level* of learning. The first heading groups together all those issues concerned with acceptance or rejection of a particular topic; which may be an academic subject, or a whole range of subjects (arts or science), or a particular small part of a subject. It also includes all those topics which young people have attitudes towards, but are not necessarily part of a school or college curriculum, such as personal relationships, popular music, films and leisure activities of other kinds.

The second heading – the *level* of learning – refers to attitudes to success and failure, and with all other attitudes that relate to the level of performance of an activity, even if it is not closely linked with formal achievement. In real life, the content of learning (often thought of as 'interest') and the level of learning (thought of as 'ambition', 'aspiration' 'achievement') are closely intertwined, but it is nevertheless both possible and useful to distinguish them conceptually.

In the following two sub-sections, we shall consider only those attitudes that are relatively stable. In a third, and final, sub-section, consideration will be given to the factors influencing the change of attitudes.

1. *Attitudes and the content of learning*

From the sociological point of view adopted by Blyth in his chapter in Volume III, the institutions shaping attitudes are both powerful and pervasive. It is possible to see the influence of specific patterns of family life, social-class factors, neighbourhood and cultural pressures – all bringing about a particular set of attitudes in each young person, or adult, for that matter. Down at the social 'grass roots', where the social psychologist works, it is more difficult to see the power of these broad institutional patterns. In fact, diversity seems to be the keynote.

This is not in any way to deny the reality of the world of social institutions. Each scale of society is real, just as (to use a suggestive but limited metaphor) each scale of map-making is real, although the space occupied by Manchester on one map suffices for the whole of Great Britain on a map of a different scale. The problem of describing social activity on the sociological scale (the scale at the more abstract end of the subject, where whole societies can be brought under a single concept) is that a whole host of individual differences in behaviour and attitude must be omitted, just as a map, even of Manchester, cannot easily show the differences in the individual buildings, and a map of Britain shows London and Manchester as dots only varying in size.

On the level of individual differences, we recognize that school children from the 'same' neighbourhood, or even the 'same' family, may show wide variations in attitude towards the school curriculum. Part of this diversity relates to differences in role, and this point will be discussed in a later section. But even within roles, diverse attitudes can readily be discerned.

The most effective way of understanding the nature of these individual differences is to reconsider the working of the self-concept, which was discussed in some detail in Volume II, Chapter 11. It will be recalled that the self-concept is a sub-system of the total personality – a system of schemata subject to strong activation, and related to the most important activities of the individual. The young child has a somewhat fluid and fluctuating concept of self, and is deeply involved in the process of learning through identification with 'significant others', typically parents, siblings and friends. By school age, the self-concept has become somewhat more stabilized and autonomous; it becomes possible, with Erikson, to talk of 'ego-identity', in something other than an incipient sense.

The attitudes of the child towards learning in general and to particular subjects or topics will depend on the expected significance of these matters to the self-concept. This is not, of course, to imply that the school child, or even the adolescent, is a self-conscious and deliberate judge of the relationship between learning and his self-concept. But if we are not implying this, then what exactly are we implying?

In simple, non-technical terms we are suggesting that the child will be attracted to those subjects which are rewarding. But we are using the term 'reward' in a somewhat unusual way, to refer to a *state of affairs* rather than a specific act (for example, an approving remark) or object (such as a prize).

The state of affairs may well be produced by a specific act or object, but only if it is connected by the child with the enhancement of the self-concept. If this seems an unduly circuitous way of putting a straightforward issue, let us consider some commonplace instances of well-meaning specific acts and objects 'back-firing'. A teacher who is disliked by a pupil may well create a conflict in the pupil by a word of approval. A way of resolving the conflict, if the negative attitude is strong, may be to reverse the behaviour that elicited the approving remark. Again, a 'prize' may be interpreted by a person as symbolizing a whole way of life that he negatively values (as in *The Loneliness of the Long-Distance Runner*; Sillitoe, 1959). A well-loved person may mean to disapprove of a pupil's act, but the attention given to the pupil in the act of disapproval may be highly rewarding, by enhancing the self-concept. This is not to say that the self-concept is more strongly enhanced by disapproval from a loved person than by approval, but the underlying common element of 'personal involvement' in both approval and disapproval may be rewarding. (Clinical studies of masochism seem to suggest that the pain of punishment and humiliation may be seen as the 'price of admission' to intense satisfactions; see, for example, Russell and Russell, 1961.)

What does all this mean for the teacher? It suggests that, from his personal experience of a lifetime of social relationships, in the family, the school, the neighbourhood, each pupil has developed a set of attitudes which are his own, though they are clearly shaped by his social experience.

It would be a mistake to forget that these individual attitudes are not only social in origin, but in every situation are expressed within socially-established limits. The problem for the teacher is to get to know his pupils well enough to know what their attitudes are. Many studies, well represented by some recent studies of Revans (Revans, 1965) bring out the greater satisfactions and higher degree of cohesion achieved in small organizations, or larger organizations with effectively functioning smaller sub-units. This greater effectiveness seems to be related to the greater likelihood that the individuality of attitudes will be recognized. It is not a paradox to note that in these effectively functioning groups, the individual is willing to 'pull his weight', and to relate his own interests to the interests of the group of which he is a part. But this readiness can easily be taken for granted as the inevitable consequence of the 'socialization process', and it would be our contention that to see the socialization process as inevitably producing acquiescence is to be tricked by one's own categories of thought.

Having made this criticism of an approach to individual attitudes that underestimates their individuality, we can return to our search for useful points that offer guidance to the teacher. One mistake that can easily be made is to forget the elaborate network of groupings that exist in every school or college. A rough distinction can be made between the 'formalsystem', charted officially by the people at the top of the system, and supported by a series of laws, rules and other sanctions, and the 'informal system' which develops spontaneously within the formal system and which expresses attitudes not allowed for in the formal system.

As Hargreaves points out, in his chapter in this volume, the study of informal systems within schools followed on the study of such systems in industry and commerce, and is still woefully undeveloped. We know enough, however, to suggest that the informal system is often a loose-knit aggregate of systems, existing at different levels of the organization and among different specialized groups. This will be briefly considered later in this chapter. For the moment, the point is that individual attitudes are not only related to the self-concept, thus giving them some measure of autonomy, and unpredictability to those who do not know the person well, but that they are also linked with a variety of groupings, not all of them known to, or officially recognized by, the teacher.

All this seems a very long way indeed from the 'table d'hôte' curriculum that still characterizes the great majority of schools. It is because of the gap between the individuality of attitudes and the uniformity of the curriculum that schools, like offices and factories, have to introduce elaborate programmes of 'incentives' to encourage the pupils to take an appropriate interest in the subjects of study. These incentives have been an established feature of the educational scene for so long that it has been easy to take them for granted as facts of life.

Despite this, there has been increasing concern in recent years with the possibility of releasing considerable energies by linking the subjects of study more closely with established attitudes. The 'progressive schools' (described, with other types of school, in an interesting recent compendium, Gross, 1966, and in the book by Neill referred to elsewhere) have pioneered the development of discretionary courses of study, in which the topics chosen are those which are close to the interests of the pupils. The organization of these individual courses of study, even in a small school, is no mean problem, and the volatility and diversity of individual attitudes to learning add to the difficulty. It may well be that the computer, and related methods of large-scale data processing and programming, will enable many of these difficulties to be overcome.

In making these points, it might be recognized that good cooking and a host who is sensitive to widely shared tastes in food may make a 'table d'hôte' arrangement acceptable to most people. It is probably because the educational system has not been wholly insensitive to the attitudes of pupils, and has traditionally left a good deal of discretion to the individual teacher, alone with his pupils in the classroom, that the apparently fixed educational curriculum has not produced revolutions before now. But there is no substitute for choice, and it is no accident that few hotels or restaurants, subject to competition from others, dare restrict the diner to a 'table d'hôte' régime. And eating is by no means the most varied of human activities, so far as human attitudes are concerned.

In this sub-section, we have been concerned with the attitudes to specific topics, emphasizing their individuality within the constraints of roles and group norms, which will be considered later in their own right. It is now time to turn to the second theme – the relationship between *levels* of aspiration and learning.

2. Attitudes, levels of aspiration and the achievement motive

Interest in the level of achievement that people set themselves in particular activities has been studied systematically by psychologists since Hoppe's experimental work in the twenties (Hoppe, 1930). Lewin and his colleagues popularized the term 'level of aspiration' (Lewin *et al.*, 1944). Hoppe showed that his experimental subjects differed from one another in their expected levels of achievement in particular tasks, and that this influenced their performance, independently of differences in ability. Later work has shown that the level of aspiration is a most complex factor, even when one omits the changes associated with increasing skill in a task, resulting from learning. The distinctively social factors influencing a person's level of aspiration are his expectations of the aspiration levels of those whose behaviour he uses as a touchstone, and his judgement of how he stands in relation to these others.

Since tasks vary, and one is not always using the same 'reference persons' as a touchstone, levels of aspiration also vary. But the personality is a system, and variations usually stay within a relatively narrow range. It is usually possible, because of this, to speak of people's levels in general terms, and in recent years, a good deal of intensive study has been made of this generalized level of aspiration when it takes the form of expecting a constant improvement in performance and seeks high standards of criticism.

Perhaps the best example of this recent work is provided by the extensive body of continuing research initiated by David McClelland of Harvard University (1953). McClelland uses the term 'achievement motive' or more technically, *n achievement* (n ach.) after Murray's classification of human needs (Murray, 1938). It is defined as a concern over performing well in relation to a standard of excellence. Studies of the conditions favouring its development suggest that this pattern of motivation develops in early life, and is fostered by parental encouragement of early achievement (not just independence, but demonstrable success in a task) and reward for achievement, particularly in the form of love and approval. The role of the mother seems to be of particular importance in this process (McClelland, 1961). As with all motivation, the persistence of a pattern is a function of reinforcement, but as the child matures, he is able to reinforce his own achievement by self-approval.

In recent work, McClelland (1967) describes successful attempts to increase achievement motivation by training in adolescence and adulthood. In one set of training courses for businessmen, four lines were followed: 1. encouraging the course to engage in forms of behaviour characteristic of people with a high achievement need (in games, writing stories in response to test questions, and so on); 2 stimulating them to set higher but realistic work goals over a two year period, with six monthly follow-up sessions during this period; 3. analysing the behaviour of the course members in group discussions, in order to increase adaptiveness to 'feedback' from work on tasks; 4. raising morale by sharing experience of successes and failures.

This brings us to a consideration of studies of attitude change, a field of study to which a considerable amount of attention has been paid.

3. *Notes on factors involved in attitude change*
There are two main lines of study of attitude change. First, the

personality congruence or balance theories, which are based on the assumption that a person's attitudes form a system, with concomitant needs for balance and coherence. Second, the group theories, which stress the importance of bringing about attitude change through acceptance of the change by all the members of a group, which then 'validates' the change for its individual members and reinforces the change once it has taken place. The first line of study is currently the most vigorous, and is connected with research work by Festinger (1957) and his associates (e.g. Brehm and Cohen, 1962), Osgood (1955) and Heider (1958). An excellent comparative discussion of these theories is given in the recent textbook on social psychology by Brown (1965).

The great value of this work has been to translate a broad concept of equilibrium between a person's attitudes into a series of precise, and sometimes unexpected, hypotheses for experimental testing. Relatively little work has been done so far on individual differences in the strength of pressures towards equilibrium, and in developmental differences. It seems probable that the drive towards integration of the attitude system becomes stronger with age. There are at least two reasons for this: (i) the adolescent and adult have developed greater skill in handling variables on different levels of abstraction, and in complex relationships with one another. Thus, contradictions and lacunae are more likely to be revealed, and resources are available for increasing the degree of integration; (ii) the attitudes of the adult are somewhat less likely to be centrally involved with the self-concept. This permits a greater ease in relating attitudes to one another formally, rather than idiosyncratically (put in Freudian terms, the mechanisms of ego-defence are less likely to be required as inputs are less emotionally charged). Among individual differences, there seems to be a difference between introverts and extroverts in pressure for integration: namely, introverts are more concerned with a coherent, stable attitude structure. Eysenck's suggestion, based on experimental studies (1967), that introverts are more sensitive to stimulation, and with higher persistence, than extroverts, would support this view, since a system which is both reasonably integrated and realistic is likely to take a great deal of time and effort to establish, but then gives greater confidence and control.

Not that any healthy system can be complete in a rigorous sense of the term. This would imply a moratorium on incoming information, or else a state of complete stability in the external and internal environments. Since environmental stability is socially and psychologically unlikely, and a moratorium suggests a kind of death, it seems that completeness is possible only at the level of routine sub-systems, dealing with stable inputs and outputs. But the total system is more likely, in health, to have the kind of completeness that comes in a good discussion when people feel that they have come to a 'natural break' and can turn their attention briefly to other things.

These comments have all been related to the first broad line of study of attitude change. But they are appropriate on the larger scale of the group, in its relationship to the attitude change of its members. The classic studies in this area were those of Lewin and his colleagues during the Second World War (Lewin, 1947). These were concerned with the relative merits of lectures and group discussion in changing attitudes to the serving of relatively unpopular foods as part of the 'war effort'. The original studies suggested that the crucial factors in accounting for the greater effectiveness of group discussion as a method of inducing change were the knowledge on the part of group members of the degree of group agreement, the participation in group discussion, the making of a public commitment to change, and the actual process of making a decision.

As always seems to happen, later work has brought out the influence of other variables, such as the specific techniques of discussion used by the group leader, the relative importance to group members of the issue under discussion (this is called technically the 'salience' of the relevant attitudes), the degree of group cohesion, the degree to which the group can reward or punish its members, and (in a sense, an on-going reward) the attractiveness of the group to its members (see Pelz, 1958). Needless to say, the most effective 'mix' of these factors seems to vary from one situation to another, and is almost certainly itself a matter of the set of attitudes and group norms regulating the appropriate ways of changing attitudes. (Cohen, 1964; Sherif, Sherif and Nebergall, 1965; Sherif and Sherif 1967)

The pioneers in a field of investigation, the people who are the first to see and state a problem in a way that suggests a method of resolving it, have the happy knack of putting the essentials of the problem clearly in the forefront. This clear view is often obscured by the complications introduced by later studies. It is worth returning to the colourful way in which Lewin presented the problem of attitude change. It is, he said, a matter of 'unfreezing' and 're-freezing', with an intervening phase of moving from the old attitude to a new one. This clearly implies a view of human activities as having a powerful tendency towards stability (called by Lewin 'quasi-stationary equilibria'). Much effort is needed to induce people and groups to move from one point of stability to another. 'Freezing' is a normal state, 'unfreezing' needs to be followed quickly by 're-freezing'.

For a warm-blooded animal such as man, freezing is close to death. But to an animal in an acute state of fear, anxiety or depression, 'freezing' can give a kind of security, a state of disappearing into the background and ceasing to be an active, and therefore vulnerable, individual. It must be added that Lewin was singularly warm, and his work among the most fruitful produced in this century. His 'field theory' stresses the subservience of structure to function, and the much-discussed mathematical presentation of his theory (Lewin, 1951; Deutsch, 1954) which strikes many as cold and impersonal, can be seen as a dramatic device for stimulating people to look at human affairs from a new perspective.

There is an interesting contrast here, between the facility and confidence with which Lewin moved to a new view of human personality and groups as dynamic systems of forces, constantly interacting and generating goal-directed activities, and the rigidity and latent anxiety in the face of change shown by the persons and groups that he attempted to understand and analyse. Lewin was clearly aware of the contrast, and devoted a great deal of effort to devising methods of increasing the intelligent understanding of people, groups and societies (see, for example, Lewin, 1948). Just as the level of aspiration of a healthy, integrated person is based on an understanding of his abilities, attitudes, and the external situation in which he is acting, and sets targets realistically to meet changes in these, and *to encourage improved performance*, so a 'healthy' group will collectively act so as to make this possible. This is, of course, largely a matter of the norms of the group, and we now turn to examine the concept of norms and some attempts to study them systematically.

IV. THE NORMATIVE REGULATION OF BEHAVIOUR IN GROUPS

In the previous section, it was seen that attitudes may change for a number of reasons. One of the most important reasons is a direct change of information about the object of the attitude. Another is an indirect change mediated through a person or an impersonal medium of communication. Since social relationships are enormously complex, and the objects of our attitudes, actual and potential, virtually unlimited, it is not surprising that many of the changes in attitude take place through group influence. As we have tried to show, there is nothing particularly sinister about this. If a person attempted to limit his change in attitudes to the results of his own personal experience, he would experience great difficulties in maintaining himself in any conceivable social role. Even that paradigm of all sceptics, the professional scientist, is dependent on the collective views of the scientific community, and as Polanyi and Koestler have shown (Polanyi, 1958; Koestler, 1959), the community rests only in part on rigorous experimentation.

We are quite naturally led, then, from a consideration of the influence of attitudes on the learning-process to a like consideration of the influence of group norms. Norms provide the limits to individual action; just as attitudes provide internal structures, derived in many instances from the norms of other groups, such as the family, the peer group, or the school class.

In an interesting discussion of the relationship between group norms and informal social influence, Jones and Gerard (1967) show that norms can be seen as a substitute for such influence. In the innumerable *ad hoc* groups of school pupils and college students used for social-psychological experiments on group processes, the group influence on individual behaviour is often exerted through personal influence. One group member will argue with another, or attempt to reach a compromise, and the structure of the group will often be clearly visible to the observer. In groups which have been together for a long time, on the other hand, the overt attempts to persuade will have changed into expectations of behaviour that can be taken for granted.

As Jones and Gerard put it, 'The existence of norms generally ensures that friction will be reduced in the relationship and, as appeals to impersonal norms replace personal influence-attempts, the (group) can function without a continual re-examination of who is capable of doing what to whom' (*op cit.* p. 645). In larger groups, the likelihood of norms replacing a good deal of informal influence is very great, and typically, in relatively stable groups, the expression of informal influence takes place in the gaps left by the general understanding of the norms.

Among the pioneering studies of group norms are to be found two particularly influential series of experiments: one by Sherif (summarized in Sherif, 1947 and developed at length in one of the classics of social psychology – Sherif, 1936) and one by Asch (1952.) Sherif used an ingenious experiment in perceptual judgement which involved a visual illusion. Not recognizing that they were making judgements of the apparent movement of a point of light that was in fact stationary, Sherif's subjects tended to make wild guesses, which then showed a spontaneous tendency to narrow down to a characteristic individual range of judgements. Sherif argued that this tendency showed the need of individuals to stabilize their judgements, even when they were based on an illusory movement. When individuals were placed in small groups of two or three, they showed a clearly marked tendency, on hearing one another's judgements, to converge on to a group standard. This standard, once formed, persisted even when the same individuals were re-tested by themselves.

To Sherif, this small experiment was a paradigm of how group norms become established. There is a strong tendency for groups, confronted by an apparently common stimulus, to form concerted impressions of it. Already, in this study, one sees certain points of difficulty if we are to think clearly about group norms. The object about which the experimental subjects were making judgements was an illusion, and this weakened the ability of the individual member to stand by a view of his own (though if these subjects had realized that they were involved in a visual illusion they might very well have agreed to differ). Another point of difficulty is that we are using 'norm' in more than one sense: as a characteristic form of behaviour of a group, a kind of average, and as a prescribed form of behaviour, supported by group rewards and punishments.

Sherif believed that there is a tendency, both in individuals and groups, to establish modal forms of behaviour as norms in the evaluative sense. In short, the typical becomes the desirable. Some aspects of this belief are brought out in a very interesting way by Asch, in a series of experiments which have been very widely discussed, and have become the centre of a certain amount of misunderstanding.

Asch used the device of a 'rigged group' to test the influence of majority opinions on a minority. He worked with college students in one of the leading liberal colleges in the United States. Unlike Sherif, Asch used a problem about which his experimental subjects could make correct perceptual judgements without the aid of the group, and could stand by these judgements if they wished. The problem consisted of comparing a line, drawn on a card, with three other lines, and judging which of the three lines was equal in length to the first line. There were eighteen sets of problems, all of this form, and the level of difficulty of these sets of problems was carefully arranged to make it possible for most subjects to make correct judgements all the time.

Groups of eight persons made public judgements on each of the eighteen sets of lines. In each group there was one subject who was led to believe that the experiment was a straightforward study of perceptual judgement. Actually, Asch had instructed the other members of each group to make prearranged false judgements on twelve of the eighteen sets of lines. The object of the experiment was to test the effect on the lone individual (the so-called 'naïve subject') of hearing unanimous false judgements by the rest of the group, after some initial correct judgements.

The result, taking the whole range of naïve subjects in the different groups, was that slightly over two-thirds of the judgements made by these isolated individuals were correct, the remaining third being affected by the false judgements of the majority, unaccompanied by any other pressure than the fact of being said aloud, in the hearing of others. (These proportions are based only on the twelve false judgements, of course.)

The third was not spread evenly over the experimental subjects. Some stood firm and made correct judgements throughout; others conformed to the false judgements of the majority most of the time. One person joined the majority in eleven out of twelve false judgements.

Asch then attempted to discover the motives of the 'yielders' and 'non-yielders'. The yielders consisted of (i) those who were so profoundly influenced by the false judgements of the majority that they claimed to have perceived the wrong lines as being correct. There were very few in this group: perhaps fortunately; (ii) those who were aware that their perceptions differed from the judgements of the others in the group, and felt that they were in some way at fault, possibly suffering from a visual defect. They chose not to reveal the discrepancy to the others, and conformed to many of the false judgements of the majority; (iii) those who did not feel that they were wrong and the majority were correct, but were not willing to call out a different judgement from the others.

The non-yielders consisted of (i) those who were completely confident that they were right, and that the others were wrong; (ii) those who were not at all confident, but stuck to their judgements in the belief that a person has an obligation to say what he believes to be right; (iii) those who felt obliged to obey the instructions given by the experimenter, and who correspondingly called out the lines as they saw them, often feeling very uncomfortable.

The findings here seem to support the belief that disagreement with a majority, even on a matter of fact, is felt to be more than a 'cognitive' disagreement: it seems to be a threat to the values of the group.

Asch then introduced a number of experimental variations, designed to test the effect of majorities of different sizes, and the effects of having a partner in making correct judgements. He found that when the experimental subjects had one 'ally' who made correct judgements before them, they were able to make correct judgements too. It should be noted that these 'allies' were also confederates of Asch, and on occasion they were instructed to go over to the majority. When this occurred, the individual who had been left behind would begin to make false judgements at about the same rate as in the original experiment. On the topic of varying the size of the majority, it was found that a majority of three was virtually as effective as much larger majorities of up to fifteen. It was as though a three to one majority seemed to be as daunting as any larger majority, while smaller majorities left open the possibility that they might be wrong, and one's own judgements might be right.

In an extension of the Asch experiments, Ruth Berenda (1950) worked with groups of schoolchildren. She brought in the teacher as a source of false judgement (a controversial example of professional ethics in psychological experiments) and found that the teacher exerted a 'pressure for agreement', but that this was less powerful, as estimated from the number of false judgements of the experimental subjects, than a group of fellow pupils.

Berenda points out that this relative lack of influence of the teacher in this particular setting is not associated with lack of respect. In fact, she believes that it is the respect for the teacher that leads to a relative lack of influence. The children were more likely to be influenced by one another than by someone out of their immediate informal circle. It is also worth noting that the children most disturbed by this experiment were not the unintelligent, passive children but the more intelligent, dominating ones, who were accustomed to being right. This study points the way towards later studies of reference groups and reference persons (well described and discussed in Merton, 1957, Chapter 9, and Sherif and Sherif, 1964).

After these early 'classic' studies there has come a flood of more differentiated studies, varying the objects, the strength of established attitudes in the persons conforming, the group structure, the 'personalities' of the group members, and the types of rewards and punishments associated with non-conformity or conformity. This work has brought out the extraordinary complexity of the relationship between group norms and the modification of individual attitudes and behaviour. Among the more important factors are: (1) the ability of the group to reward or punish the person for his compliance or non-compliance; (2) the tolerated range of variation of behaviour and attitudes within the group; (3) the availability of independent evidence on which the individual can base his judgements and (4) the degree to which the attitudes and behaviour need to be publicly expressed.

The ability of the group to reward or punish the individual is partly dependent on the value that he places on his role in the group. If a person is disaffected, the disapproval of other group members may not be a punishment. In certain instances, it could even serve as a reward, though this would create an unstable situation which would tend to change, either towards the person leaving the group or the group modifying its expectations to fit the requirements of the person (Schachter, 1951).

For the teacher, it is important to recognize the powerful group pressures for conformity that exist in groups of pupils. Not all of these pressures are norms in the more formal sense, and the 'rewards' and 'punishment' of which we have spoken must be seen in the broad sense of all the conditions which persons seek to approach or avoid, and not in the more limited sense of formal sanctions for misconduct.

Hargreaves, in his chapter in this volume, shows the contrasting norms in a high and low stream in one secondary school in Northern England. His findings are strikingly congruent with the main stream of group research in different organizations in different countries, and bring out the value of looking for the points of convergence in group activities, and some of the reasons for the intensity of convergence.

Several studies suggest that the tolerated range of variation within the group is itself a variable. It is partly a function of the tasks on which the group is engaged, and the level of achievement required by the group in these tasks. Any group activity requires co-ordination, and this in turn prescribes appropriate behaviour for each group member. This is seen most obviously in the school setting in such activities as games, athletics and theatrical performances. A rather different type of factor is the level of anxiety and aggression within the group (which may in turn be due to the persons constituting the group, or the environmental stresses to which they are subjected, or a combination of both). High levels of anxiety and aggression tend to narrow the range of tolerated variation. The contrast between A. S. Neill's account of Summerhill (A. S. Neill, 1964) and the semi-fictional account of nineteenth-century

Rugby in *Tom Brown's Schooldays* (Hughes, 1857) is striking, and the point is brought out in detail in Berkowitz's extended review of experimental investigations of aggression (1962).

So far, our discussion of social-psychological aspects of learning has focussed on the influence of attitudes and norms. When we study groups, however, it becomes clear that they are not only to be understood in terms of interacting systems of attitudes and norms. Groups simplify much of their activity by a powerful analytical device. Needless to say, this is not usually conscious or planned. They allocate a particular 'body' of attitudes, norms and related activities to particular persons and then deal with these rather than with the person in his full individuality. These simplifying 'bodies' are intensively studied by social scientists under the label of 'social roles'.

V. SOCIAL ROLES

1. *Roles and role-sets*

The study of roles is somewhat complicated by the fact that roles are both analytical concepts used by social scientists and everyday concepts used, often implicitly, by group members. Social scientists have experienced great difficulty in arriving at an agreed terminology and usage for social roles, because of this great range of traditional meanings (see Biddle, 1966, for an impressive documentation of this point). The perspectives of various specialists often sharply differ, so that one writer can include several million persons in one role concept (the role of the husband in modern family life) while another will examine a single case (the role of Mr Churchill as a war leader). A useful start, however, can be made by making the two-fold distinction between types of role-theory drawn by Banton (1965). These are the structural type, deriving from sociological inquiry (and briefly discussed by Blyth in his chapter in this volume) and the dramatic type, deriving from social psychology. Here, we shall focus on the latter.

In a play, each role is taken by a single actor at each performance. But there is no limit to the number of actors who might enact a given role on different occasions. Certain famous roles – Hamlet, Lear – have been enacted on so many occasions that traditions of interpretation become established, and a vigorous branch of criticism is devoted to examining their performance. In many ways, the theatrical role is a misleading point of reference for a social role, because it purports to be a complete person, in a situation of unusual interest. The social role, on the other hand, even when we look at it closely, as the social

I

psychologist wishes to, is on a different level of functioning. The person taking on a social role does not necessarily become a man with a mask (some social psychologists rather over-stress the etymology of the term in the Latin *persona*). But he is in a social situation, being seen from a particular point of view, as pupil or teacher or parent rather than purely as himself 'in the round'. The person in everyday life corresponds to the actor rather than the person that the actor is portraying.

Part of the charm of acting is this double aspect: the person that the actor projects is not real, so that anything that happens to him is in play, however tragic it may be. But the actor is real, and the judgements on his interpretation of the part are part of real social life. This gives rise to fascinating 'double levels' of social experience, illustrated by a French cartoonist who shows a theatre at the end of the first night of a tragedy. The audience, overwhelmed, are leaving their seats in tears. In the wings, we see the actors, equally overwhelmed by their theatrical triumph, having a wild party with champagne and cakes.

A brilliant and much-quoted pioneering study by Goffman (1959) exploits the theatrical metaphor, to show that much of the ordinary social life is based on the creation of performances for audiences. But he concludes that the stage draws on real life in a more substantial way than life draws on the stage. 'The report,' he writes, 'is not concerned with aspects of the theatre that creep into everyday life. It is concerned with the structure of social encounters – the structure of those entities in social life that come into being whenever persons enter one another's immediate physical presence. The key factor in this structure is the maintenance of a single definition of the situation, this definition having to be expressed, and this expression sustained in the face of a multitude of potential disruptions' (p. 255).

Some experiments in group psychology bring out the links between the definition of the situation in the theatre and in real life by contriving situations that come somewhere between the two. One of the clearest examples of this is a classic study by Lewin, Lippitt and White (summarized in Lippitt and White, 1947). This was concerned with studying 'group atmospheres' and their influence on social behaviour.

The experimenters trained themselves to take on three diverse styles of leadership; that is, leadership roles. These were the autocratic leader, the democratic leader and the *laissez-faire* leader. The autocrat initiated activity for his group, controlled their behaviour, issued materials for group activity at his discretion, and acted as a source of reward and punishment as well as of direction. The democrat attempted to involve members of the group in all decisions, and left the flow of activities to the group itself, becoming a group member himself as far as possible. The *laissez-faire* leader played as little part as possible in the group, and was completely permissive.

The participants in the experiment were twenty 11-year-old boys, who had volunteered to form small 'clubs' of five members to engage in leisure play-activities. They were very carefully selected to be normal in intelligence, social background and sociometric patterns of friendship choice.

The experimenters used the different styles of leadership with the same groups, and they took on different leadership roles, so as to minimize the influence of personality differences. The differences in the social behaviour of groups under different leadership conditions were striking. Groups under autocratic leadership did more work, were less aggressive, but showed rather less social cohesiveness. Further, there was some indication that their aggression was inhibited during the play session, because they tended to be aggressive after the session. The democratic groups did rather less work, though the experimenters judged the imaginativeness and quality of the work to be rather higher than under autocratic leadership (the boys were making theatrical masks of papier-mâché). Levels of aggression were higher, though much of it was joking horseplay. The *laissez-faire* groups were highest in aggression, and much the lowest in the amount and quality of work done. When the twenty boys were asked which type of leadership they had preferred, nineteen said that they preferred the democratic style. The twentieth came from a military family.

Harding (1953) has argued that this experiment has often been interpreted in a rather facile way to indicate that democratic leadership is more effective than autocratic, rather than that each pattern offers a different pattern of 'advantages' (as judged by the preferences of group members). Furthermore, the preferences of group members are likely to reflect their own 'outside' values. These were boys from a 'democratic' culture, taking part in a leisure activity. Their expectations were presumably that a good deal of freedom would be permitted. The same boys in a different activity would have readily assumed different roles, though we have no right to assume that their role-behaviour is a matter of indifference to them. In theatrical terms, they have an extensive 'repertoire' of roles, and this classic early experiment brought the point out in a very striking way.

One of the most important tasks of the growing child is to develop an understanding of social roles, as distinct from the concrete items of behaviour that make up part of a role. This process of social learning is extremely complex, and not very clearly understood. In Volume II, the chapters by Schaffer and Morris described one important part of the process; the establishment of successive identifications, initially with parents, and then with other key persons.

These identifications serve a dual function – the development of the ability to take on social roles oneself, and the understanding of the social roles of others. The games of 'teacher and pupil' still common in primary schools give the growing child some experience of the attitudes and characteristic activities of the teacher, and the appropriate reciprocal behaviour of the pupil. Let us now consider the role of the school pupil. This is a good example of the point made earlier, that some indication needs to be given of the intended level of generality of the term 'role'. Natalie Cole, for example, took on a specific role as a pupil in the school that she attended. All her school friends were also pupils. But we could also, still focussing on the role of 'pupil', look at the attitudes, norms and activities of pupils throughout the ages.

Blyth, in the last chapter in this volume, looks at the role of pupil in this more general sense. Here, we wish to emphasize the considerable degree of variability in the role, especially as it is experienced by an individual child or adolescent. As Hargreaves has shown, in his study of pupils in a secondary modern school in North West England, one can distinguish reasonably clearly between 'formal' and 'informal' aspects of the role. Many children find the distinction rather confusing, and it is often said by teachers (but not clearly established by research findings) that the ability to make these kinds of distinction is a matter of intelligence. We would rather suggest that it is a matter of flexibility, and the ability to recognize differing moods and situations, which is not so much a matter of intelligence as of social insight. In fact, many highly intelligent, introverted, rather unstable children are not able to cope with a flexible system of role expectations that an academically 'dull' child can take in his stride. It is considerations of this kind that have led to the concept of 'social maturity' or even 'social intelligence'.

It is a common observation of teachers that children and adolescents learn the informal expectations more readily than they do the formal expectations, and that more effort goes into meeting the former than the latter. The reasons for this appear to be two-fold.

First, the informal expectations are often less stringent and more readily achieved than the formal expectations (see Morris, 1958). They are closer to 'ordinary human nature' at the stage of development reached by the pupils. A second reason is that the informal expectations are closer to the actual needs and interests of the pupils.

All hierarchical systems tend to have this division into the formal and informal, and there are only two limiting instances in which the division might be eliminated. One would be a situation in which one group has total power over another, and unlimited sanctions, especially punishments. The concentration camps approached this limiting point, but many studies show that even in these extreme conditions there were signs of 'resistance movements' (see Goffman, 1961 on the characteristics of what he calls 'total institutions'). The other end of the scale would be a completely democratic system in which all members participate in making and implementing policy. Under these conditions there would appear to be no need for informal attitudes and norms. For an account of an attempt to achieve this form of organization in a small independent school, see Neill (1964); Brown (1960) describes in detail a rather complex process of changing an industrial firm towards this pattern of organization.

The almost universal arrangement for pupils is that they are grouped into age-grades, with a range of rather less than a year within each form. There is a complex mixture of seniority and ability in the placing of pupils within the school. Seniority comes first, in the sense that even the most gifted pupil will not be permitted to get far out of line with his age-group. In earlier times, an outstandingly gifted pupil could move at his own pace. It remains to be seen whether the development of individual work on teaching machines will restore this ancient possibility.

Robert Merton (1957) has coined the term 'role-set'. This is the set of relationships constituting the role. Merton's usage is somewhat different from ours: since he terms each distinguishable relationship a role. The whole set of relationships is then a 'role-set' and together constitutes a 'status'. A person will occupy a set of statuses which can be grouped into a higher-order set called a 'status-set'.

The role-set of a school pupil will include his relationships with other pupils, with teachers, and with all the other distinguishable persons that he relates to while occupying the position of school pupil. There is no guarantee that these relationships will be in balance. Recent work in the social sciences has stressed the disturbing effects of 'role conflict' and 'role strain' on those taking on roles in social groups. (Secord and Backman, 1964.) The social group, as a system, tends to a long-term balance, as a condition of its continued existence, and even conflict may be turned to integrative advantage (see Gluckman, 1955). There is some suggestion that role conflict is particularly likely to arise where there is poor communication between members of the role-set (Biddle, 1966).

Again, where there is a rapid flow of personnel through a role, due to high mobility, there is likely to be greater role conflict. Another source of conflict is the openness of the role to public debate. The role of school pupil encounters all these difficulties, and more. The growth in the size and complexity of organization of schools makes communications rather difficult. The mobility of school pupils has increased markedly in recent years. And there is a good deal of uncertainty and public debate about the aims and purposes of education, which permeates the schools.

The greatest point of role-conflict in schools probably occurs on the entry to adolescence. The school curriculum is based on the assumption of linear development of knowledge and skills, and makes little allowance for the rapidly changing expectations of the newly adolescent person. In extreme cases, the conflict can completely disrupt the learning-process. In many others it leads to dramatic contrasts in the attention given by pupils to different aspects of the curriculum.

Members of staff who are teaching subjects related to adolescent interests will find great energies available to the pursuit of learning. Those who are teaching more formal, impersonal subjects may find that an elaborate pattern of external incentives is needed, before they gain even the appearance of attention.

The complexities that can be seen in the role of the school pupil are also to be found in the role of the teacher.

2. *The role of the teacher.*

Teachers can be seen from at least three perspectives within the behavioural sciences. First, their similarities of function can be described and analysed in 'institutional' terms (as in the chapter by Blyth in this volume). Second, they can be studied as individuals in a social situation. This requires close attention to patterns of individual differences, without losing sight of the social situation in which these differences are expressed. Third, they can be individually studied as types of person, independently of their social milieu. The approach we adopt here is the second. In the social situation of the school, we can observe teachers engaging in a variety of activities. They teach academic subjects, they coach pupils in games, they act (often unwittingly) as models for instruction or identification, they attempt to influence judgements and conduct. Looking at this spectrum of activities covering the social role of the teacher, it is easy to despair of classifying them adequately.

As a first approach, we suggest that the teacher can be seen as operating in six areas of activity. These are:

(i) The communication of information to pupils in such a form that it is effectively learned. Information may take a variety of forms: words, numbers, musical notation or visual imagery. Traditionally, the communication of information is assessed by written and oral examinations, many of them given under very formal conditions.

(ii) The development of intellectual skills, that is, the ability to handle different forms of information effectively. The criteria of solution of problems, the recognition of problems, and the construction of theories which are logically coherent.

(iii) The instruction of the pupil in technical skills. We use the term 'technical' in a rather broad sense to mean the effective handling of materials in order to achieve a particular goal. The range of technical skills is so great, and the levels of achievement so varied, that individual teachers cannot tackle more than a few. In many schools, one finds concern with the skills of woodwork, metalcraft, the preparation and serving of food and drink, the decoration of homes, the maintenance and repair of vehicles, and the more academic skills of analysing chemical and physical materials.

(iv) Training in social skills. The informal arrangements of school life provide a good deal of opportunity for pupils to practice such skills on their own account, in playing games, making friends, keeping conflicts within tolerable limits and meeting strangers. Most teachers, under present limitations of time, can add only a little to these informal arrangements. But they not only can, but must, take some stand on social relationships within the classroom, in supervised play and at school meals.

Since these four levels form a relatively familiar group in educational discussion, we shall briefly consider them before proceeding to discuss the last two, which are more controversial from the teacher's point of view. They are, (v), personal understanding and (vi), self-insight.

The teacher's role is most obviously seen as relating to the first two levels. A good deal of help is available to the conscientious practitioner in developing his knowledge and skills in the communication of information and the development of intellectual abilities. He can study audio-visual aids and their uses, the techniques of programmed instruction, and the possibilities of closed-circuit television for lectures and demonstrations. The third level, too, is familiar ground. Teachers can learn, with a high probability of success, improved methods of technical instruction, in woodwork, metalwork, domestic science, laboratory techniques and, stretching the concept of technical skill to a related area, improved methods of coaching in games and athletics.

Turning to the fourth level, that of social skills, it is evident that the emphasis given to these skills in modern education is increasing quite strikingly, as social life becomes more volatile and diverse, and the chances of individual and group breakdown more probable. The development of quasi-autonomous adolescent groupings, discussed in the chapters by Hargreaves and Blyth in this volume and in Volume II, Chapter 11, by Morris, has caused much concern to adults, especially those in positions of authority. Though some of the concern may be disproportionate, it has had the effect of making the general public more aware of the problems of social education. It is true that these problems have often been narrowed to sex and delinquency (currently, drug-taking) but at least the awareness is growing. Since parents are somewhat inaccessible from the educational point of view, schools and colleges (and sometimes youth clubs) have been seen as the natural centres for social education. But are the teachers prepared to extend their role to encompass this level of learning and teaching? On this issue, there is still a continuing debate. More accurately, perhaps, a babel of discussion with everyone joining in and little agreement on the premises or the central issues. Some claim that the teacher has always been engaged in social education. Others would say that the teacher has quite enough to do already, with steadily mounting standards of entry to higher education and the professions. Yet others believe that teachers should be left to decide for themselves what should be done about social problems, and should be helped to engage in social education only at their own discretion.

Nevertheless, in some sense of the term *social education*, the teacher has always been quite deeply involved, as we have already pointed out. In this sense, all four levels of learning and teaching can be thought of as belonging to the traditional teaching role, even if social education is restricted to moral exhortation, to the arts of sportsmanship, to 'mock employment interviews' for school leavers or the teaching of dancing as a social art.

Matters are somewhat more difficult when we come to the last two levels. Personal understanding, it is true, is the extension and deepening of social skills into a unique personal relationship. But there is an individuality and warmth about a personal relationship that is not required, or even desirable, in many social relationships. Personal relationships can be seen as social relationships with a good deal of discretion left to the participants, and with strong emotional involvement. Given the strength of feeling and the uniqueness of these relationships, it is difficult to know just what the educational system can do about them in a systematic way. In the past, the system has tended to be somewhat discouraging about these relationships in the school, sensing that they are alien to the larger, more formal purposes of education. A switch to 'education for personal relationships' presents a very real challenge to this deeply rooted tradition.

Self-insight is famous for its rarity and elusiveness. The message of any moral and religious reformers, some of them the ostensible foundations of the educational system, such as Jesus and Socrates, is that 'know thyself' is a difficult, if not impossible, injunction for those who are well adjusted to established social roles. The generality of these roles stands between a person and his own uniqueness, his own personal commitment. The problem of how to reconcile, if reconciliation is possible, the growing person and the demands of social roles without threatening a sense of autonomy (to use Riesman's term) is unsolved. We are still, in the behavioural sciences, at the stage of preliminary description and conjecture. The interested reader is invited to examine this matter further in Volume II, Chapter 11, where the views of Riesman, Fromm and Erikson on autonomy and identity are considered in the light of adolescent development.

It might seem from this brief account of the various levels of learning and teaching that the teacher would do well to stick to his traditional last, and teach young people some useful information, some ways of thinking effectively, and a certain amount of technical skill. It is certainly true that each of these areas of teaching proves on closer inspection to be a fascinating and complex series of professional challenges: the challenge of devising an effective and well-integrated curriculum, close to the interests of the pupil or student; the challenge of improving existing methods of teaching, and becoming proficient in new ones; and, not least, the challenge of evaluating the effectiveness of a course of instruction.

Yet the social roles of teaching are not to be determined by the wishes of the teachers themselves, or indeed by the wishes of any single group, however well-informed and powerful. The educational system is diverse and constantly changing; the roles of teachers, even within one specific type of establishment, such as secondary grammar schools or primary schools, are extremely difficult to describe, let alone define. This is partly because of the increasing of the teacher's 'role-set', the set of social relationships that he establishes in the course of doing his daily work as a teacher.

Just as doctors work not only with patients, but with nurses, patients' relatives, consultants, orderlies, almoners, secretaries, laboratory workers and many others, so teachers work not only with pupils, but with colleagues, senior staff (including the powerful figure of the head teacher) and the parents of pupils. They may at some point make contact with members of the education committee, if only when they are selected for their post. But even if they make little contact here, they are indirectly influenced by the decisions of the committee, which have a bearing on the working conditions of teachers. Teachers also have working relationships with the maintenance and auxiliary staff of the school. It would be extremely difficult to enumerate all the distinguishable relationships that are established by a typical assistant teacher in an average-sized school.

How are these different types of relationship ordered and kept in balance? By the development of professional attitudes to the work, and by the guidance of group norms, both formal and informal. Teachers, like other role incumbents, have a conception of a 'fair day's work'. They group many relationships together, and may, for example, distinguish individually only the most acceptable and the most difficult pupils in each form, grouping the remaining two-thirds or so into a 'typical' teacher-class relationship.

Not only do different types of school vary, as Natalie Cole found when she moved from a primary to a secondary school, but there are more individual differences in climate. As Anderson and Brewer and their colleagues showed, in a series of pioneering studies now much refined (e.g. Anderson and Brewer, 1946; compare with more recent work reported in Glidewell, 1966), that individual teachers tend to have established preferences for particular styles of control of a class. Some are more dominative than others, some attempt to encourage participation in class activities in an 'integrative' manner (the terms are those used by Anderson and Brewer). The results of integrative teaching can be impressive, if the conditions are right; namely, that the teachers find the style of control compatible with their prevailing attitudes and competence, and that pupils enjoy taking part in the organization of class activities. In the early stages of enthusiasm over the virtues of 'democratic' as contrasted with 'authoritarian' teaching (to use terms that are far more frequently used than those of Anderson and Brewer), it was sometimes forgotten that the effectiveness of any style of teaching depends on more than the style itself, judged in abstraction. It depends on supportive attitudes, appropriate abilities, and expected outcomes of learning and teaching.

To return to the six 'levels' of learning and teaching discussed earlier, it is clear that the role of the teacher rarely gives equal weight to each of the six. The attitudes of the teacher, shaped by many factors other than his professional training, but clearly reflecting this training; the attitudes of the head teachers of the school, linked with governing bodies and education authorities; the group norms of the teaching staff; the attitudes and norms of the pupils; all these factors, and more (for we have not exhausted the role-set), are determinants of the contents of the teacher's role. In the kind of large, partly bureaucratic system that characterizes large-scale modern education, one might expect that the first three levels, and the first in particular, would be most compatible with the impersonality and needs for efficiency of the system as a whole. But this expectation is over-simplified. Large systems tend to be differentiated, and to create small groups of specialists with their own distinctive specialized views of life. They tend to engage in dialectic to a much greater degree than people from small, traditional, cohesive social groups. It seems no accident (to use a favourite phrase of the late Karl Mannheim) that the educational system that produces national examination syllabuses, with strong pressures for uniformity and impersonality in marking, also produces the comprehensive school, school counsellors, a school psychological service, team-teaching, curriculum development, and a booming grant-aided demand for the study of creativity.

Great attention is being paid to widening the range of educational objectives in most modern societies, including our own. (The taxonomies produced by Bloom and his colleagues have been extremely widely used; see Bloom, 1956, Krathwohl, 1964.) There is widespread interest in the encouragement of methods of discovery (Bruner, 1960, 1966) to complement the extension of methods of duplication, embodied in some of the programmed-instruction methods.

All of this can be expressed briefly and very incompletely by suggesting that education has traditionally been a series of routines, interspersed with rituals. The role of the teacher has always been potentially, and often actually, dramatic, since he has a good deal of discretion in his classroom activities. The stage is now set for the drama implicit in education to become explicit.

3. *Drama, ritual, routine and the teaching role*

One point should be made at once. The term *drama* is being used here in a technical sense, and not only as a metaphor. It is true that one commonly encountered aspect of teaching – the teacher standing alone before a mute audience of pupils, talking and gesturing – irresistibly reminds one of the theatre. But the theatre is not the main reference point here.

The role of the teacher is, like all established roles, closely bound up with an organized working day. That is, there are sequences of activity that typically involve the teacher; sequences such as a teaching 'period' of forty minutes in the classroom or the workshop, or a staff meeting with colleagues and the head teacher, or the preparation of lessons.

Some of these sequences of activity are very familiar to him. He knows exactly what will happen, and may find that much of his behaviour in these sequences is unreflective and habitual. These habitual and predictable sequences can be described as routines. It is characteristic of routines that they evoke very little feeling in themselves. If they enable a person to avoid doing something unpleasant, they will be associated with positive feeling; if they prevent a person engaging in more interesting activity, they attract negative feeling. But in themselves, they are neutral, though their outcomes may well be useful.

Routines make up a great deal of the life of many workers, and one of the most clearly marked trends in modern industry has been to turn previously variable sequences of activity into routines, which then lend themselves to mechanization. One of the best ways of seeing whether a sequence of activity has really become a routine is to ask whether anything is lost by mechanizing it, assuming that the machine produces output of the same type. It is this test that clearly distinguishes rituals from routines. At first sight, rituals look like routines in many respects. They are predictable in outward form, and are frequently repeated. But they express or evoke feeling, a feeling that is usually associated with a greatly valued person or event. Routines rarely involve the person as a whole: it is as if the person hands over the responsibility for the routine to some small part of himself – a habit. In the ritual, on the other hand, the whole person is involved. To mechanize a ritual would be a contradiction in terms, since the activity is not primarily 'instrumental' (a means to a useful outcome) but 'expressive'.

Perhaps the most obvious example of a ritual to the teacher is the institution of morning assembly, at which hymns are sung and prayers are said. Unfortunately, in many schools, if not the majority, the problems of arranging the conditions so that the assembly is experienced by its participants as a ritual have proved intractable, and we are reminded that there is a valuable distinction to be drawn between the formal social description of an event, and the significance of the event to its participants. The 'genuine' rituals of school life are usually confined to smaller groups, whose feelings and values can resonate more closely to one another than is usually possible to a whole school. Perhaps once or twice in the school year a sense of a ritual occasion is fully conveyed to most of its members; it may be an annual prize-giving, or a memorial service, or possibly a Christmas celebration.

If these are the routines and the rituals, where are the dramas? A sequence of activity is a drama if it has three elements: first, if the outcome is important to the participants; second, if the outcome is uncertain, because the situation is wholly or partly new to them; third, if they believe that their actions can influence the outcome. The uncertainty of outcome, combined with importance, produces a high state of activation (see the discussion of motivation in Volume I, Chapter 6).

If the actions of the participants are effective in achieving a desired outcome, the likelihood is that they will be repeated in a similar situation. In fact, in describing the successful completion of a drama, we are describing one form of learning. Since 'importance' and 'uncertainty' are continuous variables, we would expect dramas to range from the anecdotal to the epic. And this is exactly what happens.

In education, dramas can be deliberately contrived by the teaching staff, in order to enhance learning, or they may happen inadvertently. We have argued that the teaching role, as the individual teacher encounters it, is full of dramatic potentialities, because a good deal is left to the teacher's discretion, and the role-set is large and complex.

The problem for the teacher, then, is to attempt to develop enough competence in his work to bring the inevitable dramas to a successful outcome, and to have enough energy and self-confidence to spare to engage the pupils in planned dramas. It might be asked: why should dramas for the pupils be dramas for the staff? Is it not likely that the essence of teaching is to know thoroughly those matters which are highly important but uncertain for the pupil? This is a point that is well worth discussion.

First, it seems clear that a person who is involved in a drama can find it very reassuring to see someone else, in the same situation, to whom the situation is not dramatic. This comes close to the perennial fascination of the 'hero': he is a person who knows what is going to happen next, and is unperturbed. If the uncertainty is greater than we can tolerate, such a person may be able to help us to find the answer.

Having said this, we may add, second, that the co-existence in the same situation of a person to whom the situation is a drama and another to whom it is a routine brings about a certain tension. This is particularly likely to occur when it is realized that the person to whom the situation is routine has deliberately precipitated a drama for the other, on educational grounds. We must trace our way carefully here through the complexities of the situation. The most important point is probably the acquiescence of the person to whom the drama is happening. For example, a person being coached in cricket may ask his instructor to give him a thorough testing, to establish the limits of his competence. He is likely to find the experience quite taxing, but is unlikely to complain if the instructor regards it as all in the day's work. But if the coach does this unasked, he might well be resented for putting his pupil in a difficult situation.

Perhaps the simplest way of looking at this whole problem is to assume that uncertainty is disturbing, unless it occurs within well-recognized limits and is perceived to be resolvable into an acceptable certainty. The teacher who generates 'manageable' dramas will be highly regarded by his pupils, but he who threatens their self-confidence, and therefore their self-esteem, will be resented.

Dramas become routines, when they have been repeated often enough. Given the variability of teachers and pupils, it is perhaps not surprising that, despite the regulating effect of group norms, a programme of study that will be found challenging and absorbing by one person or group will be found unexciting to others. As mobility within society grows, and schools become more varied and comprehensive, the problem of knowing how teachers and pupils are experiencing their work will become greater than it is now, and one would guess that it is already quite intractable. The answer to this problem is likely to be found along the following lines. By encouraging a continuing dialogue, or dialectic, between teachers and pupils, by encouraging the pupil to take responsibility for his own learning, and by realizing that learning is a non-routine activity, then teachers can keep their roles fresh and dramatic. But this, of course, requires unceasing vigilance.

VI. THEMES IN THE SOCIAL PSYCHOLOGY OF LEARNING

After this outline of some of the social influences on processes of learning, it may be helpful to list some of the main themes which we have been attempting to establish. Not all of them can be regarded as proven. But they all merit serious consideration, and are supported by a good deal of evidence.

First, all learning takes place in a social context, an important part of which is specifically concerned with bringing about particular forms of learning. These 'agencies of socialization' assume that certain goals and rates of learning are desirable, and their efforts are devoted to achieving these. Each person encounters these agencies through particular persons, some of whom are in personal relationships with him, others of whom are more formal, or 'official'. The social psychologist has been particularly interested in these individual aspects of learning in a social context.

Second, from the point of view of the learner, his attitudes to the content and level of learning are of great importance. These attitudes are themselves part of a process of social learning. But, once formed, they throw much light on individual differences in learning, once differences in ability and opportunity have been allowed for. The attitude to the content of learning is not wholly determined by the content itself, but by associated factors, such as its relevance to the needs of the learner, his attitude to the teacher, and the attitudes to his peers. Attitudes to the level at which learning is to take place are linked with levels of aspiration, and the 'achievement motive'. There is evidence to show that these are functions of early childhood experience.

Third, attitudes are part of a system, both within the person as an individual 'personality system' and within the groups of which the person forms a part. The term 'norm' has been given two connotations in social psychology: first, it refers to the establishment of regularities of behaviour (for example, frames of reference both in the persons and the group), and second, it refers to sanctioned and approved (or disapproved) forms of behaviour. The first meaning of the term looks at the facts of conformity, the second looks at one of the means whereby conformity is secured. Attitudes, because they form part of a system, can change as they get out of phase with the system. Many studies have shown the tendency of an individual's attitudes to change if they are in conflict with other attitudes that he holds. Many studies also show that a person will change his attitudes (other things being equal) if they are in conflict with the norms of his group, if the group is able to sanction his behaviour.

Fourth, attitudes and norms, with their associated forms of behaviour, are socially grouped into social roles, which have systematic properties. These roles are extremely influential in determining the course of the learning-process. In schools, teachers sub-divide the areas and levels of learning into 'subjects' and 'streams'. The result of this link between learning and social roles can be to influence the learning-process quite significantly.

Fifth, the pupil in school is responding to a complex set of influences, only a part of which is under the control of the teaching staff. Many of these influences are in conflict, and an analysis of the forms of conflict throws light on obstacles to effective learning.

Although conflict can create obstacles to learning, it does not follow that effective educational planning and practice will seek to remove all sources of conflict. A very difficult and largely unexplored problem is that of establishing and maintaining intelligent control of conflict, so that it can be used constructively. In an age of worldwide, unprecedentedly destructive conflicts, it is easy to see why many people wish to keep some of the more traditional parts of social life, such as the family, education and religion, free from open disturbance. Yet a moment's reflection shows that these parts of life, being central and diverse, are in many important ways controversial. When they have been at their most healthy, they have been full of controversy (this is, admittedly, itself a controversial statement, and one that will be allowed to rest without further explanation or defence).

The social psychology of learning, then, covers an even broader range of topics than the psychology of social learning. As a systematic study, it is still in its earliest phase. But already it poses fascinating problems of its own, in helping us to look at the problems of learning in a social context, charged with powerful individual attitudes and group standards.

REFERENCES

ANDERSON, H. H., and BREWER, J. E. (1946). Studies of teachers' dominative and integrated contacts on children's classroom behaviour. *Psychol. Monogr.* **8.**

ASCH, S. E. (1952). *Social Psychology.* New York: Prentice-Hall.

BANTON, M. (1965). *Roles.* London: Tavistock Publications.

BERENDA, RUTH W. (1950). *The Influence of the Group on the Judgements of Children.* New York: King's Crown Press.

BERKOWITZ, D. (1962). *Aggression.* New York: McGraw-Hill.

BIDDLE, B. J., and THOMAS, E. J. (ed.). (1966). *Role Theory.* New York. Wiley.

BLOOM, B. S. *et al.* (1956). *Taxonomy of Educational Objectives, Handbook* I – *The Cognitive Domain.* New York: David McKay Co.

BREHM, J. W., and COHEN, A. R. (1962). *Explorations in Cognitive Dissonance.* New York: Wiley.

BROWN, ROGER (1965). *Social Psychology.* New York: The Free Press.

BROWN, W. B. D. (1960). *Exploration in Management.* London: Heinemann.

BRUNER, J. S. (1960). *The Process of Learning.* Cambridge, Mass.: Harvard Univ. Press.

BRUNER, J. S. (1966). *Toward a Theory of Instruction.* Cambridge, Mass.: Harvard Univ. Press.

COHEN, A. R. (1964). *Attitude Change and Social Influence.* New York: Basic Books.

COSER, L. A. (1956). *The Functions of Conflict.* London: Routledge and Kegan Paul.

DEUTSCH, M. (1954). Field theory in social psychology. In Lindzey, G. (ed.), *Handbook of Social Psychology.* Cambridge, Mass.: Addison-Wesley.

DOUGLAS, J. W. B. (1964). *The Home and the School.* London: Mac-Gibbon and Kee.

EYSENCK, H. J. (1967). *The Biological Basis of Personality.* New York: C. C. Thomas.

FESTINGER, L. (1957). *A Theory of Cognitive Dissonance.* Evanston, Ill: Row and Peterson.

FLEMING, C. M. (1959). *The Social Psychology of Education.* (second edn). London: Routledge and Kegan Paul.

GLIDEWELL, J. C. *et al.* (1966). Socialization and social structure in the classroom. In Hoffman, L. W., and Hoffman, M. L. (ed.). *Review of Child Development Research. Volume 2.* New York: Russell Sage Foundation.

GLUCKMAN, M. (1955). *Custom and Conflict in Africa.* Oxford: Blackwell.

GOFFMAN, E. (1959). *The Presentation of Self in Everyday Life.* New York: Doubleday.

GOFFMAN, E. (1961). *Asylums.* New York: Doubleday.

GROSS, R. E. (ed.). (1966). *British Secondary Education.* New York: Oxford University Press.

HARDING, D. W. (1953). *Social Psychology and Individual Values.* London: Hutchinson.

HARGREAVES, DAVID H. (1967). *Social Relations in a Secondary School.* London: Routledge and Kegan Paul.

HEIDER, F. (1958). *The Psychology of Interpersonal Relations.* New York: Wiley,

HOMANS, G. C. (1961). *Social Behaviour: its Elementary Forms.* London: Routledge and Kegan Paul.

HOPPE, F. (1930). Erfolg und Misserfolg. *Psychologische Forschung.* **14,** 1–62.

HUGHES, T. (1857). *Tom Brown's Schooldays.* London: Blackie. (modern reprint).

JONES, E. E., and GERARD, H. B. (1967). *Foundations of Social Psychology.* New York: Wiley.

KOESTLER, A. (1959). *The Sleepwalkers.* London: Hutchinson.

KRATHWOHL, D. R. *et al.* (1964). *Taxonomy of Educational Objectives, Handbook* II – *The Affective Domain.* New York: David McKay Co.

LEWIN, K. (1947). Group decision and social change. In Newcomb, T. M., and Hartley, E. L. (ed.). *Readings in Social Psychology.* New York: Holt.

LEWIN, K. (1948). *Resolving Social Conflicts.* New York: Harper.

LEWIN, K. (1951). *Field Theory in Social Science.* New York: Harper.

LEWIN, K. *et al.* (1944). Level of aspiration. In Hunt, J. McV. (ed.) *Personality and the Behaviour Disorders. Volume 1.* New York: Ronald.

LIPPITT, R., and WHITE, R. K. (1947). An experimental study of leadership and group life. In Newcomb, T. M., and Hartley, E. L. (ed.). *Readings in Social Psychology.* New York: Holt.

MCCLELLAND, D. C. (1961). *The Achieving Society.* Princeton: Van Nostrand.

MCCLELLAND, D. C. (1967). The urge to achieve. *New Society. Volume 9, No. 229.* 16th February, 227–229.

MCCLELLAND, D. C. *et al.* (1953). *The Achievement Motive.* New York: Appleton.

MCGUIRE, W. J. (1966). The current status of cognitive consistency theories. In Feldman, S. (ed.). *Cognitive Consistency.* New York: Academic Press.

MEAD, G. H. (1956). *The Social Psychology of G. H. Mead.* (ed. Anselm Strauss). Chicago, Ill.: Univ. Chicago Press, Phoenix Books.

MERTON, R. K. (1957a). *Social Theory and Social Structure.* (revised edn.). Chapter 9. Glencoe, Ill.: The Free Press.

MERTON, R. K. (1957b). The role-set; problems in sociological theory. *Brit. J. Sociol.* **8,** 106–120.

MORRIS, J. F. (1958). The development of adolescent value-judgments. *Brit. J. Educ. Psychol.* **28,** 1–14.

MURRAY, H. A. (1938). *Explorations in Personality.* New York: O.U.P.

NEILL, A. S. (1964). *Summerhill.* London: Gollancz.

OSGOOD, C. E., and TANNENBAUM, P. H. (1955). The principle of congruity in the prediction of attitude change. *Psychol. Rev.* **62,** 42–55.

PELZ, EDITH B. (1958). Some factors in 'group decision'. In: Maccoby, E. E., Hartley, E. L., and Newcomb, T. M. (ed.). *Readings in Social Psychology.* New York: Holt.

POLANYI, M. (1958). *Personal Knowledge.* London: Routledge and Kegan Paul.

REVANS, R. W. (1965). *Science and the Manager.* London: Macdonald.

RUSSELL, C., and RUSSELL, W. M. S. (1961). *Human Behaviour.* London: André Deutsch.

SCHACHTER, S. (1951). Deviation, rejection and communication. *J. abnorm. soc. Psychol.* **46,** 190–207.

SECORD, P. F., and BACKMAN, C. W. (1964). *Social Psychology.* New York: McGraw Hill.

SHERIF, M. (1936). *The Psychology of Social Norms.* New York: Harper.

SHERIF, M. (1947). Group influences upon the formation of norms and attitudes. In Newcomb, T. M., and Hartley, E. L. (ed.). *Readings in Social Psychology.* New York: Holt.

SHERIF, C. W., SHERIF, M., and NEBERGALL, R. E. (1965). *Attitude and Attitude Change.* Philadelphia: W. B. Saunders.

SHERIF, C. W., and SHERIF, M. (ed.). (1967). *Attitude, Ego-Involvement and Change*. New York: Wiley.

SHERIF, M., and SHERIF, C. W. (1964). *Reference Groups*. New York: Harper and Row.

SILLITOE, ALAN (1959). *The Loneliness of the Long-Distance Runner.* London: W. H. Allen.

VENABLES, P. F. R. (1955). *Technical Education*. London: Bell.

7

Interpersonal Relations and the Social System of the School

DAVID H. HARGREAVES

I. INTRODUCTION

THE PUBLICATION in 1939 of Roethlisberger and Dickson's *Management and the Worker* made a notable advance in our appreciation of the significance of interpersonal relations in an institutional setting. Prior to this study, the promotion of industrial efficiency was seen to rest mainly on the solution of two basic problems. In order to achieve the industrial organization's basic goals, especially the maximization of output with minimum cost, a rational blueprint must be constructed, involving the establishment of an administrative machine to co-ordinate different tasks: definite patterns of authority, communication and interaction; and fixed rules and procedures. Secondly, the workers must be motivated to high output by the reduction of fatigue and the stimulus of attractive incentive schemes.

The work of Roethlisberger and Dickson exposed the inadequacy of these assumptions. Within the *formal* organization of a factory develops an *informal* organization, that is, patterns of human relationships that are not part of the official organizational design. Workers and executives are not independent units executing in a mechanical or rational fashion the organization's formal purposes, but groups of persons with needs for mutual association, intimacy, security and protection. These informal groups and interactions, which occur at all levels of the formal system, and which account for a major proportion of actual interactions, develop values, customs and structures of their own, and become ends in themselves. The formal organization, being constructed on a 'logical' basis, takes no account of such relationships. In practice, the distinction between the formal and informal organization is largely analytical, for the two systems constantly interpenetrate. Yet the distinction is useful, since it brings to our attention

245

many of the most significant social processes at work within the organization. As we shall see, it is through the informal organization that the personnel can undermine, or find alternative means of achieving, the organization's formal goals.

The nature of the informal organization in one industrial setting is revealed in the famous study of the Bank Wiring Room of the Hawthorne plant of the Western Electric Company in Chicago. The workers failed to live up to the expectations of the management's 'rational' wage incentive scheme, by which the men could earn more money for faster output. The explanation was that among these 14 men patterns of friendship and interaction had grown up, leading to the formation of group values and norms, ties of solidarity and systems of mutual aid. To these men the wage incentive scheme was not logical at all, since they feared that if they worked harder the management would cut the piece rate or make some of the workers redundant. Because of this common belief and the group solidarity, the group developed an output norm – 'restriction of output' – which defined the limits of each man's work. Deviance from this norm could be punished by invoking the informal group's sanctions. Thus those who worked too hard ('ratebusters') and those who worked too little ('chiselers') would be subjected to ridicule, rejection or 'binging' (a physical blow).

Since this period enormous research resources have been poured into the investigation of informal groups in industrial organizations (see Blau and Scott, 1963), and running parallel with this work has been the intensive study of many kinds of small 'face-to-face' groups by social psychologists of the 'Group Dynamics' approach. Considerable information on the nature of small group behaviour has been obtained experimentally.

When people meet together as a small group, they usually do so because membership of the group offers some source of satisfaction to each person. The kinds of reward mediated by the group to its members vary widely, both between different groups and between different members of the same group. The group may be striving towards a goal which will benefit all the members; a member may have a specific task in which he may display special expertise or from which he can derive specific satisfactions; or the satisfaction may consist of sharing certain sorts of friendly relationships with others of similar interests. Since most groups are voluntary or self-selected, we may expect members to possess similar goals and values. Most of us actively seek the company of persons who share our own attributes, attitudes and purposes, and avoid those who in these respects are highly dissimilar to us. In institutions where membership is involuntary (e.g. schools, hospitals and prisons) the 'inmates' tend to divide themselves into sub-groups or cliques whose members share common attitudes and values.

Most groups exhibit certain central values, ideals and goals. These values express themselves in *norms* or shared beliefs about the sort of behaviour that are deemed appropriate or inappropriate to membership. These norms may be regarded as specifications of how members are expected to behave, and they may take the form of official constitutional rules and/or unwritten but none the less powerful influences on members' beliefs, perceptions and actions. Deviance, or failure to conform to the norms, invites other members to exert pressures or invoke sanctions against the deviant, since his non-conformity represents a threat to the group's values and the attainment of the group's goals. When the deviant persists in his non-conformity, he tends to become a target for ridicule or hostility, and in extreme cases he will be ostracized or driven from the group.

Thus the members are only superficially homogeneous. They vary in their commitment to the group's values; their attraction to the group; their conformity to its norms; their contribution to its goals. The pattern of interpersonal relations also differentiates the members. They do not communicate or interact equally with the other members; subgroups or cliques may evolve. Some members are liked more than others (popularity) or have greater influence over others (social power). As the members become differentiated, norms or expectations are often held about the behaviour of individual members, that is, they acquire specific *roles* within the group. Usually those members who are most committed to the group's goals, values and norms are those who attain the highest popularity, prestige and power.

In short, a small group is an elaborate network of interacting individuals, who share certain basic goals and values, who enforce regulating norms, and who become differentiated into a hierarchical structure of popularity, prestige and power.

II. INTERPERSONAL RELATIONS AND EDUCATION

Clearly such an analytical approach to the study of educational organizations should be highly productive. Among some of the basic questions would be the following:

What is the formal organization of the school?

What are the goals of the school and its teachers?

What is the nature of peer group values and structures (informal organization)?

What is the relation between the formal and the informal organization? How do they influence one another?

What is the degree of consonance between peer group values and the teacher's goals? Where there is conflict, what is the source?

How are teacher–pupil relations influenced by (a) the formal organization and (b) the informal organization?

Unfortunately, such an approach to the analysis of the school has been a rare phenomenon until recently. It is many years since William Foote Whyte in his *Street Corner Society* (1943), demonstrated how fruitful an intensive study of the structure, norms and roles of a neighbourhood gang can be, but this has remained a foundation on which few educational researchers have sought to build. The mainstream of education research (both psychological and sociological) has been concerned with learning and developmental processes, and the relation of personal and social factors to educational attainment and adjustment. Pupils, in short, have been treated mainly as individuals: the structure of social relationships of children within the school has tended to be ignored.

Of course, there have been exceptions. Perhaps the most important stream of social relations work in education is that stimulated by Moreno's 'sociometric' approach, which is based on the distribution of friendship choices within groups. Although sociometry has produced many interesting studies of interpersonal choice and popularity in children's groups, both in the United States and in Britain (Blyth 1960), it remains basically a technique not a theory of social relations. This method has been used to relate the distribution of interpersonal choice to many other variables, but too often the results lack significance because they are unrelated to the values, other structures and the larger context of the group under scrutiny. Unless we know the consequences of interpersonal choice both for the ongoing life of the group itself, and for the larger organism of which the group is a part, such data can make but a limited contribution to our understanding of the social system of the school.

A second exception stems from the sociological tradition. In spite of the suggestive and prophetic work of Willard Waller's *The Sociology of Teaching* (1932), there was little detailed empirical work until the appearance of A. B. Hollingshead's *Elmstown's Youth* in 1939. This study shows how the social structure of a small mid-western town tends to replicate itself within the High School. It is the pupils from the higher social classes who tend to take the more academic courses and achieve the highest grades; friendship and dating patterns are highly class based; and the peer culture – athletics, dancing and the Student Council – is dominated by pupils from the higher social classes.

James Coleman's later study, *The Adolescent Society* (1961), of ten High Schools in Illinois shows that peer-group status is not a simple function of social class. Despite variations between schools, a general disjunction between the dominant adolescent values and the formal goals of the school was revealed. Only a minority of the pupils aspires to an occupation which requires academic brilliance, or seeks to be remembered in the school as a brilliant student. Within the peer group, the brilliant student possesses considerably less status, that is, a lower probability of membership in the 'leading crowd', and also considerably less popularity with the same and with the opposite sex than the athlete – though the academically brilliant athlete has greater prestige and pop-ularity than the non-academic athlete.

Coleman's documentation of the dominant value orientations of High School adolescents is detailed and often ingenious. Although such adolescent value systems may be a true reflection of the social values current in American society, they represent an alienation from formal educational goals. It is this threat to educational purposes that Coleman is mainly concerned to expose and analyse. Yet the breadth gained from an investigation based on the questionnaire responses of pupils in ten schools inevitably involves a sacrifice in depth. It is thus often difficult for Coleman to account for wide variations in peer group trends in schools of different size and composition. We learn little of the details of the structure or actual interaction of the pupils' groups within any one school (cf. Newcomb, 1943 and Gordon, 1957). Teacher–pupil relationships are neglected (cf. Bush, 1954) and we have only general inferences about the impact of the formal organization on peer group structures and values. This is not to decry Coleman's contribution, which is considerable. It provides a necessary background for the more detailed study of interaction processes within the school and indicates the dan-gers of making generalizations on the basis of a study of one school.

There is no British research comparable in scope to that of Coleman in the U.S.A. – and we certainly cannot regard his findings as applicable to schools in this country. The one outstanding British contribution in this field is that of H. J. Hallworth, whose exploratory study was published in 1953. Here the central problem was the investigation of the development of stability and hierarchical structures and value systems in pupils' groups in a co-educational Grammar School, and the consonance of such value systems with the purposes of the school. Since 1953, however, most research has rejected this approach in favour of segmental analysis of more specific areas of interaction processes in the school.

III. A CASE-STUDY: INTERPERSONAL RELATIONS AMONG PUPILS

In 1964 the present writer began a study of a British Secondary Modern School for Boys (Hargreaves, 1967). The aim was to provide, in an exploratory way, an analysis of the school as a dynamic system of social relations through an intensive study of interaction processes in the school. The method of research was participant-observation. The researcher spent a complete year at the school; he undertook some teaching; he observed numerous lessons; he joined in many of the school's extracurricular activities; he held informal discussions with the pupils; he administered questionnaires and conducted interviews.

Lumley Secondary Modern School is situated in a town in the north of England. The district, surrounded by industry, consists of old terraced houses, densely packed into a residential island, and scheduled for demolition. Almost all of the four hundred and fifty pupils, aged between 11 and 16 years, live in the immediate vicinity of the school. The fathers of the vast majority of the boys are employed in manual occupations. Lumley is thus a working-class school in a decaying part of the town, though the school itself is less than a decade old.

The research is based almost entirely on the fourth year pupils, aged between 14 and 15 years, most of whom were in their last year of full-time education. It was assumed these boys would represent a crystallization of the educative process in the school.

Our initial concern is the structure of informal relations among these fourth-year pupils. The most striking fact is that friendships are largely determined by the formal organization of these boys into forms. The pupils were 'streamed' into five forms, on entry by the results of the eleven plus examination, and subsequently by performance in the school's internal examinations at the end of each term. (The fifth or 'E' stream, which contained the 'backward' pupils, was excluded from the study.) Between 60 and 78 per cent of the boys each pupil named as his friends came from the same stream. Further, the greater distance between the four streams, A to D, the lower the number of friendship choices made across the streams. Thus none of the A stream pupils names a friend in 4D, and only 1 per cent of the D stream's friendship choices is directed to 4A.

We shall examine some of the implications of the stream-specific nature of friendship choices at a later stage. For the moment, the evidence is sufficient for us to regard each form as a relatively independent network of friendship choices. Interactions are predominantly governed by the streaming system and each form perceives itself as a distinct unit within the school. By the fourth year each form has acquired a set of values and norms. That is to say, the members have arrived at a consensus about the forms of behaviour which are desirable and expected, and they have developed rules which regulate behaviour and enforce expectations. Each form is not homogeneous. The members are differentiated into those who strongly conform to the values and norms, at one extreme, and those who deviate, at the other. Those who conform tend to acquire prestige and popularity; those who deviate tend to be disliked and rejected. In short, by the fourth year these hundred boys are highly differentiated *between* streams in terms of the dominant values and norms and *within* streams in terms of high and low status cliques.

The values in 4A may be termed 'academic'. These boys perceive themselves as the intellectual elite of the school, who will achieve distinction in external examinations. Many of them intend to remain at school beyond the statutory leaving age of 15 years, in order to take a further examination, the Certificate of Secondary Education. The dominant values in this form are embodied in the boys of high informal status, that is, those boys who are perceived by others to be the leaders, the boys who 'run things', the boys who exert most influence over the others. These boys want to 'get on in life' and an essential element in this is success in academic matters. They work hard at school and approve of boys who pursue similar ideals. Whilst they naturally enjoy some 'fun' in lessons, this is secondary to the main purpose of learning. Their attendance record is good: they are absent from school only when prevented by illness. Standards of behaviour, dress and personal hygiene are high. They are proud of their good reputation with the staff and are anxious to maintain it. They are identified with the school, loyal and dependable to the Headmaster and the teachers.

The low status and unpopular boys in 4A are those who deviate from these values and norms. Such pupils are those who inhibit the form's academic progress by laziness or lack of ability; who 'mess about' in lessons; who are absent frequently; who dress untidily; who are physically aggressive to other boys.

In 4B the values and norms of the pupils are a diluted form of those in the A stream. Some academic work is essential, since some of these boys will take the external examination at the end of the fourth year, and success in this examination should qualify them for entrance to an apprenticeship. But none of them intends to remain at school beyond the age of 15 to take the Certificate of Secondary Education. Thus to work *too* hard becomes deviant. We shall refer to these values and norms as 'non-academic', since they represent a compromise between the demands of the teachers (and the examination) and the desire of the pupils to 'have fun'. Failure to join in the fun is a sign of deviance, but 'having fun' is a relief from academic work, not a replacement of it. High attendance and smart appearance decline in importance in this form.

The C and D streams may be treated as one unit, since they show a close similarity of norms and values, and the boys of high informal status in both forms comprise one united friendship group. To these boys school is a 'waste of time', an evil enforced by the law, which is to be borne with resentment. 'Messing about' is the only legitimate classroom behaviour. There is no compromise between working hard and wasting time: the values are 'anti-academic'. Undermining the lessons, and breaking the school rules by smoking and wearing jeans and long hair, become the hallmark of the high status pupil in the classroom. Absenteeism and truancy rates are high: the absence rate in 4D is six times greater than that of 4A. However, high prestige in the peer group is a function not only of anti-school behaviour but also of fighting ability. The boy with the highest informal status in 4C was the school's best fighter – 'the cock of the school'. (In 4D the boy with the highest informal status was the 'cock's' closest associate.) This position does not necessarily involve a large amount of *actual* fighting, but rather a reputation for superior fighting ability and the unwillingness of other boys to challenge the position of the 'cock'. It is retained by a systematic display of aggressive, tough and 'hard' behaviour. Yet because the 'cock' must constantly threaten others to maintain his supremacy, he was by no means the most popular pupil, whereas in 4A the boys with the highest status tended also to be the most popular.

It is impossible to examine in detail in this chapter the expression of these different norms in the daily routine of each form in the classroom. One example must suffice. Let us consider the practice of 'copying', which is generally disapproved by teachers. In 4A the pupils agree with the teachers that to copy from another pupil is to cheat. They have internalized the teachers' view that copying serves only to deceive the teacher and the pupil himself. The way to academic progress is to work on one's own and learn from one's mistakes. Copying is thus forbidden in the informal group. It is replaced by a system of *checking*, whereby it is legitimate to compare answers or to ask for advice on procedure.

'You can help someone to learn how to do it, but not copy the answer.'

In 4B the 'non-academic' norms make copying permissible. In fact, the pupils make special arrangements for the exchange of information. The boy who is good at Mathematics lets his friend copy the answers, but he expects this favour to be reciprocated in English, at which he is poor.

'Most people will let you copy. We don't mind really, 'cos we copy off them.'

In 4C and 4D we would perhaps expect, on the basis of the 'anti-academic' norms, that there would be no copying, since no one has any interest in work. In fact, copying was prevalent, but it does not stem from any desire for academic achievement. Rather, copying is an attempt to deceive the teacher into believing that *some* work is being done during the lesson. Unless the boys can write something in their exercise books, the teacher is forced to establish a rigid discipline and careful supervision of work. Copying thus satisfies the teacher's demand for written work and the pupil's desire for relatively weak discipline. However, since among the high status friends academic effort is proscribed, they cannot copy off one another as in 4B. Instead, they copy off the hard-working low status boys, whose books they 'borrow' under threat of physical assault.

'I copy off—. He's supposed to be the brainiest in the class. He couldn't stop me 'cos I'd smash him and take the book.'

Within each of these four forms the boys of similar status tend to associate together in cliques. Thus in 4A six boys form a clique of high social power, with a mean status rank of 5·5 out of thirty. Their 'academic' orientation is revealed in the group's mean academic rank, derived from examinations, of 10·2. In contrast the clique showing least conformity to the dominant norms and values has a status rank average of 18·7 and an academic average of 19·5. In 4A, where the dominant values and norms are an inversion of those in 4A, we find the reverse association between status and academic rankings. Here the dominant clique has a mean status rank of 5·9, but an academic average of 13·5 out of twenty-three. The deviant low status clique has a status average of 18·5, but an academic average of 8·4.

In short, associated with the allocation of pupils into different streams is the differentiation of norms and values between streams. We may say that the peer culture becomes split into two opposing 'subcultures' – an 'academic' pole in the A stream and an 'anti-academic' pole in the D stream. Further, status on a peer group level is related to conformity to the dominant norms of the form.

Alf, a member of the low status clique in 4A, acquired low status because of his tendency to deviate from the dominant values and norms of his peers. His academic position and his classroom behaviour as rated by the teachers were very low. The high status clique members complained that whenever the teachers left the room for a short time Alf would begin to talk or 'mess about', thus undermining the form's reputation with the teachers as highly responsible and trustworthy. His failure to produce homework regularly and to arrive at school on time was a source of constant irritation to many of his peers. When he absented himself from school during the period that the Olympic Games were televised during the day, he aroused particular antagonism, since such action was interpreted as a selfish and inexcusable attempt to sabotage the form's high attendance record. Should the form be taken out of school on a visit to a local place of interest, Alf would turn up without a tie and his best clothes. Moreover, his tendency to bully and to begin a fight represented a direct assault on the non-aggressive values of the high status boys.

When we turn to the D stream, we find that the low status peer group deviant has a set of values which in the A stream would confer high status. Dick, a member of the low status clique, was a well-built and quiet boy. He tried to work hard in lessons, since he was anxious to obtain an apprenticeship when he left school. His behaviour in the classroom was exemplary. He liked his teachers and was liked by them. Dick shunned the fashion of jeans and long hair sported by the high status boys, but banned by the teachers. To the pupils of high status in 4D, Dick was a social outcast: he was ignored except when his actions represented a threat to the dominant norms. Thus when he worked hard during lessons, members of the high status clique would try to prevent him settling down to his work by hurling various missiles or by stealing his book to copy out the answers. He was forced into a passive acceptance of these attacks, since resistance would result in a concerted physical assault outside the classroom. In short, Dick and his few deviant friends persisted in their academic orientation and conformity to teacher expectations in spite of social rejection and constant threats and reprisal.

One of the most striking consequences of the differentiation of values and norms between streams was its effects on the social relationships between pupils in different streams. The boys in 4A and the boys in 4D perceive one another in highly negative and stereotyped terms. To the boys in 4A, the 4D boys are 'scruffy', 'thick', 'lazy' and 'bullies'.

'We never sort of mix with them.'
'They're Teddy boys. They think they're tough.'
'They all *look* dumb.'

To the boys in 4D, the 4A boys are 'posh', 'teachers' pets' and 'bigheads'.

'Just 'cos they're in a higher class than us they think they're *better* than us.'
'They're all daft. Toffee-noses. You know, snobs. They think they're clever.'
'They just don't let on to you. They just look at you, you know. Just 'cos they're in a higher class. I feel like smashing them sometimes.'

This may seem strange when we remember that these boys all live in the same small district, and often in the same street. Such a view fails to take into account the influence of the school on the attitudes of its pupils. Negative stereotypes develop because the formal organization inhibits interaction between streams and promotes the acquisition of values and norms which become incompatible between streams.

IV. A CASE STUDY: TEACHER—PUPIL RELATIONS

We know from Lumley and from other studies that within the school different sub-cultures with different value systems may arise. We also know, from the classic work of Lewin, Lippitt and White (1939) on 'democratic' and 'authoritarian' leaders, and the work of Anderson and Brewer (1946) on 'integrative' and 'dominative' teachers (discussed in Morris's chapter in this volume) that the behaviour of the teacher may exert a powerful influence on the behaviour of the pupils. Further, an increasing number of important contributions to the analysis of the teacher's conception of his own role are being made (e.g. Wilson, 1962; Musgrove and Taylor, 1965). Our concern at this point is to consider the *interrelation* of a number of such factors in their influence of teacher–pupil relations. We may represent the framework of teacher–pupil interaction as structured by the teacher's and the pupil's conceptions of their roles (see Figure 7). We may consider the pupil's conceptions of his own role as a function of (*a*) the formal organization of the school, (*b*) the teachers, (*c*) other pupils and (*d*) home background, personality, etc. So far we have been mainly concerned with the influence of other pupils on the development of values and norms which specify how a pupil is expected to behave in the classroom. The teacher's conception of his own role is seen to be structured by (*a*) the formal organization of the school, (*b*) administrators, the headteacher, other teachers and parents, (*c*) the individual's background, training and personality and (*d*) the pupils. The rest of this chapter seeks to examine the interrelations of these factors, especially the ways in which they influence the nature and growth of pupil orientations to school and teacher–pupil relations.

In the early stages of interactions, the participants go through a phase of what Thomas (1920) termed 'defining the situation'. That is, each person tries to define the interaction in terms of what role he wishes to enact, what self-identity he seeks to present, and how the other participants are expected to behave. Each participant – and we may regard the pupils of a class as one participant, since they tend to act as a 'team' – will struggle to define the situation until some sort of mutually acceptable compromise or 'working consensus' (Goffman, 1959) is achieved. The struggle to define the situation is basically a question of role definitions. Each participant seeks to impose his definition of his own role on the situation and also seeks to cast the other participant into a role which is complementary to, and consonant with, his own role. Thus the way in which the teacher defines the pupil role is a function of how the teacher conceives his own role in relation to the pupil. Similarly, what the pupil expects of the teacher depends on how he defines his own pupil role.

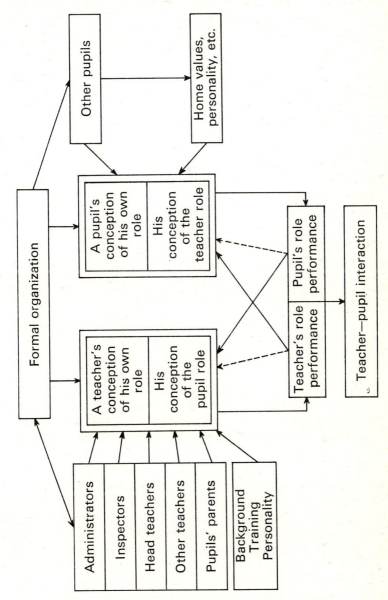

Fig. 1. The framework of teacher–pupil interaction

K

The 'working consensus' is reached through interaction. The teacher modifies his own role conception and performance on the basis of the feedback from the effects of his own behaviour and the actual behaviour of the pupils. Likewise, the pupils modify their role conception and performance when they observe the teacher's reactions to their own actual behaviour.

The process by which the participants reach an agreed definition of the situation is complicated by the fact that both the teacher's and the pupil's conceptions of their respective roles are influenced by certain 'significant others'. We have already seen that the pupil's conception of his role is subject to normative pressures from his peer group. In the case of the teacher, his conception of his classroom role is heavily weighted by the expectations of the administrators, the head-teacher, inspectors, other teachers and parents – all of whom are strictly external to teacher–pupil interaction. It is these general expectations which make certain problems common to almost all teachers, indeed which make it meaningful to speak of a *teacher role*. The individual teacher's background, training and personality allow him to improvise within these general expectations and so produce a unique and idio-syncratic performance of the role. Numerous attempts have been made to find concepts with which the teacher's classroom role may be analysed, (e.g. Sorenson, Husek and Yu, 1963; Soles, 1964; Solomon, Bezdek and Rosenberg, 1964), but I would like to suggest that almost all teachers have two basic problems. Firstly, he must establish his authority and maintain discipline and order. Secondly, he must make the pupils learn, and be seen to learn. (Both of these problems will prob-ably be less fundamental to the Infant, Junior or Remedial teacher.) The establishment of discipline and order is basic since most teachers regard discipline as a prerequisite to teaching the pupils at all. Even if the pupils learn without an imposed order and discipline, a teacher will tend to lose face before his colleagues and superiors, who frequently regard discipline maintenance as a more basic test of teacher compe-tence than getting the children to learn successfully. That the children should learn is specially important to superiors and parents, who reinforce the teacher's own tendency to rate his abilities as a teacher with the yardstick of the pupils' examination successes. In short, teachers are constrained by general expectations to perceive their classroom role in terms of making sure that the pupils both behave and learn.

This is not to say, of course, that all teacher behaviour is directed by his 'disciplinarian' and 'instructor' role prescriptions. In the process of teaching, these roles are modified in innumerable ways. Consider, for example, the 'dominative–integrative' dimension of Anderson and Brewer. The 'integrative' or 'child-centred' teacher may see the discipline problem as a matter of delegating authority, leadership and responsibility to the pupils, not of exerting his power and eliciting an unquestioned obedience. Such a teacher may regard the problem of instruction in terms of advising, providing resources and arousing intrinsic motivation. My argument is not, at this point, concerned with the various ways in which the teacher solves these problems of discipline and instruction, but with the fact that these problems of discipline and instruction do exist for teachers. I cannot conceive of a teacher who does not *in some form* have to consider how he is going to establish (and then maintain) order within his classroom, and then promote learning by the pupils. It would be wrong to supply additional connotations to the terms 'discipline' and 'instruction' as used in this discussion. A final reservation is that I am referring to interaction within the *classroom* situation. Interaction between teachers and pupils in other situations will not necessarily be structured by the same role demands.

It is of crucial importance that the teacher's conception of his own role as centrally concerned with the maintenance of discipline and the promotion of learning stems not so much from interaction with the persons to whom these roles are directed, namely the pupils, but from the formal organization and the 'significant others' mentioned earlier. Correlative to the teacher's conception of his own role is his conception of the pupil role. These are opposite sides to the same coin. In defining his own role the teacher also defines and prescribes certain roles for the pupils – roles which require acceptance of his own teacher role.

In this the teacher takes no account of the needs or expectations of the pupils, or their conceptions of the roles they wish to enact. And since the pupil's conception of his own role – and his allied conception of the teacher role – are influenced by his background and by his 'significant others', pupils as well as parents, there is a possibility of disagreement between teacher and pupil about the roles they wish to enact, and be enacted by the other, in classroom interaction. That some conflict does occur over the definition of the situation and the roles to be performed is clear from the 'testing out' to which many teachers are subjected on taking a class for the first time, especially when the class members have prior experience as a group.

This 'testing' process is rarely a direct assault on the teacher's definition. Usually the pupils' initial reaction to the new teacher is one of apparent passive acceptance. During this phase, the pupils attempt to assess the teacher's personality and the extent of the limits he will impose on the pupils' behaviour. They then begin, especially if they have grounds for the slightest suspicion that the teacher is 'weak', to make slight incursions on the teacher's definition which gradually increase in size. Once the teacher, by overlooking these early minor infractions, has allowed the pupils to undermine his definition of the situation, the reimposition of his definition on the pupils can be exceedingly difficult. For this reason, many experienced teachers regard the early establishment of their definition of the situation as being of fundamental importance, even though this may involve extreme and unjust measures which are alien to the teacher's philosophy. As one teacher, reported by Becker (1952), stated:

'You can't ever let them get the upper hand on you or you're through. So I start out tough. The first day I get a new class in, I let them know who is the boss ... You've got to start off tough, then you can ease up as you go along. If you start out easy-going, when you try to get tough, they just look at you and laugh.'

With the C and D streams, as we shall see, this attempt by the pupils to undermine the teacher's definition may persist over long periods. As one Lumley teacher reported:

'Either you murder them, or they'll murder you. Either you win or they win. And I'll tell you, mate, I'm the one that's going to win.'

This early battle over the establishment of discipline and order is illustrated in the research and fictional literature and need not be enlarged upon here (see Waugh, 1928; Braithwaite, 1959; Ellis, 1964).

The struggle over situation definition is limited by two further factors. Firstly, the pupil has little choice in the interaction. He cannot, as the teacher can, and as the participants in voluntary interactions can, withdraw and move to a new interaction which will bring greater rewards and satisfactions. Virtually his only alternative is to play truant – which is rarely more than a temporary solution. Secondly, the teacher–pupil relationship is asymmetrical. That is to say, there is a considerable power differential between the two participants. The teacher's power over the pupil resides in the traditional authority associated with his office, his adult status and his right to impose punishments. The teacher can enforce his definition of the situation on the pupils, whereas the pupils have neither the power nor the right to coerce the teacher into an acceptance of their definition. The teacher tends to present himself in such a way that the pupil is constrained to respond in accordance with the teacher's expectations. Thus the teacher usually gets what he wants; the pupils do so only when what they want is consonant with the teacher's wishes. Many techniques, less drastic than the use of punishment, are available to the teacher in the establishment of his definition. In order to promote and maintain discipline and order, he frequently creates formal and impersonal relations with the pupils, since these preserve a social distance between them. In this he is aided by the use of 'props' such as academic gowns, and by his pupils' use of the courtesy title 'sir'. He remains, in Parson's terms, affectively neutral. Two of the cardinal 'sins' of pupils are attempts to undermine the disciplinary role of the teacher. A threat to discipline, the teacher's right to issue orders and to have these orders obeyed without question, is 'disobedience'. A threat to the social distance with which he supports his authority is 'familiarity' or 'impertinence'.

In seeking to make the children learn, the teacher's second basic problem, an attempt is made to limit interaction to task-related or 'instrumental' areas, that is, the achievement of academic goals. Interaction in the classroom between teacher and pupil, and especially between pupil and pupil, is perceived by the teacher as legitimate only when it is essential or conducive to the promotion of learning. Purely socio-emotional or 'expressive' behaviour, that is, interaction which meets social, personal or emotional needs, is often perceived by the teacher as an irrelevant intrusion into the learning process, especially when this occurs between pupil and pupil. Expressive interaction is legitimate when initiated by the teacher, but illegitimate when initiated or extended by the pupil, for then it becomes intrusive and threatening. Thus only jokes made by the teacher are funny.

Much of the tension and conflict between teachers and pupils can be analysed in terms of the conflicting definitions of the situation, in terms of the incompatible projection of roles and self-identities and expectations of others. Children do want to influence the situation. Musgrove (1966) has shown that children feel that many of their expressive needs are unsatisfied by life in school. Pupils feel restricted in their desires to have freedom to put their own point of view, to have greater autonomy and self-direction, to be treated as individuals.

Let us consider the situation at Lumley School. We shall confine

K*

our discussion to a comparison of teacher–pupil relations in the fourth year A stream with those of the fourth year D stream. The pupils' perceptions of their teachers can be estimated from their responses to several items of a sentence completion test. One of the items was 'Teachers are . . .' The responses were coded as positive, negative or neutral. Fifty per cent of the A stream's responses were positive – the teacher is seen as kind and helpful – whereas only 5 per cent of the D steam's responses fell into the positive category. Seven per cent of the A stream's responses betrayed negative perceptions of the teacher – the teachers are criticized as strict, demanding, boring, unpleasant – but 45 per cent of the D stream's responses were coded as negative.

Other measures of this disjunction between streams in the perception of teachers are available (see Table 1). Seventy per cent of 4A, but only 32 per cent of 4D, express approval of a teacher who 'keeps the class quiet and under control' and there is a similar reaction to the questionnaire item concerning approval of teachers who punish boys who misbehave during lessons. Sixty-four per cent of the 4D boys disapprove of a teacher who makes the boys work hard, but the corresponding figure for the A stream is 10 per cent.

TABLE 1. *Pupils' perceptions of teachers*

Dimension	% approval	
	A stream	D stream
1. Pupil acceptance of the teacher's definition of the teacher's instructional role.		
– Teachers who make the boys work hard	57	27
2. Pupil acceptance of the teacher's definition of the teacher's disciplinary role.		
– Teachers who punish 'messers'	73	36
– Teachers who keep the class quiet and under control	70	32
3. Pupil acceptance of the teacher's definition of the pupil's instructional role.		
– Boys who get on with their work	93	45
– Boys who pay attention in class	82	36
– Boys who do not copy	77	36

4. Pupil acceptance of the teacher's definition
   of the pupil's disciplinary role.
   – Boys who obey the teachers   83   41
   – Boys who are not cheeky to the teachers   87   45

These figures demonstrate that the boys in the A stream accept the teacher's definition of the teacher's role concerning the maintenance of discipline and the promotion of learning, whereas the boys in the D stream reject the role that the teacher is seeking to perform. In other words, in the A stream there is a general consensus between the teacher and his pupils about the legitimacy of the teacher's role, but in the D stream it is a low status minority who achieve consensus with the teacher.

The other side of this coin is the extent of the pupils' acceptance of the teacher's definition of the pupil role. Once again we find high teacher–pupil consensus in the A stream. Almost all these pupils express approval, on questionnaire items, of boys who work hard in lessons, of boys who pay attention in class, of boys who obey the teacher, of boys who are not insolent to the teachers. On every one of these items it is a minority in the D stream who approve of such teacher-orientated pupil behaviour. Further, the A stream boys like their teachers and perceive themselves to be liked by their teachers. In the D stream most of the boys dislike their teachers and perceive themselves as rejected by the teachers.

In short, teacher–pupil relationships in the A and D streams are consonant with the peer group normative structure. The A stream boys accept the teacher's conception of both the teacher and the pupil role. In the D stream the predominant orientation is towards a rejection of the teacher's attempt to define the situation both in terms of how the teacher and how the pupil should behave.

The profound effects of congruent or incongruent attempts to define the situation on teacher–pupil relations in the classroom can be examined at a deeper level if we introduce Goffman's (1961) concept of *role distance*. By this term Goffman wishes to consider the fact that in actual performance of a role many actors seem to express an apparent separation or detachment from the role as determined by the expectations of others. That is, the actor adheres less strictly to the role prescriptions and introduces idiosyncratic elements which are irrelevant to the role. The new teacher, inexperienced in enacting his role, tends to restrict his performance to behaviour which is demanded by the role prescriptions (McIntyre, Morrison and Sutherland, 1966). With greater experience in playing the role, the teacher acquires greater competence and confidence in role performance, and is thus able to express role distance.

With the A stream the teacher is able to show role distance, because there is a basic consensus between teacher and pupils about the roles they expect one another to play.[1] As the teacher's discipline and teaching roles are not under threat, he is able to come out-of-role and transcend his role and become a *person* not just a *teacher*. Indeed, one A stream pupil stated that he liked his teachers because they were 'more like ordinary men'. Of course, the consensus in the A stream is not perfect. From time to time the pupils will try to assert a definition of the situation which perhaps provides greater satisfaction of their expressive needs. But since the general consensus is high, the teacher can restore his definition of the situation without returning to his basic role prescriptions or resorting to his right to apply punishments. Discipline can be restored by a joking invocation of the sanction. Rather than threatening the offenders with punishment, he can restructure the situation with a threat in the form of a joke. 'If you keep chatting, I'll have to arrange a meeting between my cane and your bottom, won't I, Tommy?' In making such a statement, the threat is masked and softened by use of the pupil's Christian name and by phrasing in terms of an appeal-question. We must note that in situations where the teacher is able to show role distance, it tends to be legitimate for the pupils to express role distance as well. As the teacher can restructure the definition with ease, he tends to grant the pupils greater autonomy and permit greater familiarity with the teacher.

In the D stream, where only a minority accepts the teacher's definition of the situation, consensus is low. The majority of the pupils are in a constant competitive struggle with the teacher. The teacher is thus unable to express role distance, since every lesson becomes a battle in which the teacher seeks to assert his basic definition. This persistent threat to his definition leads the teacher to a strict adherence to his basic disciplinary and teaching role prescriptions. To express role distance would be to exacerbate the threat, since it would imply that his demands for order and work are not to be taken seriously. A teacher with such a class may sum up his experience in such terms as 'You can't afford to give an inch to that lot.'

---

[1] The teacher's achievement of role distance is a product of teacher–pupil consensus, not of stream level.

The congruence of the definitions of teachers and pupils in the A stream is crucial to our understanding of the teacher–pupil relations in such a situation. The teacher wants the pupils to learn; the pupils want to be taught by the teacher. The teacher's basic power, in the sense of his potential ability to influence the pupils, thus consists of *reward* power (French and Raven, 1959) that is, his ability to mediate academic rewards to the pupils. The pupils conform to the teacher's demands, not simply because their values tend to be congruent, but because it is only through conformity that they can achieve their goals. Once this consensus between teacher and pupils has been attained – it is not necessarily a matter of predetermined values – the teacher's power is increased. The pupils' academic progress depends on the teacher's superior knowledge (expert power); the pupils grant the teacher the right to prescribe behaviour for them (legitimate power); the pupils grow to like the teacher and identify with him (referent power). It is because to such pupils that the teacher possesses reward, expert, legitimate and referent power that both participants can achieve role distance.

In the D stream the teacher has no reward power: the pupils do not perceive him as mediating rewards to them. Rather, the teacher's power is *coercive*, that is, the pupils perceive him as mediating punishments to them. When the pupils do accept the teacher's definition, it is merely compliance – a behavioural acceptance without private or 'real' agreement. Conformity can be elicited only under fear of the teacher's ability to administer punishments, because conformity is not, as in the A stream, of goal-attainment value to the pupils. Further, conformity will persist only when the pupils are under teacher surveillance. The teacher is thus never perceived as possessing legitimate or referent power, and is restrained from showing role distance. For the teacher to be a 'nice man' is simply to encourage the pupils to 'take advantage'. Of course, the pupils do express a form of role distance, but in this case it is a genuine disaffection or alienation from the pupil role.

Interaction reinforces these effects. In the A stream the pupils with high informal status tend to be those who are highly conformist to the teacher's expectations. Those who deviate from the teacher's expectations also deviate from peer group norms. Sanctions invoked by the teacher and the peer group tend to be mutually supportive. Members of this form are simultaneously pressured on two levels to an acceptance of the teacher's definition. When the teacher rewards the pupils for their conformity to his expectations, he confirms and consolidates peer group values and norms as well as his own power. When he punishes pupils

who reject his definition, he reinforces their deviance from the peer group. A non-conformist pupil in the A stream must be prepared to be isolated from both teacher and most of his peers.

In the D stream, the pupils with high informal status tend to be non-conformist to teacher expectations. Teacher and peer group rewards are mutually exclusive and competing systems. The pupils are 'cross-pressured'. To accept the teacher's definition is to incur peer group disapproval and rejection. Those pupils who are concerned to increase or maintain prestige in the peer group must openly exhibit their rejection of teacher expectations. When, therefore, the D stream teacher rewards the low status pupil for his conformity to teacher expectations, he reinforces the pupil's deviance from the peer group. When he punishes the high status boy for his rejection of the teacher definition, he emphasizes the coercive nature of his own power and the pupil's high status in the peer group.

When considered in this light, the allocation of teachers to streams is not simply a matter of teaching children of differing abilities. In many schools, as in Lumley, teachers tend to be allocated on the basis of qualifications and disciplinary competence to either higher or lower streams for all or most of their teaching duties. A person whose teaching is confined entirely or largely to upper streams achieves role distance from the consensus about the definition of the situation which exists between himself and the pupils. This role distance allows the teacher to be less bound by the basic role requirements, with the result that he is able to express himself as a *person*, not just as a role-performer. Through these personal satisfactions, such a teacher becomes increasingly attached to the role, in the sense that the role is attractive to him and the performance of the role is supportive of his self-identity. When such a teacher takes the low streams, he falls back on his basic role requirements, since he needs to enforce his definition of adequate discipline and instruction. The resistance of these low stream pupils to his definition reduces the personal satisfactions he derives from the interaction, with the result that he tends to complain about the pupils' behaviour and attitudes, and avoids contact if possible. Thus he tends to resist any attempt to increase the proportion of his teaching load given to low streams, not only because of the implied insult to his teaching competence, but also because of the diminished personal satisfactions.

The teacher at Lumley who is assigned entirely or primarily to low streams, where a low consensus between teacher and pupil exists, is faced with a difficult problem of adjustment, especially if he has been allocated to low streams because his discipline is already weak. Because of the low consensus, he is restricted to a performance of his basic role requirements. Life becomes an uphill struggle to establish discipline. The battle to maintain order, to promote learning, and to enforce his definition of the situation in numerous small ways, may be so demanding, exhausting and demoralizing that he becomes less attached to, and less personally involved in, his role. As performance of the role offers so few rewards, the role ceases to be a medium for self-expression, but acquires a routine, custodial nature. Such a teacher's alienation from his role expresses itself in many ways. He begins to compromise with the pupils over the definition of the situation. Instead of trying to enforce his definition according to the basic role requirements, he will lower his level of acceptability of both teacher and pupil role performance. That is to say, he will establish new levels of adequate performance which will reduce the fatigue resulting from adherence to his basic role prescriptions. He is able to justify these lowered standards, both to himself and to his colleagues, with the statement, 'These are low stream boys: you can't expect much from them.' The teacher thus accepts as normal a level of noise and indiscipline which would be intolerable to the high stream teacher. Further, because of the great effort needed to persuade the pupils to learn, he tends to let each individual work at his own rate and makes little attempt to ascertain the nature and rate of either individual or class progress. He knows that copying is prevalent, but he punishes such behaviour only when it becomes blatantly obvious. In all this he is aided and abetted by the fact that the pupils are not entered for external examinations, which eliminates the danger of any check on academic standards. In short, the teacher reduces his standards of behaviour and academic performance and expects little. The pupils live up to these expectations and become progressively indisciplined and retarded.

V. THE PROCESS OF SUB-CULTURAL FORMATION

So far we have considered the differentiation of values, norms and attitudes among the fourth-year pupils at Lumley School and also some aspects of teacher–pupil relations in different streams. How is it that two opposing sub-cultures, the academic and the anti-academic, arise within this school? In fact, there is no evidence of normative differentiation among the second-year boys at Lumley: the divergence of pupil values seems to take place during the third and fourth years. It is a *process* to which numerous factors contribute.

One obvious factor (see Diagram on p. 257) may be the home background of the pupils. It is indeed true that upper stream pupils come from smaller families than do lower stream pupils. Further, A and B stream boys perceive their parents as showing greater social ambition for them, more concern over academic attainment, and greater control over their activities. As we shall see, the formal organization tends to facilitate differentiation by concentrating boys with similar pre-disposing home values into the same stream. As indicated in Table 1 (page 262) the in-school and environmental factors interact and reinforce one another.

Perhaps one of the most important, but least recognized, of such factors is the way in which the teachers perceive their pupils. The teacher's perception of his pupils is conditioned by two facts. Firstly, the interaction between the teacher and the pupil is largely task-related and confined to the classroom situation. Secondly, the reaction of the teacher to the pupil is dependent upon the extent of the pupil's acceptance of the teacher's definition of the situation. The teacher thus tends to see the child as a *pupil*, not as a whole person with individual needs, motives and feelings. The teacher, in a word, will tend to evaluate the child in terms of the appropriateness of his behaviour to the teaching situation.

In taking a class of pupils for the first time a teacher divides the pupils into three categories (Bruner, Goodnow and Austin, 1956): the 'good' whose behaviour strongly conform to his expectations; the 'bad' whose behaviour strongly deviates from his expectations; and a residual, intermediate category whose behaviour is unknown or at neither extreme. It is the pupils in the last category whose names the teacher learns last. The teacher's categorization is thus based upon the degree of the child's expressed support for the teacher's basic role problems of control and instruction (see Ausubel, Schiff and Zeleny, 1954; Hallworth, 1961; Williams and Knecht, 1962; Lambert, 1963). The 'good' have ability, work hard and behave well. The 'bad' show no industry and tend to be ill-mannered, disobedient and disruptive during lessons. As the child passes through the school he tends to settle in the eyes of the teachers, into one of these categories. He acquires a 'reputation'. Informal gossip about the pupils among the teachers – and such gossip forms a substantial proportion of teacher–teacher interaction – may lead a teacher to categorize a child prior to actually teaching him. This structuring of future interaction on a preconceived basis may lead the teacher to expect certain kinds of behaviour from a pupil and it may also lead the pupil to a *fulfilling* of these expectations.

More central to the process of normative differentiation is the fact that the categorization also extends to streams. High streams are perceived to consist mainly of 'good' pupils, and the low streams mainly of 'bad' pupils. At Lumley the teachers thus tended to favour the boys from high streams in many ways, but most obviously in the selection of prefects, sports teams and in eligibility for school visits and holidays. They come to *expect* certain forms of behaviour from certain streams. The teachers may thus aggravate incipient normative differentiation. We cannot be surprised if the pupils increasingly conform to these expectations, in the manner of a self-fulfilling prophecy, so that the low streams get 'worse' by means of a vicious circle effect and the high streams get 'better' by means of a virtuous circle effect.

The formal organization also contributes to the process of normative differentiation. The value systems associated with high and low streams can become increasingly concentrated over the years by means of the school's 'promotion' and 'demotion' system. At the end of each term, boys in the highest positions in the form's examinations are promoted to a higher stream, and the boys in the lowest positions are demoted to a lower stream. In time the higher streams thus acquire boys whose orientations to the goals of the school and the expectations of the teachers are positive. In the low streams congregate the boys with poor attainment and anti-academic attitudes. Because interaction among the boys is confined by the formal organization to members of the same stream, the concentration of boys with similar values, in each strengthens their alienation from others.

'I wouldn't go in [a high stream]. I'd stay off [school]. I don't like them from what I've heard of it. All my mates would call me snobby and that.'

The teachers' assumption that the higher streams contain the most able pupils is thus false, for low stream pupils with a fairly high measured IQ depress their examination performance in order to avoid promotion. The teachers tend to regard attainment and orientation as synonymous with ability.

The pupils in the lower streams are faced with acute problems. In terms of the dominant values of our society they are failures, since they stand at the bottom of the educational and achievement ladder.

These boys are excluded from any sort of external examination, so they possess none of the formal qualifications which in our society are a passport to skilled jobs with higher pay and social prestige. Whilst in the first two years at the Secondary School membership of a low stream may not be perceived as involving restrictions on occupational choice, by the fourth year, when the question of their future occupation becomes important, such boys are forced to accept that the dice are loaded against them. They must face the fact that most of the skilled occupations are closed to them, since entry to an apprenticeship requires qualifications or good references from the headteacher – neither of which they possess. They are thus finally compelled to a realistic appraisal of their futures and the renunciation of their financial and occupational aspirations.

From this point of view their contempt for the school's emphasis on academic achievement is understandable, for their rewards for academic efforts are minimal. Even within the school they must accept a lack of status in the eyes of the teachers. They are considered the academic failures and are not even given the special attention accorded to the 'backward' E stream boys. They are frequently taught by the least qualified and the least competent of the teachers, since the 'best' teachers are allocated to the pupils of academic promise in the higher streams. This lack of status is enhanced by the tendency of the teachers to favour the high stream pupils in numerous ways, as we have already noted.

The solution of many of the pupils in low streams at Lumley is to reject the pupil role and turn to a delinquent orientation. They initiate a system of values which inverts those of the teachers, school and society. High status becomes a matter of embracing and exhibiting anti-academic, anti-teacher and anti-social values. They aspire to roles beyond those of the schoolboy, namely those of the adult male. They make a show of smoking and drinking; they aggressively assert their independence and resent any form of control or supervision; they seek out clubs and activities which grant them autonomy, adult status and prestige in their own group.

We are all – teachers, researchers and the general public – often only too willing to blame the failures of our educational system on factors external to the school: bad heredity, defective personality, adverse home conditions. All of these may be contributory factors, as ample research evidence in recent years has indicated. Yet there is a real danger that we may use the results of psychological and sociological research on the determinants of scholastic attainment and school adjustment as a defence against the examination of in-school processes. In so doing, we underestimate the influence and strength of the factors which have been central to our analysis of Lumley School: the effects of the formal organization of the school, the effects of teacher–pupil perception and interaction; the effects of peer group values and pressures. Nor is it enough to imagine that the problems of low stream pupils will be solved simply by curriculum development or the provision of school counsellors or finer buildings and more adequate aids and facilities. The production of pupils with anti-academic and anti-social values may well be a permanent price we shall have to pay for schools with an academic elite and for a society in which occupational prestige and economic gain depend on academic ability and achievement. Whilst it may not be within our grasp to cure our social and educational ailments, I would suggest that until we divert more of our research resources into a deeper investigation of the social system of our schools, and until we can convince our teachers and educationists of the crucial importance and often unrecognized effects of social relations and social processes within the school, our attempts to improve the education of our children will constantly fall short.

REFERENCES

ANDERSON, H. H., and BREWER, H. M. (1945, 1946). Studies in teachers' classroom personalities. *Applied Psychol. Monogr.* **6, 8** *and* **11**.

AUSUBEL, D. P., SCHIFF, H. M., and ZELENY, M. P. (1954). Validity of teachers' ratings of adolescents' adjustment and aspirations. *J. Educ. Psychol.* **45,** 394–405.

BECKER, H. S. (1952). Social class variations in the teacher-pupil relationship. *J. Educ. Sociol.* **25,** 451–465.

BLAU, P. M., and SCOTT, W. R. (1963). *Formal Organizations.* London: Routledge and Kegan Paul.

BLYTH, W. A. L. (1960). The sociometric study of children's groups in English schools. *Brit. J. Educ. Stud.* **8,** 127–147.

BRAITHWAITE, E. R. (1959). *To Sir With Love.* London: Bodley Head.

BRUNER, J. S., GOODNOW, J. J., and AUSTIN, G. A. (1956). *A Study of Thinking.* New York: John Wiley.

BUSH, R. N. (1954). *The Teacher-Pupil Relationship.* New York: Prentice-Hall.

COLEMAN, J. A. (1961). *The Adolescent Society.* Glencoe, Ill.: The Free Press.

ELLIS, H. F. (1964). *A. J. Wentworth, B.A.* Harmondsworth: Penguin Books.

FRENCH, J. R. P., and RAVEN, B. H. (1959). The bases of social power. In Cartwright, D. (ed.). *Studies in Social Power.* Michigan: Ann Arbor, University of Michigan. Reprinted in Cartwright, D., and Zander, A. (1960). *Group Dynamics: Research and Theory.* London: Tavistock Publications.

GOFFMAN, E. (1959). *The Presentation of Self in Everyday Life.* New York: Doubleday Anchor Books.

GOFFMAN, E. (1961). *Encounters.* Indianapolis, Ind.: Bobbs-Merrill.

GORDON, C. W. (1957). *The Social System of the High School.* Glencoe, Ill.: The Free Press.

HALLWORTH, H. J. (1953). Sociometric relationships among Grammar school boys and girls between the ages of 11 and 16 years. *Sociometry.* **16**, 39–70.

HALLWORTH, H. J. (1961). Teacher's personality ratings of High School pupils. *J. Educ. Psychol.* **52**, 297–302.

HARGREAVES, D. H. (1967). *Social Relations in a Secondary School.* London: Routledge and Kegan Paul.

HOLLINGSHEAD, A. B. (1942). *Elmstown's Youth.* New York: John Wiley.

LAMBERT, P. (1963). The 'Successful' Child: some implications of teacher stereo-typing. *J. Educ. Psychol.* **56**, 551–553.

LEWIN, K., LIPPITT, R., and WHITE, R. K. (1939). Patterns of aggressive behaviour in experimentally created social climates. *J. Soc. Psychol.* **10**, 271–299.

MCINTYRE, D., MORRISON, A., and SUTHERLAND, J. (1966). Social and educational variables relating to teachers' assessments of primary school children. *Brit. J. Educ. Psychol.* **36**, 272–279.

MORENO, J. L. (1934). *Who Shall Survive?* Washington D.C.: Nervous and Mental Diseases Publishing Company.

MORENO, J. L. (ed.). (1960). *The Sociometry Reader.* Glencoe, Ill.: The Free Press.

MUSGROVE, F., and TAYLOR, P. H. (1965). Teachers' and parents' conception of the teacher's role. *Brit. J. Educ. Psychol.* **35**, 171–178.

MUSGROVE, F., and TAYLOR, P. H. (1966). The social needs and satisfactions of some young people. *Brit. J. Educ. Psychol.* **36**, 137–149.

NEWCOMB, T. M. (1943). *Personality and Social Change.* New York: Dryden Press.

ROETHLISBERGER, F. J., and DICKSON, W. J. (1939). *Management and the Worker.* Cambridge, Mass: Harvard Univ. Press.

SOLES, S. (1965). Teacher role expectations and the internal organization of secondary schools. *J. Educ. Psychol.* **57**, 227–235.

SOLOMON, D., BEZDEK, W., and ROSEBERG, L. (1964). Dimensions of teacher behaviour. *J. Experimental Educ.* **33**, 23–33.

SORENSON, A. G., JUSEK, T. R., and YU, C. (1963). Divergent conceptions of the teacher role: an approach to the measurement of teacher effectiveness. *J. Educ. Psychol.* **45**, 287–294.

THOMAS, W. I. (1920). *The Unadjusted Girl.* Little, Brown & Co.

WALLER, W. (1932). *The Sociology of Teaching* (1932). New York: John Wiley. (Reprinted 1965, Science Editions.)

WAUGH, E. (1937). *Decline and Fall* (1928). Harmondsworth: Penguin Books.

WHYTE, W. F. (1943). *Street Corner Society.* Chicago: Chicago Univ. Press.

WILLIAMS, J. R., and KNECHT, W. W. (1962). Teacher's ratings of High School Students on 'likeability' and their relation to measures of ability and achievement. *J. Educ. Res.* **56**, 152–159.

WILSON, B. (1962). The teacher's role: a sociological analysis. *Brit. J. Sociol.* **13**, 15–32.

8

Social Contexts of Development and Learning

W. A. L. BLYTH

I. INTRODUCTION

THIS final chapter takes the form of an essay on the social contexts of development and learning, written from a sociological point of view. It is intended to take a more general view than the chapter by Hargreaves, which focuses on a single school, and a more institutional standpoint than the chapter by Morris, which stays close to individual attitudes and behaviour.

Space does not permit an adequate introduction to the sociology of education, still less a survey of the technical literature in this field.[1] The attempt, then, is solely to extend this section of the book into the sociological range of considerations. Before beginning on this task, it might be appropriate to emphasize the similarities, rather than the differences between the perspectives taken by the main specialist disciplines in education and child development.

When considering these topics, a sociologist covers much of the same ground as a psychologist. In the social sciences, as in other branches of human knowledge, it is not entirely appropriate to speak of boundaries between subjects, but rather of perspectives, which result in the concentration of some problems and some methods of study in the foreground of one academic discipline while they occupy a more peripheral position in another. For example, when a sociologist looks at children learning in a classroom, he is likely to think first of the significance of this process in the school viewed as a social institution, or in society as a whole. A psychologist might be more prone to think of individual differences in rates of learning, interests and abilities. A social psycho-

[1] See, for example, Ottaway (1965); Halsey, Floud and Anderson (1961); Musgrave (1965); Swift (forthcoming).

274

logist would be trying to take a point of view between those of the psychologist and the sociologist, giving due weight to individuality but recognizing the play of social variables in learning. All of them would be studying the same scene, and interested in other perspectives; but each would concentrate on a different aspect. The distinctive sociological aspect is the study of social institutions, and of the inter- action between institutions in society.

The term *institution*, as used by many sociologists, deserves some clarification. It does not necessarily mean something founded or instituted in any explicit sense. Rather, it refers to all the relatively enduring, socially sanctioned features of collective behaviour within a society. These range from practices such as Bonfire Night to basic features of social organization such as monogamous marriage, but include many with a legal basis, such as County Councils. One thing they all have in common: they can be thought of without reference to particular individuals or groups. One category of institution can be designated as education, and within this category, the most significant institution is the school.

Sociologists do more than identify and classify social institutions. They also analyse and interpret them. Thus, a classroom in a school represents one part of the 'formal' structure of the institution, a part whose function in relation to the whole can be defined in a generally agreed way. At the same time, it is a scene of social interaction, in- volving social processes some of which are recognized as normal func- tions of a school, such as the learning of skills and cognitive data and socially-approved behaviour, and some of which are less immediately apparent such as the inculcation of general social values and the development of individual personalities. Finally, it can be a scene of social change. Over the weeks and months, children and teachers alter in response to their innate equipment, their mutual interactions and their response to the world beyond.

All these matters are the concern of psychologists also, but the main interest of sociologists is in the social institutions and pro- cesses themselves, rather than in their impact on individuals. The difference between the two disciplines is, as was previously emphasized, essentially one of perspectives.

Within institutions and their subdivisions, particular importance attaches to the *roles* played by individuals and groups (as indicated in Chapters 6 and 7; see also Banton, 1965). The distinction between a person and a role is an important one. A famous historical cartoon shows this in an amusing fashion. Louis XIV of France, *le grand monarque*, was in fact a little man, and the first of three sketches shows him as Nature made him (or almost): LUDOVICUS. The second portrays the vacant trappings of his resplendent office: REX. The third suggests the synthesis of the little man in the big office, as his leading subjects encountered him, *le roi soleil;* LUDOVICUS REX. The Louis XIV of history, like the rest of us, was a person fulfilling or discharging a role. Sociologists would say that Louis was the *incumbent* of that particular kingly role.

Social institutions imply roles. This can be illustrated from an educational context outside the classroom, namely the football field. A football team does not just consist of eleven unassorted players, as 7-year-olds have to realize. It requires that the members should be distributed in a particular way – a goalkeeper, two backs and so on. There are eleven roles, each of which may be discharged with varying degrees of orthodoxy and of success. Even if he scores a goal, a back does not become a forward: his role remains defined. Roles, too, imply a correlative *status*. For example, one of the eleven players in a football team is, in addition to his positional role, captain, and in that capacity has the right to wield authority and the obligation to bear responsibility. Military hierarchies illustrate this relation between role and status with particular clarity. In addition, roles may carry informal status, for example when small boys all want to be centre-forward and, as football nowadays shows, they may change.

Previous chapters have shown how these concepts of role and status can be useful when considering the functioning of educational institutions. In the U.S.A., and to some extent in this country also, the roles of teachers have been subjected to systematic analysis, and some attention has also been paid to roles and status within families (e.g. Parsons and Bales, 1956; Brim, 1957; Bott, 1955) and other institutional contexts of child development.

American sociologists such as Linton (1936) and Parsons (1952) have evolved elaborate classifications of role and status, and some of their terminology has passed into general currency. This is particularly true of the distinction between *ascribed* and *achieved* roles, the differentiation between *specific* and *diffuse* roles, and the contrast between emotionally charged and emotionally neutral roles (in Parsons' terminology, between 'affectivity' and 'affective neutrality'). Each of these pairs or terms represents opposite poles of a continuum or dimension on which a role can be classified and, since they help to illuminate the

ways in which roles are important in children's learning and development, each merits a brief explanation.

Ascribed roles are those to which we are born. An heir to a throne is
a clear instance of this, but almost everyone has some ascribed roles to
play: boy, son, brother, pupil, citizen and so forth. We cannot with
impunity contract out of these, or their correlative status-positions. But
we can, and almost must, add to these a series of relatively achieved
roles which arise from the sequences of response which we make in
particular social situations. The boy who appears brave, or the girl
who appears kind, two or three times, soon acquires a reputation for
consistency of behaviour which is exaggerated and, by affecting other
people's expectations, facilitates further behaviour of the same kind and
consequently the 'achievement' of a new role. Of course, other patterns
of role-achievement may also have less desirable results. On a more
sophisticated level, adults continue to achieve new roles throughout
life.

The second role-distinction, the dimension from specific to diffuse,
may be less familiar but is easy to understand. A specific role is closely
defined. For example, a policeman on point duty has a highly specific
role to discharge. However intricate and exhausting his ceaseless gestures may be, he does exactly what is expected of him, within agreed
and clearly delineated limits. If he were to wink at a girl pedestrian, or
swear at a driver, or experiment with new signals invented by himself,
that would be incompatible with the specific role of the wonderful
English policeman. By contrast, a mother has an endless, bewildering
and demanding series of functions to fulfil. Her work is never done,
and she never knows, in verbally definable terms, whether she has done
any of it completely. The policeman's role is highly specific; hers is
highly diffuse.

A third distinction may also be made, as already indicated, between
emotionally-charged and emotionally-neutral roles, that is, between
those involving close personal contact and those associated with
generally impersonal behaviour. The policeman and the mother exem-
plify this contrast also. In fact, specific roles tend to be emotionally
neutral, and diffuse roles tend to be emotionally charged. But that is
not always the case. For example, a nurse in a children's hospital has to
confine herself to quite specific roles, carefully hedged about by hospital
regulations; but the expectation is that she will discharge them with
warmth and understanding.

It is through role-playing, with its various characteristics, that a role-incumbent makes a series of adjustments to his social environment. In some instances of collective behaviour, the same can be true of groups. By accurate perception of *role-expectations*, individuals and groups come to apply their social learning effectively, and thus to achieve and define their membership within a society. This is the way in which a sociologist might elaborate an expression often used by psychologists and educators: adjustment to environment.

But what is *environment*? This too requires some comment. To psychologists, it tends to mean the total external pressures brought to bear on an individual: everything 'out there', to adapt the Bishop of Woolwich's phrase. This leads sometimes to the habit of thinking of the individual and the environment as two mutually exclusive entities. On the other hand, a sociologist is likely to emphasize that the environment is not an entity at all, but a whole series of interacting influences of various kinds and on various levels. Moreover, he is liable to add that the individual is really a part of the environment, or rather that a symbiosis of individual-in-environment, delineated through the individual's role-structure, is a more basic social fact than the individual considered in isolation. There is nothing logically incompatible between these points of view, although they have in practice given rise to quite important and lively controversies (see, for example, the discussion in Wiseman, 1964). More fruitfully, they have led to an increasing readiness to consider the dimensions of environment as well as those of personality, and to realize that these include geographical, ecological and social elements. A child's development is largely influenced by the social roles which he learns and, although these may be affected by his genetic equipment and its consequences for his skeletal, glandular and cerebral development, they are also largely an outcome of his social relations with his family and the associates whom he meets in his neighbourhood, his school and his church, and they may even be modified by the physical configuration of the world in which he grows up.

To summarize: a sociologist considers child development as the interaction, largely through role-learning, of individual children with their spatial and social environments, the latter being principally defined in terms of personal relations and social institutions. These spatial and social environments open out as a series of contexts, a series both in space, like radiating ripples in a pond, and in time, for the growing child gradually increases the range of his social experience until he participates in them all. They can be epitomized in a diagram:

SOCIAL
(personal and institutional)

SPATIAL
(physical)

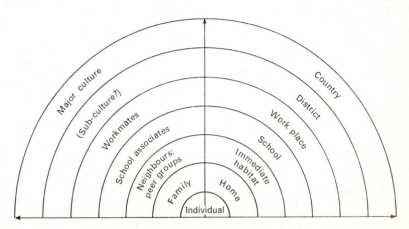

Fig. 1. The Dimensions of Children's Environment

These contexts are not, of course, dimensions in the statistical sense, but levels of generality, ranging from the most immediate, where personal relations bulk biggest, to the most general, where sociology merges into cultural anthropology. Viewed from the individual's point of view, the horizon gradually expands, without the foreground ceasing to be important, as on a misty morning when the sun begins to break through. Only one or two of these contexts are non-simultaneous; and even these are tending to merge to some extent, for example, in the linkage between school and work (see the recommendations of the Newsom Report, 1963). So the contexts are not discrete, but it will be convenient in practice to consider them in turn, except for the work situation, which really lies outside the scope of this book and is included in the diagram only in order to complete the sequence.

II. INFLUENCES OF FAMILY AND HOME ON DEVELOPMENT AND LEARNING

The experience of belonging to a family is primarily a psychological one, for it is there that an individual's personality is in one sense constructed. Yet a family is also a social institution, and in many ways it has a social significance which could escape psychologists. For one thing, the very concept of adult roles in society is first learned in the family context. The first roles to be learned are relatively diffuse, ascriptive and emotionally charged, that is, they are bound up with the whole cognitive and emotional complexity of family living, into which children are expected to fit according to the generalized expectations of their society. Incidentally, these roles are also prominent in relatively simple adult societies, for the differentiation of roles, as of most other cognitive and social phenomena, is characteristic both of increasing maturity in individuals and of increasing complexity in societies.

Male and female roles are in fact learned differently. 'Daddy' is a perceived and known individual, but soon all men are 'daddies', that is, the adult male role is quite soon differentiated from the individual person. But 'Mummy' has a unique significance for girls and boys alike, and so the learning of the adult female role is a more complicated process, one in which the nursery or infant teacher is well qualified to play a leading part, encouraging the separation of role from person here also, though at a rather later stage, as Parsons suggests (in Halsey *et al.*, 1961). If we substitute 'Dad' and 'Mum', the sociological processes remain similar, for this is something almost unrelated to social background, though the actual mechanisms by which it is carried out vary considerably within, and still more between, societies.

In addition to these generalized adult roles, children learn within families the role and status of *child*. This is itself in some ways a product of modern industrial society. St Paul doubtless 'thought as a child' (I Cor. xiii, 11), but he was not classified as a child in the same inclusive fashion as children today, and would not experience the same long, institutionalized immunity from work, or the combination of dominance and indulgence that accompanies it. But children today have none the less to learn to be children, as distinct from egocentric babies, and this they do differently according to whether their family is large or small, and if it is large, according to the place which they occupy in the 'sibling series'. Nisbet (in Halsey *et al.*, 1961) has shown how this may affect measured intelligence, which tends to be lower in large families, while Lees and Stewart (1957) though they only studied a fairly small population, put forward a more systematic consideration of the effect of family position on achievement. They suggested that, for example, 'intermediate' children were likely to be more dependent than eldest or youngest children on the company of other children in the family, and therefore also less open to adult verbal influences. Because of this, they may perform rather less well in tests of formal education.[1] However tentative these comments may be, they do serve to indicate the ways in which family circumstances may affect children's role-learning, and the educational consequences which this may have.

Children also learn to be girls or boys, that is, they are 'sex-typed'. Natural endowment does, of course, predispose children broadly towards sex-appropriate behaviour, but in detail much has to be learned in any specific society, and it is in the family, from parents and siblings, that the first determining influences are brought to bear. Sex-roles are usually accepted readily, and with increasing enthusiasm as children grow older.

The family does more than provide an arena within which generalized role-learning develops. In addition, each family is a small-scale social institution of its own, with its own structure of roles and status, and a range of social and emotional experience which becomes the prototype of all that follows, and which continues to influence what follows in a remarkably persistent way. The experience of being overshadowed by a brilliant elder sister, or of being an only child prematurely sophisticated in adult conversation, or of being rather overlooked within a large family unit, can have life-long consequences. At the same time, however, this family interaction is the first process in which children evolve their own achieved roles, as tomboy, bookworm, Stoic or clown, with all the implications that this may have for subsequent personality development. In the course of the same experience children also learn the distinctive lore and attitudes of their family as a whole, its 'culture', so to speak, and the behaviour appropriate to its members.

Hitherto in this chapter it has been assumed that a family consists only of a father, mother, sons and daughters. However, it may extend further. A small proportion of families have other relations living in the same household, though probably this proportion is nowadays lower than it used to be. For nearly all other families, there are other homes in which it is possible to visit grandparents, uncles, aunts and cousins, and to learn further lessons about adult and child roles. It is hardly necessary to add that it is also possible to gain some insight into social conflict. In one particular case, that of grandparents, children

---

[1] The surveys conducted for the Plowden Committee suggest that the degree of parental supportiveness for school learning is in fact more important than the acutal family size (Central Advisory Council for Education (England) 1967, Vol. I, p. 33) though the family-size variable was not extensively considered in the actual investigations.

L

may not only learn about the generalized 'old person' role, but may also find quite readily that the old tend to be allies of the very young against the intermediate generation, being once removed from the immediate responsibilities of child-rearing. This situation is one which the children may soon learn to exploit, using their extensive reserves of winsomeness with considerable skill, and thus gaining a further initiation into social experience.

It is hardly necessary to point out that adolescence introduces a new element into family relationships. Teenagers, where role-learning is concerned, do not merely elaborate upon the patterns established in childhood. They assume new, more specific roles, often incompatible with each other and collectively requiring a marked discontinuity with the roles already learned. The demands of present physical developments, future occupational aspirations, and general social pressures, are potentially in conflict. The chance of actual disharmony is heightened by confusion and uncertainty about the definition of roles in general nowadays, while an outbreak of conflict is rendered still more likely because of the widespread social prescription in our society that the teenager role itself should be emotionally charged, so that its incumbents are almost encouraged to indulge in bouts of individual and collective expressivity. Adults, themselves rendered inescapably conscious that their own youth is over, are in their turn liable to interpret the 'moodiness' and extravagant demands of their adolescent children consciously as a piece of outrageous effrontery, and subconsciously as a criticism and a threat directed at their most vulnerable point, namely where the inherited value-systems have given way, and nothing coherent or widely accepted has emerged to take their place. Yet the family, however torn with conflict, usually holds together. Despite the increasing social distance between generations, the family remains the basic social context and, since the wider social influences are largely filtered through and conditioned by it, the family has some claim to be regarded as the basic institution in English society. Where it is impaired, or absent, child development is almost inevitably stunted.[1]

In addition to the influence of this first social environment, the corresponding spatial environment, that of the home, can be important in its own right. It is only possible here to mention in passing the kind of influence which it can exercise, depending on the size and shape

[1] Musgrove (1966) emphasizes that the social potency of the family may be actually increasing, and suggests that one role of the school may be that of counteracting the various kinds of pressures that families may exert on children.

of the home and its subdivisions, its contents with their potential range of cultural stimulus (Blyth, 1965, Volume II, pp. 52-4) and its proximity and relation to other homes. Within this context, sensory experience can take place, varying in extent and richness both according to the physical properties of the home and of course also according to the ability and readiness of parents to enable and encourage children to make use of it.

III. DEVELOPMENT AND LEARNING IN THE IMMEDIATE HABITAT

The first extension of the spatial environment outside the home is a very limited one, almost the logical rounding-off of the home itself. It reaches into the immediate surroundings, a geographical area much smaller than anything that could be termed a 'neighbourhood', but it gradually and irregularly expands as the children's experience increases, and as their cognitive structures develop. They get to know accurately the layout of the surrounding houses, their gardens and entries, the way to the nearby shops, then perhaps a park or a recreation ground, or a field and a lane; and within this small world they weave webs of cognitive experience whose potential for the development of further experience varies, with the result that their patterns of development vary too.

Within this area of spatial experience, as within the home, they meet social experiences too. 'Significant others' outside the family begin to people their worlds. One child may encounter them in the traditional culture of the congested city district, another in the more stylized manner of the suburban lounge or garden, a third in the possibly intense interaction of the nucleated village, and a fourth in the more distant, dilute relationship of the open countryside. As is shown in novels and autobiographies, as well as in more scientific studies (e.g. Kuper, 1953), this is added to family experience to form the very stuff from which social attitudes emerge, and within whose influence their subsequent development to some extent remains, however much they are overlain and modified.

Some of the persons encountered outside the family are adults, whose presence assists the children in learning about adult roles and in dissociating these from their own parents and relatives. But probably the contact with children outside the family is more important. Just as adults are no longer identified with parents, so children are no longer identified with siblings. What is more, it becomes customary to meet, where possible, as this immediate habitat expands, substantial numbers of other children of approximately the same age. This enables most children to experience, as their social development proceeds, membership of what sociologists call a *peer group*, a social institution already discussed in the preceding chapters. The exceptions are those who live in sparsely-populated districts, or in decorous neighbourhoods principally characterized by big gardens and old people, and those whose parents, believing that the local child population includes a number of undesirable elements, restrict their children's participation, a procedure which has more apparent justification in some places than in others. But usually there is some form of local peer life, and in childhood and early adolescence it may absorb most of a child's loyalties and interest. At that stage it is mostly monosexual in character, encouraging the consolidation of sex-roles prior to the 'heterosexual revival' in adolescence when, first collectively and then in quartets and pairs, with the girls chronologically in the lead, for the first time since infancy boys and girls come together again.

These peer groups are all the more important because they are the first social institutions within which children learn to play roles on a *primarily* achieved basis. In the family, a child is essentially a son or a daughter, a brother or a sister. To adults outside the family, children whom they know are primarily children from particular families. But in the peer group a child is literally nobody except what he makes himself. He may start with a trace of ascribed status because he is someone else's sibling or friend, but in no time at all he comes to be valued only for what he himself is and has and does. Then, owing partly to chance and partly to natural aptitudes, each member of the group develops characteristics which mark him out as a leader or a fighter, a clown or a 'brain', or whatever it may be. For girls, the range of normally approved roles is somewhat, but not very different. Very soon this reputation becomes generalized and almost stereotyped, so that the child's own personality begins to take on the colouring of the achieved role, as has already been indicated. It is this type of social process that sociologists have in mind when they speak of personality as a social product.

Later, the web of local experience is widened to include formal institutions such as local churches and their youth organizations, and the various other bodies that cater for children and young people, whether under a religious aegis or otherwise. These include the familiar uniformed organizations, and some less familiar ones too, together with the whole range of children's clubs and play centres, youth clubs, and branches of political, pre-military and community-service organizations. Some children are drawn to one or more of these; others remain determined non-joiners (Morse, 1965). For those who do, sometimes under heavy pressure, elect to submit a part of their leisure to organized activities within one or more of these institutions, the process of role-learning is further developed there, while in addition the values overtly promoted by the organizations are absorbed with varying degrees of alacrity and completeness.

Thus there are several distinct ways in which the immediate habitat is important in learning and development. Still another way may be mentioned briefly. As in the home, the various persons and objects in the child's vicinity may also acquire some symbolic significance. This is a matter which depends substantially on psychological functioning at the subconscious level as well as on cultural experience (Madge, 1949), but the potential importance of ideas and motives derived from interaction between unconscious mental processes and objects in the environment should not be overlooked.

IV. DEVELOPMENT AND LEARNING IN SCHOOL

It is in school that the first virtually universal formal learning environment is encountered. The term 'formal' is here used to imply not formality of teaching method but the fact that schools are legally established as social institutions, unlike peer groups which are not.

First, schools themselves are physical contexts, whose size and structure are expected to evoke particular responses in children as they grow. That, at least, must be an assumption behind any specific planning of school buildings. Early memories of schooldays, like those of home, are often associated with the formation of enduring attitudes derived from the physical shape of some particular infant school or private school, or even from the seating plan used within it. The possible enduring effects of physical structure in schools on the learning and social behaviour of children have been thoroughly considered by the Plowden Committee (Central Advisory Council for Education (England) 1967, ch. 28). But the physical configuration of a school has hitherto been, in general, less important than its social structure as an institution, which can be considered under two main headings, formal (official) and informal, with some 'semi-formal' activities such as games and societies in an intermediate position.

The formal organization of the child population in a school increases in complexity as children grow older (Hoyle, 1965). Large secondary schools are very different in structure from infant or nursery schools. The first principle of classification that one usually notices in English schools is by age. In general, children work with other children of the same age, or as nearly the same age as possible. This means that the prospect of 'going up' is held before children at each annual milestone, thus emphasizing that they are on the road to maturity. Only in a few primary schools is there a deliberate modification of this principle namely where vertical grouping has been introduced, and where social stability has thus been given priority over the annual ratification of growth.

Sometimes, mostly at the secondary level, the sexes are separated. The consequences of this are often discussed, and it does in general appear likely that the consequent intensification of sex-role learning has two disadvantages. First, it hampers and occasionally, if notoriously, distorts the central aspects of sexual development. Also, it causes some exaggeration of certain aspects of both masculine and feminine roles, and most conspicuously of what amounts to a cult of uncouthness among boys, which an exclusively male staff may be prone to countenance rather readily.

Recently, controversy has become focussed on a third feature of the formal structure, namely grouping by ability, or rather by a combination of ability and attainment. This gives rise to streaming or its equivalent. Increasingly (see, e.g. Daniels, 1961; Jackson, 1964; Douglas, 1964), research is showing that at least at the primary level allocation to a particular stream tends to stereotype children, irrespective of the reason for their original placement, and to lead teachers and others to make particular assumptions about children's intellectual and social potential, so that movement from stream to stream becomes increasingly difficult. At the secondary stage the issues are more complex, since abilities and roles become more differentiated, and some form of setting is often introduced to mitigate the rigidity of streaming, but it is necessary here also to appreciate the potential significance for individual development implied in these differing structures of educational expectation. (In Chapter 7, Hargreaves has graphically demonstrated the social consequences of streaming in one secondary school.)

One other aspect of the formal structure, overlapping into the semi-formal aspects, is important for some children. Through selection as prefects, monitors, team members or the cast of a play, they learn some of the roles associated with delegated status. The quality of these roles varies from school to school, as does the method of selecting their incumbents, but it is never without significance, especially since some children are not chosen at all. For this is yet another way in which schools select and classify their pupils, marking out different paths for them, and modifying their development through constant and complex interaction between the children and the formal structure of their schools. Meanwhile, they learn from their school's organization something, perhaps too kindly or too restricted or too authoritarian a view, but something nevertheless, about the working of social institutions in general.

Within their formal organization, schools also play an important part in promoting the learning of other roles, and as a pre-condition of this, the learning of the generalized role of pupil, within which the necessary further learning can be accomplished. Having learned to be children, they learn to be schoolchildren. Having responded gradually, often cautiously, and variously according to circumstances, to social pressures to do what other schoolchildren do, a child then learns in succession how to be, perhaps a nursery pupil, certainly an infant, a junior, and a secondary pupil (or the corresponding independent-school equivalents) with an increasing range of permitted academic, athletic and social functions as he goes. Girls appear to learn these pupil-roles better than boys, at least until adolescence, when there may be an abrupt tacking to meet the storm. Or perhaps it would be more accurate to say that, before adolescence, the consensus of girl opinion about the pupil role coincides more closely with adult wishes than does the consensus of boy opinion. Moreover, as already suggested (p. 280 above) in school a child learns also a new conception of the roles of adults, especially women. An English boy may have considerably more difficulty in differentiating male roles than female roles, because of his relative lack of men teachers in the primary school, though here perhaps he is likely to be more fortunate than his American counterpart. In any case, by meeting an annual succession of partial mother-substitutes, he at least comes to realize that for him the role of teacher is not necessarily tied to one person, as the role of mother is. After that, the way is open to the realization that most other adult roles must be similarly separated from their particular incumbents, and so a child begins himself to be something of a sociologist, forming viable ideas about the society in which he lives.

For older pupils, and more dramatically in the case of girls, this process of role-learning becomes more problematical in school, just as it does simultaneously at home. Teachers come to symbolize tutelage. They are often resented if they exceed their more specific roles, yet at the same time they are also criticized for their lack of general, diffuse interest in their pupils. Apparently they cannot win. But, since society sets adolescents such contradictions in their own role-learning, as they come to distinguish between their sexual, social, economic and civic selves, it is small wonder that they tend to find convenient scapegoats in the nearest available adults, namely parents and teachers, especially since these also represent the perpetuation of childhood relationships.

However, at the same time, the formal organization of a school can give a specific kind of assistance to young people in their development. By giving some experience – the amount varies greatly from child to child and from school to school – of social responsibility and 'democratic' organization within the school's own concerns, teachers can assist, especially at the secondary stage, in the building of suitable social attitudes and assumptions. If some aspects of school life, such as academic excellence or athletic prowess, or school drama, are given unique or excessive emphasis, this too has implications for attitude-building. But if young people and their needs are taken seriously and courageously by teachers as they are, and if they are allowed and even required to take some responsibility for the conduct of at least some of their own affairs as well as for their own impending entry to adult life, then they are more likely to respond positively, in school and afterwards. They may, especially if the school is seen to offer genuine life-chances to its pupils, display quite extensive departures from the patterns of teenage role-assumption which are otherwise likely.

Anyone who reflects on his own schooldays will soon realize that much of a school's permanent influence depends on the *informal* relations between its members. Children's peer groups develop inside the school as well as outside, and may exercise quite an important influence on the motivation of individuals and their response to the academic and social purposes of schools (Blyth, 1961). Even in mixed schools, this peer society is mainly monosexual, as it is in neighbourhoods, and serves to reinforce the consolidation of sex-roles. Within these monosexual groups, pairs of children may develop intense and occasionally passionate friendships, while during the junior-school years and in the early part of secondary education the groups may sometimes coalesce into larger gangs for limited purposes. Later, all of this group experience merges in the 'heterosexual revival', though the sexes never seem to merge so readily in the formal context of the school as in the informal situation in the neighbourhood. Perhaps this is another argument against the further intensification of this type of sex-role development through a single-sex formal organization in schools.

Often there is a positive relationship between peer groups inside school and those outside, especially at the junior and secondary stages and particularly when pupils hail from distinctive cultural backgrounds which render them less ready to absorb the school's majority values. This can sometimes render possible quite an illuminating explanation and even prediction (Blyth, 1961) of social processes within schools. But reference to 'cultural backgrounds' brings into the discussion a type of social context which is on a larger scale than that of the immediate habitat, and merits separate attention.

V. DEVELOPMENT AND LEARNING IN THE SUB-CULTURAL CONTEXT

During recent years there has been increasing recognition that English society can be regarded as including a series of 'sub-cultures', some more geographically discrete, and some more socially distinctive, than others. The worlds of Bethnal Green (Young and Willmott, 1957) and 'Crown Street' (Mays, 1962) and other less familiar localities have come to be recognized as important influences on the children who grow up there, and also to some extent on their reactions in school. Some districts are conspicuous for sub-cultures whose adherents comply readily with schools' requirements; some try to take the school in tow; some are ignorant or suspicious of what goes on within its walls; some are deeply divided in their attitudes. Jackson and Marsden (1962) in their portrait of 'Marburton' bring out poignantly, if sketchily, some of the contrasts that can exist, and other research work, including some of my own (Blyth, 1961), substantiates in broad terms the type of social process that Jackson and Marsden specified, and so indeed does the cumulative experience of a host of teachers and others. Hargreaves' chapter embodies an example of it, and the Newsom and Plowden Reports lay emphasis on it. (Central Advisory Council for Education (England) 1963 and 1967.)

It is customary, though perhaps rather patronizing, to describe the more distinctive sub-cultures as 'deviant' from the national norm or average. The principal areas of difference from this norm are to be found in the use of language, in the nature of social interaction, in the social goals (or 'levels of aspiration') which individuals and groups set for themselves, and in the concepts of social and moral behaviour which prevail within the sub-culture. Every locality and every sub-division of English society has some distinctiveness in these respects, but in some places this is more recognizable than elsewhere.

Language, for example, varies in its structure and also in the richness and universality of its vocabulary. Where there exists a sub-culture with little need for rich or subtle, or official and formalized, communication, it is not unlikely that children will grow up with only what Bernstein (in Halsey *et al.*, 1961) formerly called a 'public' language and in his more recent terminology refers to as a 'restricted code', with its simple structure and limited capacity as a vehicle of abstract thought (Bernstein, 1965). It can itself be regarded as affecting the structure of thought and the individual's capacity for thinking, quite apart from the genetic equipment which is his by heredity. So, especially when school work begins to make more extensive demands on children, as often happens in the middle years of secondary schools and especially in grammar schools or their equivalent, the linguistic environment of the sub-culture can begin to figure as a limitation on educability. Children find it more difficult to undertake what comes next in the course, or even to understand the point of it. At the same time, perhaps, this linguistic handicap is related to an inability or unwillingness to learn the panoply of specific, emotionally neutral roles characteristic of fully-organized adult society as we know it. If this is true, then in a sense they may be sociologically fixated in early adolescence, with their social perspectives limited to a teenage-eye view. The roles which they learn with ease are well adapted to living within the sub-cultural context but not to emerging from it.

The comparatively unsophisticated social structure and role-relations of the local sub-cultural community may also reinforce the effects of verbal limitation. For the adequacy of this sub-cultural system, the richness of its personal relations, and even its apparent defiance of the less savoury aspects of society as a whole, can act as a powerful deterrent to those, such as the 'scholarship boys' (Hoggart, 1957) who are given the option of climbing the ladder of meritocracy. Or, at least, this was true until very recently; for the distinctiveness of sub-cultures may be giving way before the economic and cultural pressures of mass (not necessarily middle-class) society.

Closely linked with these issues is the question of levels of occupational aspiration. In homes where the use of language is restricted, and partly for that very reason, people are less capable of understanding the purpose and value of prolonged education, which is the normal built-in expectation of many middle-class families. This is particularly true in the case of girls. In addition, such homes, especially those in the more distinctive sub-cultures, are often understandably associated with a belief that the dice are heavily loaded against their children achieving much in the way of social mobility. This makes academic effort appear not only difficult, but ultimately pointless; a mockery imposed from without. Probably this combination of distaste and disbelief has been strengthened through the corporate experience of the Great Depression, still so vividly alive in folk-memory, when so many doors seemed open to the few and closed to the many; but even now, when economic circumstances and educational opportunities are at least formally more favourable, the same pattern persists. Some places simply don't produce doctors, especially women doctors.

Finally, this pattern of deviance and restricted cognitive capacities can be linked with markedly different social and moral values. The most conspicuous instances of these, the ones that usually figure in public discussion, concern sexual behaviour and attitudes to property. Of the latter, it seems that a community can establish distinctive attitudes to the property both of its own members and of society as a whole. The conventional patterns of the wider society may be rejected with evident contempt, though it does not follow that they are necessarily replaced by anything less mundane or more admirable. Where this takes place, children may in their turn come to evaluate goods and services at home, in school, in the street or elsewhere in ways that may cause conflict or necessitate re-learning, especially if they move outside their own area.

Ideals of sexual behaviour, too, may vary from the national norm, although this norm is itself too unstable to permit clear contrasts, and although indeed some sub-cultures are praised, in a patronizing way, because they adhere conspicuously to the traditional norms, and others because they do not. However, during adolescence there may be a particular importance in discrepancies in sexual mores between teachers and pupils. Whether they inherit a sub-cultural code, or whether they adopt it, at least negatively, as a symbol of protest against the Establishment, young people may come to identify some of their teachers with the majority, traditional, view, especially in secondary modern schools which may themselves symbolize institutional rejection. In that case these teachers, perhaps already cast in the role of scapegoats, as has previously been suggested, may come also to symbolize conformity and perhaps timidity or lack of success in sexual experience. At an age when 'sex' matters so much, this may predispose girls and boys alike to belittle their teachers' opinions on other matters also. In other words they may set a sharp limit to the specificity and emotional neutrality which they will permit in their teachers' roles.

Hitherto it has been assumed that most deviant sub-cultures must be handicapped in some way, and isolated from the main stream of society; 'way-out' is a possible translation of 'deviant'. Slums, mining communities, and rural villages come to mind. But strictly the term 'deviant' can also be applied to any numerically inferior group, and thus to the more privileged and affluent sectors of society too, though here perhaps it would be more accurate to speak of dominance than of deviance. These sectors also diverge from the normal pattern, but in general their divergence takes the form of exceeding the normal goals and competences, rather than of misunderstanding and rejecting them. If they have a pattern of disdain, it is for undue timidity and lack of adventure in goal-setting. At the same time, their adherents often assume that it is right and proper for their children to be educated in schools outside the national system, an assumption which is, for a variety of reasons, also made on their behalf by many outside their own circle. It is also widely expected that, partly because of their different style of education, their basic patterns of learning and development will show distinctive characteristics; indeed, much of their domestic life and all of their children's school life tends to ensure this. The roles they learn are to a large extent appropriate to some form of social elite, while the social factors of language use, group solidarity, occupational aspiration and general mores serve to reinforce their prestige, rather than their separateness as in the case of less fortunate sub-cultures.

Sub-cultural influences interact in different ways with the other social contexts already mentioned. Within the family there is likely to be broad agreement, at least until adolescence, so that children are not likely to experience much culture-conflict in this closest environment, though it is not impossible. Within some local habitats, however, one can find smaller-scale patterns of deviance. (Kuper, 1953; Mitchell *et al.*, 1954). Some families could be termed 'right deviants', who regard their neighbours as unambitious and intrusive and who are regarded by those neighbours as 'stuck-up'. Others could figure as 'left deviants' problem families whose standards of domestic efficiency and propriety mark them off from the rest. For children in either of these types of deviant family, life and learning must be slightly complicated. Much the same is true of peer life, at least in the earlier years of growth, for peer groups tend usually to reinforce the major value-systems of an area, and may thus involve the children from deviant families in additional difficulties. In middle and later adolescence this issue may in fact become more involved, for then peer groups often distinguish themselves both from the local culture and from the wider society, though in their opposition to the latter they may contrive to display some of the characteristics of the former, transposed into another key. For example, a gang of motor-cyclists with leather jackets may be the despair of its members' Mums (or 'old ladies'), but the gang would be less likely to form in the first place if those Mums had not come from a particular type of sub-cultural background. Meanwhile, some peer groups, like some families, may find themselves in a minority position within a particular culture-area, rejected either on account of their collective aspirations towards social mobility and the roles they learn as a means of paving the way – 'anticipatory socialization', as it is sometimes called – or else because of their opposite behaviour, namely an extreme rejection of the conventions of the wider society (Cohen, 1955; Cloward and Ohlin, 1961; Matza, 1964; Downes, 1965). In either case, as in the family context, the process of development and learning will be rendered more complex, and in either case the distinctiveness of the peer group is likely to be facilitated through the learning of a group role, as well as of individual roles within the group. The existence of such group supportiveness can render more effective the collective mobility of the members, whether upward in the course of improving their social status, or outward beyond the bounds of legally permitted activity.

There are also obvious differences between sub-cultures in the nature and degree of the collective social weaning of peer groups in childhood and adolescence. Any observer can see the contrasts in forms of association among boys, and rather differently among girls, in a slum, a housing estate, a rural village, a middle-class suburb, and an independent boarding school. From one of these to another, there is considerable variation in assumptions about what constitutes maturity, though this variation is probably declining under the impact of the collective, autonomous 'youth culture' which is taking shape.

It is however in school that sub-cultural differences operate most significantly. From the work of Hargreaves (Chapter 7) and others, we have already seen that, for a few children, they are decisive, determining the extent to which prolongation of formal education and especially its verbal content is acceptable. For many others, too, this may be marginally important. Since such influences depend substantially on membership of groups, they are closely related to the informal peer group structure of schools, especially secondary schools. And, since the groups from the less educationally favourable sub-cultures tend to gravitate into the less esteemed parts of schools, such as the lower streams, they affect the formal structure too. Moreover, though public debate has centred round its working in grammar schools (e.g. Jackson and Marsden, 1962; Davies, 1965), this type of social process can operate to some extent in schools of any type (e.g. Holly, 1965. There is also much similar research material in the American literature). For it is in society as a whole, rather than in particular patterns of school organization, that the roles and values and attitudes associated with distinctive sub-cultures must be adapted and accommodated.

In fact, schools are at least potentially less subject than the wider society to these social determinants. At primary and secondary levels alike, they can break partly away from social pressures. They can refuse to be a mirror-image of society; indeed, they are expected to do better than that and to be initiators of social improvement. Each school can, and perhaps must, develop a quality of intrinsic, autonomous culture (Blyth, 1965, Volume I, pp. 20–21 *et passim*), which does not favour any one section of its pupils but transcends the expectations of them all. This requires all the skill and determination and devotion that a school can muster. Without it, a school wastes its creative potential and cannot be described as truly educational or truly democratic. With it, schools can promote the integration into society both of the long-standing rural and urban sub-cultures of British society but also, and perhaps critically, of the newer immigrant communities that might otherwise degenerate into ghettos. They can in addition ensure that children from the hitherto more privileged 'sub-culture' may continue to progress educationally without disparagement, but that their progress is based on achievement rather than ascription.

VI. DEVELOPMENT AND LEARNING IN THE MAJOR CULTURAL ENVIRONMENT

Some consideration must now be given to the wider society itself. When we consider the outcome of studies of learning and development in different countries (e.g. Mead and Wolfenstein, 1955; Whiting and Child, 1953), we can hardly fail to be impressed by the extent of the variations associated with the major cultural differences between them. The whole pattern of development and learning can here be viewed from the point of view of *socialization*, that is, the process of learning to participate effectively in a particular society. Anthropologists have for a long time appreciated the importance of this, and titles such as *Becoming a Kwoma* (Whiting, 1941) and (more familiar) *Growing up in New Guinea* (Mead, 1930, 1942), are frequently encountered in anthropological literature. It is more difficult to think in similar terms about our own culture, though American writers have tried to do this in their still more complex situation. Yet there is no lack of general discussion about individual processes of socialization that take place within the total culture in England. Values in schools are perpetually examined: it is only necessary to consider the claims made for, and against, religious education or comprehensive schools to appreciate that instruments of socialization in the major culture are the object of lively discussion and research. This extends also to what the Americans would call 'non-school agencies' of socialization, such as the uniformed organizations, whose impact in the immediate habitat has already been mentioned. The various mass media of communication, and especially television, are constantly cited as good or bad influences on the development of children's values and attitudes, and here too there has been serious research to find out how formative, and how socially beneficial or harmful, these mass media are (Himmelweit *et al.*, 1958; Halloran, 1964).

The general impression which emerges from these investigations is that they are neither so beneficial nor so harmful as partisan opinion might suggest, but that they do result for a variety of reasons in a further concentration of interest and demand on the already popular types of passive entertainment. This could result in a stereotyping of popular taste, even when that taste is expressed in virile idioms which appear more full-blooded than the faded conventions of the concert hall and the art gallery (Hall and Whannel, 1964). It could also result in the perpetuation of a cultural class-division between the mass and the minorities, operating at every age-level from the primary school to adulthood (Blyth, 1965, Volume II pp. 127–30; see also Bantock, 1963).

Less attention is usually paid to the degree of separateness or specificity which characterizes English society as a whole, or to the

consequent specific pressures which are brought to bear on English children. This is largely the result of historical developments: British priority in industrialization, the growth (and decline) of the British Empire, the nature of urbanization in Great Britain, the degree of immunity from foreign invasion over the centuries, the peculiarities of British constitutional development, and even the unique role of the leading public schools. It would require a whole volume to trace the impact of any one of these, but together they have produced a distinctive environment, one whose influence on learning and development provokes the admiration, and also the censure, of the rest of mankind.

Like all other social processes, however, socialization in England is changing. As the apparatus of government, industry and trade becomes more complex and mechanized, new skills and new patterns of learning are in demand. First, clerical and mechanical competences were required; now technology and automation make the principal demands. Each is translated into particular terms for schools, and in the long run the schools respond, but in so doing they alter the children's environment and their cognitive development. Here, the question arises of the optimum encouragement of the nation's resources of talent, and it is necessary to consider the definition of talent in sociological terms.

When a psychologist speaks of talent, he tends to define it in relation to innate abilities, though allowing a considerable variation in development according to environmental motivation, as in the Parable of the Talents, where the effect of innate differences is palpably reinforced by environmental pressures. However, a sociologist is often more sceptical, as we have seen, about regarding individuals and environments as discrete entities. He is more likely to think of a talent as a response to a social situation, though allowing a considerable variation in that response according to the genetic equipment of individuals. There is nothing essentially incompatible between these two points of view, although the differences between their relative emphases does tend to lead some sociologists to overemphasize the capacity of children and young people to channel their talents maximally wherever society requires, while some psychologists remain distinctly sceptical in their turn about this cognitive cornucopia. Needless to say, the resultant attitudes can carry over into social and political thought, both among specialists and among the population in general, and affects their expectations in relation to education and their preferences for different patterns of curriculum and organization. But on one issue there is growing agreement, namely that the accelerating pace of social and technical change leaves little room for complacency about either the organization or the curriculum. This applies throughout the age-range. It would be particularly unfortunate if it were to result in action only at the secondary level because the main controversies are centred there, for piecemeal modifications at that stage cannot be fully effective unless they are considered in relation to what precedes and what follows it. Otherwise the mobilization of talent, however defined, will be hampered, and the development and learning of children will remain imperfectly adjusted to future needs. To this problem the Plowden Committee has drawn attention.

Meanwhile, as the general values prevailing in society undergo change, so this change percolates through into childhood and more particularly into adolescence, accentuating thereby the social distance between generations and thrusting each newcomer into a position of more conscious social isolation than his forebears knew, so that he is more than ever dependent on the support of his peer group, and more than ever prone to assume roles that are developed there.

It would be impossible here to discuss the full implications of these major social processes in the light of the very extensive research and theory which now exists, while to do so without reference to them involves little more than speculation. However, they must be borne in mind, especially when interpreting foreign investigations and applying them to the British scene. They should also be remembered when the roles of the young today are considered and evaluated. For, to express a personal view, contemporary British society offers them little in the way of agreed model, guide or precedent. Instead, they are confronted by a mixture of new and unrelated stimuli together with the relics of traditional attitudes, all transmitted in a climate of opinion which appears to combine short-term hedonism and acquisitiveness with a sophisticated, wordly-wise resistance to any rhetorical call to action, in case it should turn out to be naïve or insincere. Either we have heard it all before, as in the case of appeals for pre-marital chastity, or as in the case of nuclear armaments, we cannot do anything about it anyhow: so goes the line of thought, and in the light of it politicians, social workers, ministers of religion, novelists and playwrights with a social conscience are all regarded with suspicion. Either they are in the game for what they can get out of it, in which case they are knaves, or they are not, in which case they are fools. Such attitudes are widespread, though fortunately far from universal. Nor are they confined to the United Kingdom; and they may be preferable in any case to those prevailing in China. But they are not an ideal backcloth for adolescence, nor an ideal prelude to the future that adolescents are expected to usher in (Musgrove, 1964).

VII. THE DEVELOPMENTAL SEQUENCE OF SOCIAL LEARNING

Each child in turn moves through this sequence of social contexts, modified by cultural and sometimes sub-cultural influences. To some extent, the particular phases of development and learning are determined by physical factors and innate stimuli, but even these apparently physiological determinants are in part accelerated or retarded by the nature of the society in which children grow up. What is more, the actual age-span of 'infancy', 'childhood' and 'adolescence' is partly affected by the assumptions of a particular society, and markedly so by the age-structure of its organized system of formal education, just as the role of 'child' is itself partly a social product. The significance of this age-structure is apparent if, for example, in England one compares the use of the term 'junior' with that of the expression 'prep-school boy'. In either case there is a tacit assumption that something belongs especially to that age-span; but the two age-spans are not identical. Each however has its own significance in a particular context. Now, with the age-span of different educational stages under widespread reconsideration, the discrepancies are quite likely to increase within the public sector of education, as well as occurring between the public and the private pattern.

This may lead in its turn to a less precise definition of stages, and thus to an increase in confusion about the learning of roles during childhood and adolescence. A 10-year-old in one place may be cock of the walk in a primary school, and in another, somewhere in the middle of a middle school: a sixth-former may be at the dignified summit of a full secondary school in one town, and already a student of a sixth-form college if he moves to its neighbour. An unintended by-product of the diversification of educational administration may be that it becomes increasingly more necessary to unlearn and re-learn the roles associated with various stages of development as pupils move from place to place, a process which is itself liable to become more widespread as society changes.

Even apart from this, there are considerable possible variations in the developmental sequence encountered by individuals. The various social contexts may be in harmony, or in conflict, as has already been mentioned, and this may also result in discontinuities and abrupt alterations as children encounter new contexts for the first time. The move of village children to a town secondary school is one example of this type of change; entry to work constitutes another. Thus the particular patterns of learning and development established in one part of childhood and youth may be reinforced, or modified, in the next, with consequent need for changes in roles. Some patterns indeed may be truncated, or abruptly terminated, as for example when a boy goes for the first time to a boarding school and finds that his favourite activities have no place there, or when a girl becomes a member of a peer group that is incompatible with her family's values.

VIII. THE ROLES OF TEACHERS AS AGENTS OF SOCIAL DEVELOPMENT AND LEARNING

For a sociologist, as for anybody else, a study of learning and development must include some reference to the roles of teachers. They are themselves a part of the social structure of their society, a professional group whose functions are, to some extent, and perhaps to a rather indefinite extent, laid down by society and differently interpreted in different social situations. Moreover, teachers differ among themselves in their personal circumstances and their psychological characteristics. Nevertheless, they all teach. That is, they mobilize their stimuli in such a way as they think will promote their pupils' learning, and they organize their classes as social units in such a way as to foster cognitive and social learning and development.

In so doing, they are themselves subject to a number of influences. As a professional group, one which admittedly has many levels of qualification and organization, teachers share the characteristics of other similar groups – techniques of organized social control over their own members and activities, a recognizable self-consciousness as an occupation, and even a characteristic repertoire of gesture and behaviour of which the layman is traditionally aware, for laymen have been through school. For some teachers too, especially those from humble origins, their occupation is a symbol of personal achievement and social mobility, which perhaps predisposes them towards those few of their pupils whose patterns of learning and development, and whose levels of aspiration and method of role-assumption, appear most similar to their own. At the same time it may actually reinforce their latent hostility to other pupils if these appear, either through a further widening of the door to social mobility, or on the other hand through their scornful rejection of the 'mobility ethic' itself, to constitute a threat to their teachers' hard-won status. For other teachers, school-teaching may represent something of a *pis aller*, almost an index of downward mobility when compared with their previous ambitions. Such teachers are likely to seize any chance of proving, in their general pattern of role-assumption, that they are more than 'mere' teachers. Thus in all of these ways, teachers tend to be oriented towards the values of the professional middle class in general, even if they do not all quite qualify for membership of it; and this again influences the patterns of social learning in school which they are likely to reinforce.

That in turn may imply that they have, by aspiration if not by ascription, more in common with their middle-class than with their lower-working-class pupils (Jackson and Marsden, 1962), especially if these come from a deviant sub-culture which erects barriers against schools and their values and fosters the scornful rejection of the 'mobility ethic' which has already been mentioned. In this case teachers may bring about a situation in which insecurity and mutual uncertainty develop and in which, indeed, the association in some children's minds of school learning with rejected social norms and standards may be intensified. In other cases, however, teachers may encounter different conflicts of social assumption among pupils whose socio-economic status is equivalent to, or superior to, their own, but whose families sustain rather different educational and social goals.

Conversely, other teachers may adopt something of a 'rebel' role, identifying themselves with different categories of pupil, and perhaps facilitating the social and even academic adjustment of the otherwise rejected, or perhaps assisting them towards the explicit formulation of an unconventional occupational choice, which sheer ignorance might otherwise have obliged them to set aside. Teachers in this mould act, as it were, as catalysts in another type of social reaction.

Other factors may render the position of individual teachers more complicated. These include the psychological qualities which predispose them to become teachers in the first place, and to spend their days with the young (and many of their evenings preparing to spend their days with the young). They also include the patterns of social pressure in different places which affect their role-expectations.

There are variations, too, according to the type of school. As we have seen, it is the teachers of younger children whose roles are most evidently diffuse. They stand nearest to parents in the range of their concern with the children, seeing their development as a whole, whereas the teachers of older adolescents are, and are expected to be specialists in narrower and more specific fields. For the same reason, the teachers of younger children have more emotionally-charged roles (see Wilson, 1962).

Teachers in general are at the meeting-point of pressures from many sources; from parents, from employers, from the churches, from central and local political authorities, from local community influences, from examining bodies and so forth (e.g. Merton, 1957). The social consequences of this exposed and focal situation lie rather outside the scope of this chapter, but it is important to realize that teachers' impact on their pupils' development is likely to reflect their conception of their own roles and the correlative status-positions which they occupy. The more uncertainty and dissatisfaction they feel, the less stable and welcoming is the atmosphere in which children are taught.

One particular source of uncertainty and perhaps also of dissatisfaction among teachers is that they, too, are experiencing the consequences of social change. The roles and valuations associated with traditional modes of teaching are no longer so acceptable as they were. The transition from older to newer patterns of authority leaves considerable gaps in the clearly-expected nature of teachers' behaviour. The introduction of automatic devices such as teaching machines and unconventional modes of organization such as team teaching may all conspire to undermine a teacher's confidence in taking his inherited (and stereotyped?) roles. A consequence might be that teachers would fall back on more authoritarian methods of instruction and control until a new style of teacher roles and behaviour, adapted to the new situation, emerges and becomes accepted (see Gardner and Cass, 1965).

The actual classroom interaction through which these roles are discharged is also of crucial importance, but it will not be discussed here, since it has already figured in Chapters 6 and 7 in this volume.

Teachers, then, are a part of children's environment. But they themselves are in an environment which influences them in turn. It is therefore probable that the role of formal education in learning and development is qualified by an almost infinite regress of social circumstances. It is in the consideration of situations of this kind that a sociological analysis of environment is necessary, if a realistic picture of social processes is to be drawn, and therefore if the scope of positive education in schools is to be gauged with any degree of accuracy. But it must be reiterated that, when this analysis is complete, it reveals with enhanced clarity that there *is* a place for positive education. Indeed, if there is one social institution which stands out from the rest as the place where society can be improved, it is the school, and if there is one social role without which any hope of social amelioration must be abandoned, it is that of the teacher.

IX. CONCLUSION

It has been possible here to give only a sketch of the way in which a sociological approach can be made to the study of children's development and learning, and to outline the social contexts within which it takes place. By virtue of its selection of material, and indeed of its style and the structure of its assertions and opinions, a sketch of this type is bound to be personal and subjective. This must be borne in mind, and perhaps corrected through a reading of other material, some of it indicated in the references in this chapter, which may suggest other points of view. Meanwhile it is hoped that this sociological perspective appears reasonably compatible with the material presented in the earlier chapters. Where it does, it will help to fill out the picture of the children and young people in our schools and in our midst. Where it fails to do so, it may thereby serve to call attention to some of the points where the psychology and sociology of education still await reconciliation in a wider synthesis.

REFERENCES

BANTOCK, G. H. (1963). *Education in an Industrial Society.* London: Faber & Faber.

BANTON, M. (1965). *Roles.* London: Tavistock Publications.

BERNSTEIN, B. (1965). A socio-linguistic approach to social learning. In *Penguin Survey of the Social Sciences.* Harmondsworth: Penguin Books.

BLYTH, W. A. L. (1961). *Children's Groups and their Social Background.* Unpublished Ph.D. thesis: University of Manchester.

BLYTH, W. A. L. (1965). *English Primary Education: a Sociological Description.* London: Routledge & Kegan Paul.

BOTT, ELIZABETH (1955). Urban families: conjugal roles and social networks. *Hum. Relat.* **8**, 245–284.

BRIM, ORVILLE G., Jnr. (1957). The parent-child relationship as a social system: 1 – Parent and child roles. *Child Development.* **28,** 343–364.

CENTRAL ADVISORY COUNCIL FOR EDUCATION (ENGLAND). (1963). *Half our Future.* London: H.M.S.O.

CENTRAL ADVISORY COUNCIL FOR EDUCATION (ENGLAND). (1967). *Children and their Primary Schools.* London: H.M.S.O.

CLOWARD, R. A., and OHLIN, L. E. (1961). *Delinquency and Opportunity.* Glencoe, Ill.: The Free Press.

COHEN, A. K. (1955). *Delinquent Boys.* Glencoe, Ill.: The Free Press.

DANIELS, J. C. (1961). The effects of streaming in the primary school. *Brit. J. Educ. Psychol.* **31,** 67–98, 119–127.

DAVIES, H. (1965). *Culture and the Grammar School.* London: Routledge and Kegan Paul.

DOUGLAS, J. W. B. (1964). *The Home and the School.* London: MacGibbon and Kee.

DOWNES, D. (1965). *The Delinquent Solution.* London: Routledge and Kegan Paul.

GARDNER, D. E., and CASS, J. E. (1965). *The Role of the Teacher in the Infant and Nursery School.* Oxford: Pergamon Press.

GROSS, N. (1965). *Staff Leadership in Public Schools: a Sociological Enquiry.* New York: John Wiley.

HALL, S., and WANNEL, P. (1964). *The Popular Arts.* London: Hutchinson.

HALLORAN, J. D. (1964). *The Effects of Mass Communication, with Special Reference to Television.* Leicester: Leicester Univ. Press.

HALSEY, A. H., FLOUD, J. E., and ANDERSON, C. A. (ed.). (1961). *Education, Economy, and Society.* Glencoe, Ill.: The Free Press.

HIMMELWEIT, H. T., OPPENHEIM, A. N., and VINCE, P. (1958). *Television and the Child.* Oxford: O.U.P.

HOGGART, R. (1957). *The Uses of Literacy.* London: Chatto and Windus.

HOLLY, D. N. (1965). Profiting from a comprehensive school: class, sex and ability. *Brit. J. Sociol.* **17,** 150–158.

HOYLE, E. (1965). Organisational analysis in the field of education. *Educ. Research.* **7,** 97–114.

JACKSON, B. (1964). *Streaming: an Educational System in Miniature.* London: Routledge and Kegan Paul.

JACKSON, B., and MARSDEN, D. (1962). *Education and the Working Class.* London: Routledge and Kegan Paul.

KUPER, L. (1953). *Living in Towns.* London: Cresset Press.

LEES, J. P., and STEWART, A. H. (1957). Family or sibship position and scholastic ability. *Sociol. Rev.* (New series.) **5**, 85–106, 173–190.

LINTON, R. (1936). *The Study of Man.* New York: Appleton-Century.

MADGE, C. (1949). Public and private spaces. *Hum. Relat.* **2**, 187–199.

MATZA, D. (1964). *Delinquency and Drift.* New York: John Wiley.

MAYS, J. B. (1962). *Education and the Urban Child.* Liverpool: Liverpool Univ. Press.

MEAD, M. (1942). *Growing Up in New Guinea.* Harmondsworth: Penguin Books (first published: 1930).

MEAD, M., and WOLFENSTEIN, M. (1955). *Childhood in Contemporary Cultures.* Chicago: Univ. Chicago Press.

MERTON, R. K. (1957). The role-set: problems in sociological theory. *Brit. J. Sociol.* **8**, 106–120.

MITCHELL, G. D. *et al.* (1954). *Neighbourhood and Community.* Liverpool: Liverpool Univ. Press.

MORSE, M. (1965). *The Unattached.* Harmondsworth: Penguin Books.

MUSGRAVE, P. W. (1965). *The Sociology of Education.* London: Methuen.

MUSGROVE, F. (1964). *Youth and the Social Order.* London: Routledge and Kegan Paul.

MUSGROVE, F. (1966). *The Family, Education and Society.* London: Routledge and Kegan Paul.

NEWSOM REPORT. See Central Advisory Council for Education (England) (1963).

NISBET, J. (1961). Family environment and intelligence. In Halse A. H. *et al.*, *Education, Economy and Society.* Chapter 23. Glencoe, Ill.; The Free Press.

OTTAWAY, A. K. C. (1965). *Education and Society* (revised edn.). London: Routledge and Kegan Paul.

PARSONS, T. (1952). *The Social System.* London: Tavistock Publications.

PARSONS, T., and BALES, R. F. (1956). *Family, Socialisation and Interaction Process.* London: Routledge and Kegan Paul.

SWIFT, D. F. (ed.). (in press). *Reader in the Sociology of Education.* London: Routledge and Kegan Paul.

THODAY, M. (1965). Genetics and education. *New Society.* 22nd July, 13–16.

WHITING, J. W. M. (1941). *Becoming a Kwoma: Teaching and Learning in a New Guinea Tribe.* New Haven, Mass.: Yale Univ. Press.

WHITING, J. W. M., and CHILD, I. L. (1953). *Child Training and Personality*. New Haven, Mass.: Yale Univ. Press.

WILSON, B. (1962). The teacher's role: a sociological analysis. *Brit. J. Sociol.*, **13**, 15–32.

WISEMAN, S. (1964). *Education and Environment*. Manchester: Manchester Univ. Press.

YOUNG, M., and WILLMOTT, P. (1957). *Family and Kinship in East London*. London: Routledge and Kegan Paul.

INDEX

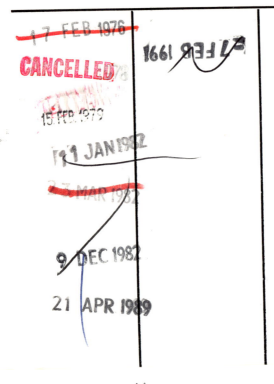